Ursula K. Le Guin's
Journey to
Post-Feminism

Ursula K. Le Guin's Journey to Post-Feminism

AMY M. CLARKE

CRITICAL EXPLORATIONS IN
SCIENCE FICTION AND FANTASY, 18
Donald E. Palumbo *and* C.W. Sullivan III, *series editors*

McFarland & Company, Inc., Publishers
Jefferson, North Carolina, and London

Portions of Chapter Four appeared as "Tales from the Distaff: The Parallax View of Earthsea" by Amy M. Clarke in *Paradoxa* 21 (2008).

Selections from *Dancing at the Edge of the World* Copyright © 1989 by Ursula K. Le Guin. Used by permission of Grove/Atlantic, Inc.

Selections from *The Language of Night: Essays on Fantasy and Science Fiction* by Ursula K. Le Guin, ed. Susan Wood (New York: Berkley, 1979) reprinted by permission of the author's agents, the Virginia Kidd Agency, Inc.

"Danaë 46" Copyright © 1981 by Ursula K. Le Guin; first appeared in the author's own collection, *Hard Words and Other Poems*; reprinted by permission of the author and the author's agents, the Virginia Kidd Agency, Inc.

"Invocation" Copyright © 1977, 2005 by Ursula K. Le Guin; first appeared in *Speculative Poetry Review*, no. 2; from the author's own collection, *Hard Words and Other Poems*; reprinted by permission of the author and the author's agents, the Virginia Kidd Agency, Inc.

"On Sappho's Theme" Copyright © 1960, 1988 by Ursula K. Le Guin; first appeared in *Husk* 39; reprinted by permission of the author and the author's agents, the Virginia Kidd Agency, Inc.

LIBRARY OF CONGRESS CATALOGUING-IN-PUBLICATION DATA

Clarke, Amy M., 1961–
    Ursula K. Le Guin's journey to post-feminism / Amy M. Clarke.
    [Donald Palumbo and C.W. Sullivan III, series editors]
        p.   cm. — (Critical explorations in science fiction
    and fantasy ; 18)
    Includes bibliographical references and index.

    ISBN 978-0-7864-4277-5
    softcover : 50# alkaline paper ∞

    1. Le Guin, Ursula K., 1929– — Criticism and interpretation.
2. Feminism in literature.   3. Science fiction, American —
History and criticism.   4. Fantasy fiction, American — history
and criticism.   I. Title.
PS3562.E42Z594   2010
813'.54 — dc22   2009047857

British Library cataloguing data are available

On the cover: Ursula K. Le Guin (photograph by Marian Wood Kolisch); background images ©2010 Shutterstock

Manufactured in the United States of America

*McFarland & Company, Inc., Publishers
    Box 611, Jefferson, North Carolina 28640
    www.mcfarlandpub.com*

For Joyce Clarke
Sleep Well

Table of Contents

Preface

Ursula Le Guin is beyond question one of the great science fiction and fantasy writers of our time. She stands alongside J. R. R. Tolkien and C. S. Lewis for the quality and mythic status of her Earthsea series, while *The Dispossessed* and *The Left Hand of Darkness* are among the most important science fiction novels of the twentieth century. She has been both prolific and consistently inventive for nearly half a century; her most recent novel, *Lavinia*, based on a character in Virgil's *Aeneid*, shows no diminishment of her powers and indeed is among her best work. Le Guin has also been a central figure in feminist theory. She has frequently said that her writing was utterly reshaped by a feminist awakening she experienced in the late seventies when she responded to criticisms that her work was anti-feminist by immersing herself in the feminist debate. Once having accepted feminist principles, Le Guin evolved a poetics of non-linear narrative, emphasizing "female" values and experimentation with language and syntax. This feminist reshaping is most obvious in her fiction of the eighties, reaching its peak in *Always Coming Home*. It forms the basis of her influential essays, especially "The Carrier Bag Theory of Fiction" and "The Fisherwoman's Daughter." In her own reckoning, this feminist conversion is the pivotal event of her writing life.

Remarkably, despite much fine work on Le Guin by academics such as Marlene S. Barr, James Bittner, Mike Cadden, Elizabeth Cummins, Richard Erlich, and Warren Rochelle, no book-length treatment focused on Le Guin's feminism has yet been published. My 1992 dissertation, *A Woman Writing: Feminist Awareness in Ursula K. Le Guin*, did have such a focus, and at the time, my premise that Le Guin's work exhibited the feminist conversion she self-reported seemed quite valid. After all, it was based on a thorough reading of Le Guin's canon and of the relevant feminist theory, it was critiqued by the preeminent feminist scholar Sandra

1

Gilbert, and it featured input from Le Guin herself, who patiently read sections of it and answered my many questions. While I did present conference papers derived from the dissertation, I opted against publication, perhaps instinctively knowing that the story of this feminist awakening was incomplete.

For some years, teaching full time and raising my sons took my attention away from Le Guin. Then the surprise appearance of a number of new stories from Le Guin's old worlds — Earthsea, Orsinia and the Hainish Ekumen — snapped me back to attention. Like many Le Guin readers, I had long since given up hope that she would return to these much-loved places. When she did, I was surprised to feel so immediately at home in these works. Where was the feminist poetics so evident in the unsettling *Tehanu*, the non-linear *Always Coming Home*, or the Woolf-inspired *Searoad*? This new work was in many ways like her old: challenging to social complacency, as always, but not out of keeping with stories like "Vaster than Empires" or "Two Delays on the Northern Line." Here again was the impeccable characterization, the deft narrative curve, and the pure ending note. Notably, men as rounded characters had returned to Le Guin's worlds. As grateful as I was to again roam the streets of a Hainish planet, reading this new work made me question the premise of my dissertation. If feminism had so changed Le Guin, where was the lasting evidence of this? Had she moved on from feminism? Had feminism itself moved on?

This book attempts to answer these questions. To do this, I take a broad, chronological look at Le Guin's writing career, crossing genre lines freely to include not only her fantasy and science fiction but also her mainstream fiction, her poetry and her criticism. I argue that Le Guin's canon does indeed show a feminist reshaping at its midpoint but that she was never as "masculinist" as has been argued. I also examine feminism's recent evolution into post-feminism, considering what this might mean for Le Guin. Having followed the feminist tide, does she now emerge as post-feminist? Can she help us define this still-ambiguous term? I argue that Le Guin has in fact moved into next-stage feminism. Her return to the imaginary lands of her earlier writing is marked not by feminist essentialism and narrative experimentation, but by her seeming rapprochement with traditional forms. Her recent writings represent Le Guin at another artistic height, but they also indicate a narrative journey back to her own beginnings, her own "native" content and style. Yet, she returns with the express aim of shifting paradigms and breaking with the literary rules of engagement, a legacy of her feminist empowerment.

Because my focus is on Le Guin and feminism, except where they closely pertain, I leave discussion of her other core themes to more capable hands. Le Guin scholarship is ongoing; 2008, for example, saw two new collections on political issues in *The Dispossessed* first published in 1974. My approach, while career-spanning, is necessarily narrow. "The Return of the Native" introduces the study, establishing my argument that the shape of Le Guin's career is more circular or spherical than linear. After briefly considering the feminist movement that so influenced Le Guin, I show that not only has she entered a post-feminist phase, but also that she can be read as a perfect model for how a literary/political movement like feminism can shape the artist. Chapter One, "Contrary Instincts," covers Le Guin's early career through the enormously productive period from 1966 to 1979, when she dramatically claimed her place as a major genre writer. To put into context the negative criticism leveled at her by gender theorists who felt *The Left Hand of Darkness* and *The Dispossessed* had failed as "thought experiments," I place Le Guin in the fantasy and science fiction traditions, especially to show how she plays with the constraints of these genres. I conclude that while she was inhibited to some degree by the conventions of science fiction and fantasy, Le Guin is given less credit than she deserves for having stretched the boundaries of both genres.

Following Le Guin's career chronologically, Chapter Two, "The Voyage Out," considers Le Guin's "loss of faith" in science fiction and fantasy, as well as the beginnings of her feminist awakening. In her writing of the late seventies, Le Guin struggles to express a feminist poetics. "The Fisherwoman's Daughter," Chapter Three, finds Le Guin as at the height of her feminist period, which spanned the eighties and early nineties. After her long hiatus from science fiction, Le Guin returned to the genre with *Always Coming Home*, where she plays with narrative form and establishes an essentialist, separatist, eco-feminist ethic. She also produced the experimental story suite *Searoad* and the bleak Earthsea novel, *Tehanu*. I argue that while this period marks her most direct attempt to embody feminist theory in fiction, it did not always produce her most successful work.

Chapter Four, "Repairing the Sequence," discusses Le Guin's return in the last two decades to Earthsea and to the Hainish universe. I place Le Guin as post-feminist by analyzing her recent writing, which exhibits post-feminist influences in its focus on story, diversity, and non-gendered life choices. I also look at how in the newer Earthsea books, she entirely remakes the male-dominant paradigm that underpins them, creating a world of unlimited possibility regardless of gender. I conclude that Le Guin has returned to her "native" style and indeed to her "native lands," updating her early work to reflect her feminism but striving for balance and unity rather than separatism. The final chapter, "Landing on Middle Ground," looks at Le Guin's reconciliation of her contrary instincts to subvert and to play by the rules. More than that, however, it examines how recent events, including the wars in Iraq and Afghanistan, as well as Le Guin's increasing attention to her own mortality, have steered her the philosophical direction of her writing. It discusses *Changing Planes*, the "Western Shore" books and the novel, *Lavinia*. I reinforce my position that Le Guin, now a post-feminist, follows the natural trajectory of the feminist evolution and so fully exemplifies the impact of feminism on the work of a significant writer.

A portion of this book is based on my 1992 dissertation, *A Woman Writing*, for direction on which I must thank Jack Hicks, Sandra Gilbert and Gary Snyder. Ursula Le Guin was astoundingly sweet to the hapless graduate student who pestered her with questions. George Hersh was amazingly generous with his time. He questioned some of my feminist assumptions, and even if I did not always "hear" his critiques at the time, they stayed with me and directly influenced the present work. The Academic Federation at the University of California, Davis awarded me a professional development leave that helped me make the leap from dissertation to book proposal. More recently, Sylvia Kelso included me in the Le Guin *Paradoxa* issue, despite my coming on board late in the game, and David Willingham allowed me to use material that appears there. The Virginia Kidd Agency and Grove Press both granted me permission to quote extensively from Le Guin's writings, including from her poetry. The wonderful Donald Palumbo helped me get this book published and was both funny and accommodating. Marijane Osborn, easily the best mentor at UC Davis, has graciously encouraged my writing as has another UC Davis colleague, Helen Raybould. To those who have most directly supported my writing this book — my brother Paul, my parents John and Joyce, and especially Larry, Harrison and John Greer — thank you.

Introduction: The Return of the Native

If fiction tells the truth about the human experience, what does it mean for a writer to experience a paradigm shift mid-career? What if this change is so fundamental it alters not only this writer's perspective on the world but on her writing too? For many writers who experienced it, modern feminism caused such a paradigm shift. As a social and political movement, it challenged laws and lifestyles. In its academic role, it forced a re-examination of the received knowledge and standard curricula. For literature, this meant rethinking semantics, syntax, narrative form, and the standards used to judge literary worth. Feminism challenged the canonical tradition in particular, asking why tales of heroes and adventure were so favored: where were the stories about women, the household, the mundane? The writer who experienced a feminist awakening might question not only how to tell her stories but what stories to tell. Her altered sensibilities would also color the work she did previous to this paradigm shift. Is the early work any less legitimate? Moreover, if we consider modern feminism to be continually evolving, we have to ask how the feminism by which this writer was shaped relates to the feminism she later practices. Has she become post-feminist?

A writer who beautifully illustrates the effects of feminism on a literary career is Ursula K. Le Guin. Widely acclaimed, Le Guin has written important works of science fiction, fantasy, children's literature, feminist literature and literary theory. In her forty plus years of publishing, she has written twenty novels, ten collections of short stories, six volumes of poetry, four volumes of translation, thirteen children's books, four collections of essays, and some screenplays. She has won many awards, including the National Book Award, the Kafka, the Pushcart, the Newbery, and the Pen/Malamud. Within the science fiction community, she has been honored with multiple Locus, Hugo and Nebula awards. She has been short-listed for the Pulitzer and has begun to collect "lifetime achievement" awards.[1] Academics have written a dozen monographs, compiled essay collections and published countless articles on her work.[2] Le Guin has taken a public role as well, giving commencement addresses and lectures, leading writing workshops, and serving on editorial boards.

As a major contemporary author, Le Guin is an interesting test case for asking how feminism has shaped modern fiction, in part because she was slow to embrace feminist ideals. In 1970 she said that she was taking no part in the movement. It was too general, too often anti-male, and too middle-class. Sexism, moreover, seemed "an injustice which is less evident than many others."[3] Yet well before she made these statements, she published *The Left Hand of Darkness* (1969), a "thought experiment" on life without gender distinctions. The book, while quickly recognized as a major work of science fiction, was faulted by early feminist critics for pro-male bias.[4] These critics argued that Le Guin's androgynes seem like men because she uses the pronoun "he" and fails to depict the androgynes in female as well as male roles. She also focuses on a human male protagonist and makes sexist comments. Le Guin defended herself in her essay, "Is Gender Necessary?" Here she takes issue with the critics, defending her use of the male pronoun by stating that she "utterly refuse[d] to mangle English by inventing a pronoun for 'he/she'."[5] Her next major novel was 1971's *The Dispossessed*, another thought experiment, this time on anarchy and equality. Again she was praised in some quarters but roundly criticized by feminists. The bitterness and personal nature of some of these attacks shook Le Guin:

> First I was mad; Then I let myself listen to them, and decided some of them were simplistic (they wanted a tract and not a novel) but all of them were to some extent right. I remain defensive only to this extent: OK, sister, so you do it in 1967, and then tell me what I did wrong![6]

Nonetheless, by 1974 she would call herself a feminist. She couldn't see "how you can be an intelligent woman and not be a feminist."[7] She described feminism as having "liberated me from ways of thinking and being that I didn't even realize I was caught in. But I was caught. And now I'm free of certain rigidities — for instance, the fact that all my early books are about men, and women are very secondary."[8]

Vibrant, interesting women characters do appear in Le Guin's early fiction, yet most of her early stories are about men. These are not your usual heroes (broad-shouldered hunks are not Le Guin's type), but they are the characters who "do" things, who are at the center of the narrative action. She was writing, as she describes it, the typical hero story: linear, conflict-oriented and centered on a heroic male. When her mother, the author Theodora Kroeber, asked her why she didn't write about women, she replied, "I don't know how."[9] Once Le Guin began to consider feminism valid, she read widely in feminist theory. Central to her emerging feminism was the work of critics who were re-examining literary canons, rediscovering lost women writers, and revolutionizing the concept of "woman's writing." Woman's writing, as it pertains to Le Guin, means stories about women, told in non-linear fashion, about non-heroic people, and using what Le Guin calls the "mother tongue,"[10] the language of the household.

Her wealth of reading, however, seemed to stymie her own work. Throughout the seventies, Le Guin struggled to incorporate these ideas into her writing. This is evidenced by her relative lack of productivity. She wrote mainly short stories, many of which give witness to her readings in political and literary feminism. These stories are often grim narratives of oppression under totalitarian regimes. They are anti-romantic, featuring women who never marry or are widowed early and don't remarry. She often tells the story of a quiet female revolutionary, as she did with Odo, the founder of the anarchist rebellion at the heart of *The Dispossessed*, in the short story "The Day Before the Revolution" (1974). By degrees Le Guin edged toward a novel, *The Eye of the Heron* (1979), a book she describes as a turning point. She repeatedly got stuck while writing it because the male hero seemed to insist on getting killed. She says she didn't know, "the hero was actually a girl [Luz] from the aggressive culture, only she isn't really a hero either."[11] *Eye* is still rather conventional in structure and does not stand out as one of Le Guin's most interesting novels, but the male hero's early death indicates that feminism had made an impact. The male voice steering the narrative gives way to the female. Instead of fighting the dominant culture, Luz urges her people to sneak off and establish a hidden colony. Le Guin was, as Virginia Woolf describes it, "breaking the sequence,"[12] departing from the expectations of the reader about narrative continuity, conflict resolution, and the fate of the hero.

When she wrote *Eye*, Le Guin also turned serious attention to the issue of language — by the mid-seventies a significant concern of feminist scholars. Mindful of the semantic critiques of *The Left Hand of Darkness* and *The Dispossessed*, she proceeded with more caution in *Eye*. She didn't experiment with language. Instead, she called attention to its power and for the first time seemed to argue that we can, indeed must, change it. Luz recognizes early on the need to give the new place new names, as the old names carry with them old attitudes. She says that they should give the planet, Victoria, a new name, "One that doesn't mean anything. Ooboo, or Baba."[13] If these sound like baby words, it is because she is starting from the beginning, constructing a new language for a new order. She is remaking language, inventing or discovering the mother tongue. In *The Eye of the Heron*, Le Guin shifts narrative focus to the female, reconsiders the effects of language, and breaks expectations about what being a "hero" means.

Eye marked Le Guin's transition into a fully feminist mode. In 1985, she published *Always Coming Home*, about a far-future society. This is easily Le Guin's most experimental work, composed of story fragments, poetry, song and recipes collected by a meta-fictional archaeologist of the present. It is the essence of Le Guin's feminism: non-linear, inclusive of the non-heroic details of life, essentialist and eco-feminist. Her 1991 collection of linked stories, *Searoad*, is more mainstream, but it is equally intent upon breaking the sequence to tell about women's lives. In this period she also wrote essays, many of them given as lectures. "The Fisherwoman's Daughter" and "The Carrier Bag Theory of Fiction" are two of the more influential of these essays, marrying French and American–style feminism, as will be explored later. In 1986, she published a revision of "Is Gender Necessary?," reversing her view on the male pronoun, which she now feels "does [...] exclude women from discourse."[14] As evidenced by her writing, lectures and activism, she clearly felt a duty to add her voice to the public dialogue, in some cases angering and alienating readers. She seemed indeed to adopt the persona of the "Space Crone," a postmenopausal woman who because of her marginal social position can comment openly about her society. Whereas Le Guin once said that her duty was to rock the boat without offending, she became willing to offend, to speak openly about her core beliefs.

This became clear in 1990 with her sudden return to Earthsea, a place she seemed to have finished with years before. Her return was jarring because the new book, *Tehanu*, was radically different from what readers might have expected. Though by no means completely masculine, the early trilogy fits easily into the tradition of high fantasy with its heroes, wizards and quests. The main character of *Tehanu*, on the other hand, is a middle-aged farmer's widow who adopts a little girl raped and mutilated by her own relatives. It is an unsettling book, shifting Earthsea's compass distinctly toward the feminist. Revisiting Earthsea, however, allowed Le Guin to align the world she invented in her earlier career with her feminism. This was her place, what would she make it stand for? As explored in Chapter Four, she would subsequently go to great lengths to rebalance the power structures and shift the narrative focus of Earthsea. Much the same thing happened when she returned to Orsinia, her invented European country, where in "Unlocking the Air" she liberated its citizens from communist rule. Perhaps most tellingly, though, she returned to her Hainish universe, the site of so much of her early science fiction success. Again, she seemed to be working out how to bring this universe in line with the feminist paradigm.

But this brings me to a turning point because in comparing her early, pre-feminist work to her most recent fiction — and indeed the comparisons are quite direct as she is returning to places and characters she had created much earlier — we might expect to see a radically different style, narrative form, content, language. But we do not. In comparison with the experimentalism and inventiveness of *Always Coming Home* or *Searoad*, this recent work looks and feels much like vintage Le Guin. Is she being restrained by returning to science fiction and fantasy, genres with such clear boundaries? Or, has her feminism evolved in recent years into something else? Has she moved past the high feminist and into the post-feminist?

Let me illustrate with a specific point of focus, Le Guin's science fiction set in her Hainish universe, or as she prefers, the Ekumen.[15] Science fiction, despite its seemingly radical nature, is a surprisingly tradition-bound genre, one Le Guin has had an ambivalent relationship with from the beginning. She first "read science fiction in the early forties: *Thrilling Wonder*, and *Astounding* in that giant format it had for a while ... I liked 'Lewis Padgett' best."[16] She also began her sf [17] writing career at this time, at age 10 submitting a time travel story to *Amazing*. Le Guin would take her first hiatus from sf soon after.[18] In her essay "A Citizen of Mondath," she says, "I got off science fiction some time in the late forties. It seemed to be all about hardware and soldiers ... I did not read any science fiction at all for about fifteen years, just about that period which people now call The Golden Age of Science Fiction."[19] In 1961 though, a friend loaned her Cordwainer Smith's "Alpha Ralpha Boulevard." It came as a revelation, an indication that science fiction had evolved away from the limitations she had seen in it earlier. Having made this discovery, in the next 13 years she established herself as an influential writer of sf, producing seven sf novels (including the Nebula- and Hugo-winning *Left Hand of Darkness* and *The Dispossessed*), many short stories and some theory.

At the end of this enormously productive period she was both exhausted and disillusioned with science fiction; again, she disengaged from the genre: "Space was a metaphor for me. A beautiful, lovely, endlessly rich metaphor for me [....] until it ended quite abruptly after *The Dispossessed*. I had a loss of faith ... I don't seem to be able to write about outer space anymore."[20] The loss of faith she describes was a direct result of Le Guin's feminist awakening; it shook her belief that science fiction could tell the stories that most concerned her. Feminist theory revealed to her the limitations of the genre: it allowed only for a man's story told in a linear, conflict-oriented fashion. It also showed her what she characterizes as her own collusion with that paradigm.

Eventually, Le Guin returned to the genre, slipping in through the back door with the sf-inflected utopia *Always Coming Home*. Insofar as it is science fiction, *Always Coming Home* radically breaks the mold of the sf novel. It is also deeply embedded in feminist essentialism. It breaks the sequence, as Woolf describes it, of expected storytelling in its pastiche of story, poem, anthropological notes and recipes for stewed chicken. But it also has the feel of a separatist experiment, with the concomitant suggestion that it is easier to break with tradition when outside the influences of the traditional form. The true test comes when Le Guin returns to her Ekumen, where she applies her feminist principles to her own traditionally conceived universe. Here the question of how much feminism has changed the way she tells stories becomes problematic, for her most recent sf, collected in works like *A Fisherman of the Inland Sea* (1994) and *Four Ways to Forgiveness* (1995), shows no significant changes in narrative technique and little semantic experimentation. There are, in fact, remarkable continuities between her earliest work and her most recent.

Le Guin's newest sf is concerned, as was the oldest, with freedom, justice, connection, balance, and especially the role of the exile. She retains, too, her focus on the function of story, on how we use story to make meaning of the world. This is illustrated this by briefly comparing three of Le Guin's short stories. The first is her very first, written when she was around ten years old. It no longer exists, but Le Guin remembers it as being about scientists who travel back in time to discover how life evolved on Earth:

> they bring wood with them for a campfire, but they use some local rocks to make a fireplace with. And the rocks they used had the seeds of *life from another planet* on them (that's the old "panspermia" theory of the origin of life on Earth), and the fire sterilizes the rocks, right? And so when they come back to the Twenty-First Century ... the Earth has no life on it! So what did they do? They got out of it by going back earlier in time and saving the rocks, or something.[21]

The story, ingenious for a ten-year-old, resonates with standard Le Guinian themes. There is, of course, the idea Le Guin here calls "panspermia," the seeding of the universe by a single race (her trope of connection underlying difference). There is the characteristic sense that science should be in the service of discovery and not exploitation. There is an insistence on taking resonsibility: these scientists have made an impact and must restore the natural order. Finally, and most importantly here, there is the time travel element that she will play with in later time dilation and Churten theory stories. For Le Guin, the theory of relativity lends itself to a metaphor of exile. The space traveler, in leaving his or her planet, will not find the same reality upon return. As she has said, and many critics have noted, Le Guin's writing is often about an exile.[22] At ten years old, she easily solves the problem. Though we do not know how these journeyers move through time, clearly they can; in particular, they can go back in time to correct their own mistake.

Some 25 years later, when Le Guin returned to writing sf, the themes listed above are mostly intact. A rock shows up too, in one of Le Guin's earliest published sf stories, "The Dowry of the Angyar" (1964). This story, which would later become the prologue for Le Guin's first sf novel, *Rocannon's World*, is essentially a Nordic myth in sf drag, with a time dilation twist. A young noblewoman, Semley, bargains to regain her family's treasure — a sapphire necklace that will bring honor to her beloved husband and child. Her fixation on this jewel will lose her everything that she has. What Semley does not understand is that the necklace is housed on another planet, in a museum under the control of the League of All Worlds. While the journey there will seem to take only one long night to Semley, due to time dilation, sixteen years pass for those she left behind. When she returns home, her husband is dead and her child is the same age as she. For the now more savvy Le Guin, interested not in ignoring the laws of physics

11

but in using them to the story's advantage, there can be no heroic return for Semley; she runs off into the marshes to die by her husband's grave. "The Dowry of the Angyar" is not ostensibly about Semley at all, but about an ethnologist, Gavarel Rocannon, who returns Semley's necklace to her. His narrative, marked by his perplexed sense that he has stumbled onto some tragic story he will never know the whole of, opens and intersects the story. An omniscient narrator asks, "How can you tell fact from legend, truth from truth?"[23] In the next ten years Le Guin would write many stories exploring both exile by space travel and the manner in which storytelling tries to capture an exile's truth. Her mobiles — ambassadors to other worlds who are displaced by time dilation — make their reports to the Ekumen in the form of stories. Like Rocannon, they struggle with what story can reveal and what it leaves unsaid.

After her second disillusionment with sf, Le Guin returned to the genre with a story that closely mirrors "Dowry." "Another Story" was published in 1994, a full 30 years after "Dowry" and some 56 years after her first time travel story. Yet it begins with a remarkably similar premise. A mobile of the Ekumen, Hideo, is making his report in the form of a story. But rather than begin with himself, Hideo relates a traditional Terran narrative, "A Fisherman of the Inland Sea," about a young man who is seduced by the beautiful goddess of the sea. After passing with her what seems to him only a long night, he goes back to shore to find that generations have passed and everyone he knew is long dead. In Hideo's world, this cautionary tale is a warning about the consequences of traveling offworld. Hideo ignores the implications of the story, leaving his idyllic home and the woman who loves him to study on a planet four light years away. His story directly parallels Semley's: like her, he leaves behind those who love him for what seems a larger prize. Unlike Semley, though, he knows the price he will pay when he climbs into his spacecraft. But this price is far dearer than he could have imagined. He achieves his goal of studying physics, but his homesickness and loneliness eventually lead to a breakdown.

While "Another Story" is clearly the superior narrative, the product of a highly skilled writer, the stories described show no dramatic changes in theme, narrative structure or characterization. Le Guin seems to be telling only a much better version of her own earlier stories. There is a difference though. Unlike Semley, and indeed unlike any of Le Guin's exiles since her very first story, Hideo gets to go back and start from the beginning, to correct his mistake, restore balance, and rewrite the ending to the story. A physicist, Hideo is working out the problems of churten theory, which promises space travel without time loss. Churten drive, once perfected, would move humans instantaneously through space in a universe-reducing leap from place to place, much like Alfred Bester's jaunting or Cordwainer Smith's planoforming. Le Guin keeps the technology unclear by telling us that the physicists themselves do not really understand how it works. They do know that if it can be made to work consistently, it will end exile by time dilation, the consequences of which Le Guin has written about so often. While churten drive is a mode of travel from place to place, in this story it also allows travel through time. Whether through his experiments or his own mistaken choice to leave home, Hideo has created an imbalance in himself and in the fabric of the universe, created a wrinkle in time. While running experiments, Hideo is caught in this fold and finds himself eighteen years in the past; he is almost magically returned home to correct his original error. His lover is startled to see him since to her Hideo has only recently left (though he returns much older). They live, all things considered, happily ever after, an atypical Le Guin ending. She has come round again to the ten-year-old's solution, an unexplainable leap through time.

Since Hideo has gone back in time, he reinvented his future and will never become a physicist for the Ekumen. They are not expecting his report, yet he knows he must tell it anyway. He writes, "So, now: I hope the Stabiles will accept this report from a farmer they never heard of ... Certainly it is difficult to verify, the only evidence from it being my word."[24] Hideo's story is received by the Ekumen but in a form that is garbled and unintelligible due to the fold in time. Nonetheless, churten drive is tied directly to the act of storytelling. In "The Shobies' Story," where Le Guin introduces churten theory, the crew of the first ship to experiment with the drive finds it has gone hopelessly awry. They become trapped in a limbo of disconnection where all experience different realities. They survive by sitting in a group, sitting around the proverbial campfire (that should remind us of the scientists in her first sf story) telling each other their stories, trying to make meaning out of chaos. Throughout Le Guin's Ekumen novels, story is a powerful way to transmit truth. Her narrators frequently begin with the standard explanation that rather than give a report, they will tell a story. This implies that story gets at truth better than "fact" and that objectivity is impossible. Churten drive solves not only the abiding Le Guinian problem of exile but is actually powered by collective storytelling, the building of consensus reality. The radicalism of these recent stories is not in their experimental form, their play with language, or their focus on female characters. Rather, they break with the sf tradition by ignoring the laws of physics to provide happy endings, resolution and reconciliation.

If this closer look at Le Guin's sf proves anything, it is that her career does not break easily into a neat before-and-after-feminism dichotomy. For one thing, she was never as tradition-bound and hero-oriented as has been described. In fact, with *The Left Hand of Darkness* and *The Dispossessed*, she was an early feminist voice even before she aligned herself with the movement. Moreover, Le Guin continues to evolve. Her writing has taken distinct turns into the more experimental, separatist, and angry, following the shifting tides of feminist thought. It now seems that Le Guin has entered a mode of return and reconciliation. Whether this is specific to Le Guin or a reflection of next-phase feminism is a question to be considered in depth toward the end of this book. In general, however, I take a career-spanning view of Le Guin's writing, examining how, where, and sometimes if feminism has influenced her. In that way, this is both a history of Le Guin's involvement in the movement and of the movement itself, assuming as I do, that feminism has made its own next paradigm shift.

The Wave Gathers

The women's movement that would eventually so influence Le Guin was not a new phenomenon.[25] Theorists and activists championing women's rights to vote, to own land, to be educated, employed and paid equally have appeared at different times over the centuries. Women such as Aphra Behn, Mary Wollstonecraft, Margaret Fuller, Margaret Sanger, Virginia Woolf, and Simone de Beauvoir had written on feminist issues; some of them and many others had agitated — often at great personal cost — for women's rights. Some of these battles, most famously the right to vote, were won. Yet much of this work was forgotten or distorted, so that it was unavailable in the mid to late-sixties as women came again to examine the nature of their lives.[26] The reawakening of the women's movement in America began somewhat slowly in the early sixties, but picked up speed until it emerged full-blown by the early seventies. In 1963, Betty

Friedan's *The Feminine Mystique* brought to light the profound dissatisfaction and undirected anger of many middle-class housewives. Friedan's influential book was important primarily for giving a voice to women who had hitherto felt they had no right to complain about what should have been perfect lives. *The Feminine Mystique* has been criticized, but it was a groundbreaking contribution.[27]

In the ensuing years, the popularity of the pill, the growing number of women in the workforce, and the participation of women in the various movements of the sixties contributed to the rise of feminism. Women's activism in the free speech, civil rights, and anti-war movements brought them face-to-face with their own double standard. While they were working for the freedoms of others, they recognized that these freedoms did not extend to themselves. Within these supposedly radical, society-altering groups, women activists found they were expected to perform the usual "female" functions and nothing more.[28] A century earlier, women working within the Emancipation Movement had similarly begun to consider the nature of their own "enslavement," thus initiating a movement for women's rights. The same process seems to have been at work in the 1960s.

By 1966, women were mobilizing, holding demonstrations and distributing broadsheets.[29] This activism was given added force in what proved a banner year for the women's movement: in 1970 a cluster of important feminist documents appeared, giving the movement a strong body of theory on which to build. This work, for the most part, looked closely at what Friedan had left unexamined: the prevailing power structure and how it oppressed women. Kate Millett's *Sexual Politics*, Germaine Greer's *The Female Eunuch*, Shulamith Firestone's *The Dialectic of Sex*, Eva Figes' *Patriarchal Attitudes*, and Robin Morgan's anthology *Sisterhood is Powerful* examined in detail different aspects of the male power structure and proposed various methods for toppling it. These early theorists were all primarily concerned with the nature of women's oppression, with the way in which virtually every social system then in place colluded in keeping men dominant, women subservient. Their work formed a base from which women could draw, making possible Women's Studies courses, specific political platforms, and more feminist theory.

Women were breaking the silence that Friedan saw as an essential part of their oppression and were coming together to discuss their feelings. Consciousness-raising groups were an integral element of the movement and of the growth of feminist theory. The groups facilitated self-awareness and social activism, bringing into the open issues like rape, battery, and incest, questions of interpersonal relationships and problems in the workplace, as well as matters of female sexuality, including lesbianism. Women thus began to free themselves from the shame they felt about these "taboo" topics. Where authoritative statements on women had hitherto been the domain of men, women were gaining access to a good deal of information based on the lived experience of other women. Consciousness-raising sessions helped to expose patterns of behavior such as sexual harassment used to control and subordinate women. These behaviors could thus be analyzed and resisted. The women participating in these groups also gained a sense of personal empowerment in that the validity of a woman's experience was taken for granted; for most women this was a marked change from an atmosphere in which they were not allowed to speak as experts about their own lives.

In the years that followed, the base of the women's movement grew. Groups like the National Organization of Women and mainstream publications like *Ms.* formed while women joined the abortion debate and established local support centers focused on such issues as rape and crisis pregnancy. Theoretical treatises proliferated, as did journals, magazines, and women's conferences. Feminist inquiry spread to more arenas, addressing mental illness, women's medicine, domestic violence, and sexism in education, the workplace, and the media. On the academic front, women began to reexamine literature, history, religion, psychology and other arts and sciences to identify the mechanisms of oppression, to reinterpret data, and to rediscover the women working in these fields who had been forgotten. Feminist literary criticism, discussed in more detail below, was an outgrowth of this academic industry.

Despite the common goal to end oppression against women, feminism had many faces and many dissenting voices. Hester Eisenstein distinguishes between:

> radical feminism, which holds that gender oppression is the oldest and most profound form of exploitation ... socialist feminism, which argues that class, race, and gender oppression interact in a complex way ... [and] a liberal or bourgeois feminist view, which would argue that women's liberation can be fully achieved without any major alterations to the economic and political structures of contemporary capitalist democracies.[30]

To this list Eisenstein adds a "cultural feminist position, which eschewed an explicit political or economic program altogether and concentrated on the development of a separate women's culture."[31]

The categories Eisenstein describes, though, only begin to convey the variety of ideas spawned by the women's movement — as evidenced in its activism, its theory, its art — or of the sometimes acrimonious sentiments expressed among the broad ranks of feminists. Perhaps the most common complaint against the mainstream feminist movement at the time was that it was white and middle-class; women of color and of lower classes argued that their pressing concerns were not the same as those of so-called mainstream feminists.[32] There were also severe differences about the nature of the "revolution." Some feminists advocated working within the system, either co-opting male power or working to bring feminist ethics into male spheres of influence. At the other end of the spectrum were feminists like Mary Daly, who argues in *Gyn/Ecology* that there can be no compromise, no collusion with man the enemy.[33]

At the heart of the disputes among feminists is the fundamental matter of how gender is constructed.[34] Whether behavior is biologically determined or a result of social conditioning has enormous consequences for feminist theory and feminist practice. In its earliest manifestations, the women's movement tended to espouse nurture over nature, arguing that men and women are socialized into the roles we play. A goal, then, could be an androgynous society in which men and women shared equally in everything. Theorists considered the possibility that women could be reconditioned — particularly through consciousness-raising — to become more aggressive and thus less likely to be victimized. Some theorists looked to reproductive technology to free women from the "tyranny of biology" and so erase what they took as the essential source of women's oppression, their role as bearer of children. Freed from what had been their defining social role, women would be on equal footing with men to chart any life course. The androgynous ideal came quickly into question by those who resisted the assumption that women should become more like men in order to succeed in a man's world; there seemed to be no suggestion that men themselves should change.[35] Those who favored a theory of nature over nurture, referred to here as essentialists, sought recognition of what was inherently valuable in women. Men and women are different, essentialists claim, and women should celebrate and explore what nature has given them as particularly female qualities. At one extreme, gynocentric essentialism posits that not only are women different than men, but that the traits or values that define women (nurturing, communication, compassion) are better than those that seem to define masculinity (logic, competitiveness, aggression). This theory is book-ended on the theoretical spectrum by androcentric essentialism: a belief in the biological basis for gender, except considering men, or the traits used to define maleness, as better, making men morally, physically, and psychologically superior to women. At the farthest reaches of gynocentric essentialist theory is what Eisenstein calls "cultural feminism," the belief in the utter incompatibility of men and women and thus the need for separate cultures. Many feminists take some middle ground. Jean Baker Miller, for example, does not argue that women's values are inherent, but rather that women have developed valuable strategies for coping with life during their socialized subservience. These strategies should be retained and taught to men as women and men become equal. Though Le Guin describes her own beliefs as having always tended toward androgyny, over the course of her long career she can be located at different points along this spectrum.

Women's Literary Tradition Resurfaces

Literary criticism, a cross-disciplinary endeavor that has long been relatively friendly to women, became center stage for exploration of feminist theory. Kate Millett's *Sexual Politics* (1970) was both a political tract and a work of literary criticism. Millett examined the dynamics of sexual power in works by popular and lauded male writers. She thus launched the first phase of a specifically feminist literary criticism arising from the women's movement.[36] In comparison to later work, Millet's analysis can seem unsophisticated, in particular because she connected what was on the page with real life. Elaine Showalter describes early feminist critics as intent on "exposing the misogyny of literary practice: the stereotyped images of women in literature as angels or monsters, the literary abuse or textual harassment of women in classic and popular male literature, and the exclusion of women from literary history."[37] However naïve such a critical approach now seems, particularly in contrast to French feminism, at the time it came as a powerful awakening.

Distaste for the misogynist and/or male-centered text was part of the impetus for a next phase of feminist criticism that focused on women's literature.[38] Critics like Patricia Meyer Spacks, Ellen Moers, Showalter, Sandra Gilbert and Susan Gubar, and Jayne Tompkins began wondering what literary analysts like Woolf had long wondered, where were the women writers, the "damned mob of scribbling women"[39] whose texts seemed nowhere in evidence? Why had they all gone out of print? These critics and others began to recognize that our literary heritage, the canon of Western literature passed down through college courses and collections like "The Great Books,"[40] excluded women. These books were only infrequently about women; they were even less frequently written by women and were almost never about the lives that the majority of women had led over the centuries. Feminist theorists began to question the critical heritage wherein predominantly white male intellectuals decided what constituted great writing and what did not. Could their gender and their cultural biases have colored their perceptions? If our sense of literary greatness is taught and not innate, can it be refashioned?

From this questioning of critical practice came the unearthing and reconsideration of long unread texts. This recovery of an ongoing women's literary tradition both spurred and facilitated a reading of these texts as artifacts of the female imagination.[41] In *Literary Women*, Moers showed how women's texts bear evidence of the writer's gender. She argues, for example, that Mary Shelley's traumatic experience of the death of her infant is reflected in *Frankenstein*. In *Madwoman in the Attic*, Gilbert and Gubar examined the subtexts of nineteenth-century novels by women and found that they reveal feelings of confinement and repression. The idea of a specifically "female" literature again posed the dilemma of essentialism versus androgyny. If women and men wrote differently, is it because of socialization? Or is there an innate difference? Is there even such a thing as a woman's sentence as Woolf suggested, a woman's writing? [42] These increasingly complex investigations of literature and language necessitated a more sophisticated and more widely-based theory. Feminist critics became increasingly interdisciplinary as they explored and defended their ideas, bringing concepts from linguistics, sociology, history, anthropology and psychology to this examination of the sexual politics of writing.

For the most part what has been described is the work of so-called American or Anglo-American feminists. In relation to the French school of criticism, Anglo-American critics appear relatively simplistic, little more than historical revisionists.[43] Largely ignoring the work of American feminists, French critics took the question of women's language and women's literature to increasingly abstract reaches. Critics like Julia Kristeva, Hélène Cixous, and Luce Irigaray — to name a few of the most prominent — focus on language above all else.[44] Their great discovery is *l'écriture feminine*, female or feminine writing. Opposite the ostensibly linear, rational, and dispassionate discourse "natural" to men, this is radically passionate, non-linear, non-sense, writing that conveys the rhythms and multiply erogenous sexuality of the female body. While this seemingly essentialist identification of the female with irrationality and even incoherence appears a great step backwards towards misogynistic definitions of woman as inferior to man, French feminist critics see it as a site of extreme disruption of the male hegemony, an occasion for massive subversion. This criticism is notoriously difficult. Much of it is written in artful and slippery puns and as such is not completely translatable, while to appreciate it in the original necessitates a very good knowledge of French. This style is playful and subversive, meant to demonstrate that the seeming hegemony of male-controlled language is a fallacy: language is inconstant, unfixable. Unlike American criticism, which generally is accessible to the interested reader, much of French criticism depends on neologisms and theory taken from diverse disciplines. Writing like Cixous', which attempts to embody *l'écriture feminine*, can be disconcerting to readers used to linear and dispassionate prose. The changes of mood, frank discussion of female sexuality, and loose conjoining of ideas can be both refreshing and bewildering.

That the French and American versions of feminism have been at times estranged is illustrated in feminist surveys of criticism that defend or deride either school. It is, for example, interesting to compare Toril Moi's pro-French *Sexual/Textual Politics* with Janet Todd's Anglo-American–based *Feminist Literary History*. Some critics have openly decried the effects of French style feminism as contributing to a sense of women's studies as both elitist and incomprehensible.[45] Over time, critics, of course, have managed to span the divide that separates these theoretical and political stances. French criticism remains for the most part untouched by the work of their Anglo-American counterparts. On the other hand, few American critics write without some recognition of French-originated theories. Gilbert and Gubar, for example, merge historical and sophisticated linguistic analysis in *No Man's Land*.[46] Le Guin, herself fluent in French, uses both.

After the Movement

As did feminism's earlier incarnations, the movement that emerged in the sixties would eventually lose momentum, for a wide variety of reasons. Inevitably, once some of its aims were achieved, even partially, the perceived need for continued activism waned. The movement's sometimes anti-male rhetoric, particularly from feminist essentialists, turned away some women and otherwise supportive men who found this stance objectionable or counterproductive. Racial tensions, particularly charges of solipsism against white feminists, contributed as well, as did the movement's core disagreement as to whether gender differences should be embraced or eliminated.

If the seventies were about rallying together, focusing on commonalities to build a force for change, the eighties shifted to an emphasis on difference, in particular on the effects of race, a factor largely overlooked by the predominantly white and middle-class theorists on the early front lines. In *Modern Feminist Thought*, her engaging overview of feminism, Imelda Whelehan discusses the forces that would eventually pull second wave feminism apart, at least on the academic front. She cites the friction between feminism as a political force and its role in the academy as theory not practice, and the effects of emphasis on differences of race, class and sexual preference. She writes, "There seemed to be a tendency to attempt 'ownership' of feminism by the hostile discrediting of another's perspective, particularly through invidious hierarchies of identity politics."[47] Susan Gubar, in "What Ails Feminist Criticism?," agrees with Whelehan that a focus on difference contributed to a decline in feminist studies. She describes personal attacks that sometimes had a racist aspect. The other side of this argument is represented by theorists like Gayatri Spivak, cited by Gubar as a perpetrator of racist insinuations, who argues that not only were women of color excluded from seventies-style feminism, but that it ignored the multiple effects of misogyny, racism, and poverty on Third World women.

> In the matter of race-sensitive analyses, the chief problem of American feminist criticism is its identification of racism as such with the constitution of racism in American. Thus, today I see the object of investigation to be not only the history of "Third World Women" or their testimony but also the production, through the great European theories, of the colonial object.[48]

21

The debates, however heated, could have indicated that the movement was strong enough to extend its theoretical boundaries; instead, they signaled the decline of women's studies as an academic pursuit. By 1997 in "The Impossibility of Women's Studies," Wendy Brown would question how effectively women's studies programs could be delivered in a university system that seemed to have moved beyond them. Indeed, she concludes the discipline has reached the end of its viability. Gubar, while not forecasting the demise of women's studies, nonetheless laments the growing use of arcane discourse by feminist academics. She contends that the rhetoric of high criticism has made feminism less accessible and more seemingly out of touch, robbing the movement of some of its political force and disaffecting the next generation of scholars and activists.

As much a factor as any, however, in the undermining of women's studies were the concerted efforts from anti-feminist groups to feed a public perception of feminism as both unneeded and extremist. Phyllis Schlafly, the public face of the fight against the Equal Rights Amendment, gave way to political commentators like Ann Coulter who would ridicule the feminist agenda. Even women who both benefited from feminism and in most ways embraced the basic feminist ideal of equality would disavow feminism, leading to the standard disclaimer, "I'm not a feminist, but..." Indeed, "feminist" has taken on the qualities of terms like "liberal" or "socialist," bandied about in the media as a pejorative. The 2008 vice presidential candidate Sarah Palin answered one interviewer in the affirmative when asked if she was a feminist, but in a later interview answered the same question with a refusal to be "labeled," doubtless heeding the advice of campaign managers fearful of alienating conservative voters. Ironically, Palin embodied some of the gains of feminism as a working mother, a governor who ran for vice president with a baby in her arms. But she also espoused views, on the right to life for example, which would be anathema to most avowed feminists. While the Bush administration used feminist rhetoric to publicize the plight of Afghan women and so rally support for war against the Taliban, under its leadership women saw a roll back of abortion rights and little progress on the issue of equal pay. In fact, as in the early 1960s, other social problems — the wars in Afghanistan and Iraq, gay rights, the economy, and immigration policy — claimed the energies of those who might otherwise have worked on behalf of women's rights.

The Waves

Does this mean that feminism has run its course? In a reframing of that metaphor, current feminists sometimes evoke the image of feminism as running in waves — a continuous presence that sometimes gathers intensity, pulls together energy, and creates change before dissipating temporarily. The first wave is commonly thought to have emerged at the turn of the twentieth century in the fight for women's voting rights. After that movement's decline, feminism was mostly out of the public eye until the mid-sixties as women involved in the civil rights and peace movements learned the value and means of mobilization and gathered forces to form the "second wave." Now, according to a good number of theorists,[49] a new wave of feminism has gained momentum, a "third wave" populated mainly by younger women who are moving on from the political and theoretical stances of their feminist mothers. The wave model is useful in evoking continuity, motion, power, and return. But it insinuates that the second wave of feminism, like the first, has passed. It is something of a false cognate or is at least an imprecise model; the first and second movements had more in common with each other — were more militant, more separatist, more divisive — than they have with the third, which is more widely encompassing, particularly in its embrace of diversity, femininity and sexuality. The wave model also fails to recognize earlier attempts to gain rights for women.

Stacy Gillis and Rebecca Munford argue against the metaphor of "waves" because it invites a sense of generational conflict, the third wave daughters against their second wave mothers. Yet this conflict certainly exists.[50] Third wave feminists are both the literal and figurative daughters of feminists. This generation came of age watching their mothers balance career and family, in households where men shared the work of child rearing. They watched *Buffy the Vampire Slayer* not *I Dream of Genie*, played basketball rather than cheered from the sidelines, and began to outnumber males in college. Astrid Henry writes that because of the social and political gains of the second wave, this generation was born into a world where women's rights were somewhat secured. "Third-wave feminists assume a certain level of individual and political freedom."[51] Their sense of security allows them to reopen some of the behavioral borders their mothers had fenced off. Thus the menswear business suit gave way to more traditionally feminine attire — as made notorious in the nineties by the television character Ally McBeal, a corporate lawyer in miniskirts and high

23

heels.[52] The grrrl power movement — embodied in bands like Hole and in the popular media where characters could be beautiful and yet fight like a man — stretched the boundaries of where power and sexuality meet.[53] Men are less like the "enemy" and more like partners. While second-wave mothers worry that the hard-won victories of the seventies are being subsumed in a haze of Victoria's Secret's ads, their daughters subtly but steadily co-opted, the daughters practice a different brand of feminism. The younger generation claims that their mothers are constraining them to a single model of womanhood; more than that, they argue that feminism has succumbed to caricature. Henry writes that this new generation finds collectivity not in "sisterhood" but in "a *shared generational stance* against second wave feminism."[54] This generational conflict is famously embodied in the rift between Alice Walker and her daughter Rebecca. Rebecca Walker is as ardent a supporter of equality as her mother, yet she takes a different tack, arguing that the world has changed and that feminism needs to keep up. Though she has not found a useful replacement, Walker rejects the term "feminism" altogether:

> the left is getting our collective ass kicked because of ... this kind of romantic, naïve attachment to movement narratives and aesthetics of 20 and 30 years ago. [...] I still do not believe that the use of the term Feminist galvanizes, unifies, or inspires at themoment. I think it did at one time and that was fantastic. But not now.[55]

Ironically, some of these third wave feminists feel patronized by their feminist elders. In "Generations, Academic Feminists in Dialogue," Diane Elam concurs that some:

> senior feminists insist that junior feminists be good daughters, defending the same kind of feminism their mothers advocated. Questions and criticisms are allowed, but only if they proceed from the approved brand of feminism. Daughters are not allowed to invent new ways of thinking and doing feminism for themselves.[56]

Rather than embrace this generation's insistence on its own paradigm, some feminists see a danger in letting up too soon, letting their collective guard down when so much injustice still exists and while women are losing rights that the second wave thought were secured. They see erosion by forces attempting to return to a pre-feminist state, not an evolution in feminist thought.

Post-Feminism

Other than the term "third wave," the other name widely given to this new generation of scholars and activists is "post-feminist," like its prefix-free counterpart, a highly embattled term.[57] "Post-feminism" has two generally used but diametrically opposed meanings. In academic circles, post-feminism is akin to "post-colonialism" or "postmodernism." "Post" connotes an evolution past the embedded term (colonialism, modernism, feminism), but it is still of and about that term. Post-colonialists, for example, do not assume that colonialism and its effects have vanished, but they recognize that a new order has emerged and warrants scrutiny and definition. In some arenas, however, the term "post-feminism" is worse than an insult. It denotes a weapon, wielded by forces on the right, created to end feminism itself: this is sometimes called "media post-feminism."[58] Angela McRobbie describes this kind of post-feminism as an active process by which feminist gains of the 1970s and 80s are undermined by elements of popular culture made to seem well-intended. Susan Faludi describes this phenomenon at length in her bestseller *Backlash: The Undeclared War Against American Women* (1991).

> The truth is that the last decade has seen a powerful counterassault on women's rights, a backlash, an attempt to retract that handful of small and hard-won victories that the feminist movement did manage to win for women. This counterassault is largely insidious: in a kind of pop-culture version of the Big Lie, it stands the truth boldly on its head and proclaims that the very steps that have elevated women's position have actually led to their downfall.[59]

This offensive takes as one premise that feminism, having achieved its goals, is no longer needed: women have achieved career equity and men take responsibility for child rearing. At the same time, feminism is painted as having made women unhappy, forcing them into overdoing it at work and at home, or paradoxically into having no home life at all. Under feminism, women over-focus on their careers and run down their biological clocks, leaving no chance of marriage or children. This critique of feminism comes from a variety of sources, including from within feminism itself. Imelda Whelehan points to work by popular theorists like Naomi Wolf (*The Beauty Myth*, 1991), Camille Paglia (*Sex, Art and American Culture*, 1992) and Katie Roiphe (*The Morning After*, 1994) who seem to be working from a feminist platform, but who blame feminism and women themselves for problems they encounter, from discrimination to date rape.

The media certainly has a central role in promoting the end of feminism. One of the earliest uses of the term post-feminism was in Susan Bolotin's 1982 article "Voices of the Post-Feminist Generation," published in *New York Times Magazine*.[60] Bolotin interviewed women who mostly agreed with the goals of feminism but who did not or would not self-identify as feminist because of the negative connotations attached to the term. As soon as the term "post-feminist" appeared in the popular press, its use exploded exponentially. Coppock, Hayden, and Richter argue: "Post feminism happened without warning. It seemed to arrive from nowhere. One minute there were feminisms, identified by their diverse political standpoints and their contrasting campaign strategies, the next ... it was all over."[61] Smelling blood, those invested in dismantling feminism, primarily the growing conservative movement of the 1990s, took the opportunity to declare its demise. Whether arguing for feminism's end or arguing, as did Paglia, that feminism was actually bad for women, these forces took to using the term "post-feminism" to mean that the movement was over. Yvonne Tasker and Diane Negra, in their introduction to the entertaining and insightful *Interrogating Post-Feminism*, write that the term post-feminism is "inherently contradictory, characterized by a double discourse that works to construct feminism as a phenomenon of the past" while simultaneously suggesting "that it is the very success of feminism that produces its irrelevance."[62]

To complicate the matter, the term is also used to describe a growing body of theory and practice representing a quite dissimilar view of feminism; it is often differentiated from "media post-feminism" by being called "academic post-feminism." Teresa Hubel concurs that the "post" in post-feminism indicates a "reaction to as well as a step further in a theoretical and activist movement. Far from proclaiming the death of patriarchy, this feminist post-feminism vigorously suggests that the old liberal and maternal tools can't work to vanquish the enemy."[63] In *Postfeminisms*, Ann Brooks argues for post-feminism as "a stage in the constant evolutionary movement of feminism... [its] 'coming of age'."[64] That feminism needs some realignment, repositioning, and even some new terms for itself is clear. Post-feminists argue that feminism needs reshaping not because it has met all its aims, but because it has not kept pace with the changes it has wrought in the world. Misha Kavka points out that as early as 1985 the pre-eminent feminist scholar Toril Moi used the term "post-feminism" in *Sexual/Textual Politics* to describe a movement past binaries of equality and difference feminism.[65] Donna Haraway's often quoted "Cyborg Manifesto" sketches out a plan for just such an advance. Haraway suggests taking the cyborg as a metaphor or paradigm for feminist reunification; as does the cyborg, feminism needs to integrate its many and sundry elements to form a working but not homogenized unit. According to Brooks, post-feminism is both porous and comprehensive, a "non-hegemonic feminism capable of giving voice to local, indigenous and post-colonial feminisms."[66] The post-feminist embrace extends as well to theories like post-structuralism, especially in rejecting singular, master narratives and instead seeking out the individual story, accepting multiple points of view. Unlike the storytelling of the early women's movement used in consciousness-raising sessions, the goal is not collectivity by seeing sameness, but instead by accepting difference. Along those lines, post-feminism rejects the essentialism inherent in much feminist theory. Taking lessons from gender studies, post-feminism is more male-inclusive, building as it does on the belief that gender lies upon a continuum. This inclusiveness extends to matters of personal choice as well, including those of work, dress, and sexual practices. Some choices post-feminists make might be considered regressive or capitulatory by second wave feminists, like choosing marriage and child rearing instead of a career.

Le Guin Among the Feminists

To some feminists, particularly in the heat of the 1980s, when feminism merged with multiculturalism, a white, middle-class, heterosexual, married woman like Le Guin had no place calling herself a feminist; she was too much a part of the power structure to have any objective distance from it. For such feminists, the more marginal one is — by class, race, sexual preference, sexual or physical victimization — the more truly feminist one could be.[67] Le Guin responded angrily to this exclusion:

> Some of the women I respect most, writing for publications that I
> depend on for my sense of women's solidarity and hope, continue to
> declare that it is "virtually impossible for a heterosexual woman to be a
> feminist," as if heterosexuality were heterosexism; and that social marginality ... "appears to be necessary" to form the feminist. Applying

27

these judgments to myself, and believing that as a woman writing at this point I have to be a feminist to be worth beans, I find myself, once again, excluded — disappeared.[68]

Though Le Guin recognized that her understanding of feminism must be differ from that of someone of a minority race, once she identified herself as a feminist, she refused to allow herself to be pushed out. Of course, the fact that it took her some time to discover her own absolute need for feminism may indeed derive from her upbringing and her earlier, unexamined comfort with the status quo. If Le Guin did not identify with the movement for some time, it could be because she did not "need" feminism in its early years. She was well educated and was a professional writer with a supportive partner, so she was insulated from many of the conditions that propelled women into the movement. Her gender, by her own report, was never an issue in terms of publication. Nonetheless, Le Guin's feminist awareness seems to have arisen in great part around her art. If we are to take as evidence her own writings on the subject, she came into feminist consciousness as she recognized that as a woman writer she was being censored, was in fact censoring herself.

Of course, the "woman question" was so pervasive in the 1970s that there is no way of knowing exactly how Le Guin came to feminism. Certainly, some part of Le Guin's conversion came as a result of the attacks against *The Left Hand of Darkness* and *The Dispossessed*. In answering her critics, she had to look to the possibility that she was upholding traditional literary standards. In retrospect, she realized that she was accepting literary traditions that excluded her personal truths and discouraged her awareness of that exclusion. As she explains in an early version of her essay "The Fisherwoman's Daughter,"

> By the luck of race, class, money, and health, and by the grace of parents, family, partner, and friends, I have lived freely as a woman writing. For years that personal freedom allowed me to ignore the degree to which my writing was shaped and controlled by an internalized masculinist judgments and assumptions. Even when subverting the conventions I disguised my subversions from myself. I did finally realize that I chose to work in such despised genres as science fiction, fantasy, juvenile, precisely because they were excluded from critical, academic, canonical sanction, leaving the artist free: but it was another ten years before I had the wits and guts to see and state that the exclusion of the genres from "literature" is unjustified and unjustifiable. And in my fiction until the mid-seventies, in the choice of subjects, heroic adven-

ture, high-tech futures, men in the halls of power, and in the dominance of male characters, I was a dutiful daughter of the patriarchate.
Didn't I have all my fathers to think back through?[69]

What did being "a dutiful daughter of the patriarchate" imply for her art?
This internalization of "masculine" values includes an emphasis on male
characters and heroic adventures and a tacit devaluation of women and
female spheres of activity. For Le Guin it also meant a degree of acceptance of traditional rules of narrative that preach conflict as the central narrative element and linearity as the proper narrative form. The degree to
which Le Guin herself actually wrote within this tradition is one focus of
Chapter One. She had internalized these rules to the extent that they constrain much of her early writing, though with some important subversions.

The rise of the women's movement and the evolution of feminist theory gave Le Guin tools for reassessment. She began to question not only
her adherence to rules of fiction decided upon by men, but also to the
underlying notion that a woman, if she writes at all, shouldn't write about
what she knows. Le Guin became deeply immersed in feminism in the
mid–1970s, when she underwent the feminist awakening that reshaped
her writing. She had by then already written the books that established
her reputation in the fields of science fiction and fantasy. Nonetheless, her
conversion had remarkable and visible effects on her writing. She began
to write more and more about the lives of women, to pay greater attention to issues of language, and to move further and further from standard
narrative techniques. Chapter Two details Le Guin's struggles to break free
from the literary models that had so firmly shaped her work. In Chapter
Three, I discuss her emergence as a confident feminist writer, looking at
works like *Always Coming Home* and *Searoad* to illustrate her full embrace
of *l'écriture féminine* as well as of essentialist, eco-feminist models of sustainability.

By the 1990s, however, Le Guin's writing had again begun to shift,
as indicated by her return to the Ekumenical worlds of her earlier science
fiction as well as to Earthsea. As discussed earlier in this Introduction,
with her return to these lands came a movement away from the high feminism of the 1980s. Whereas she had been writing almost exclusively about
women, in a sometimes experimental narrative style, she once again
included complex, sympathetic male characters and used more linear storytelling. At the same time, she takes more chances, in particular by ignoring the laws of physics in her sf. These stories emphasize strategies of

engagement, rapprochement, and as the title of a story collection from this time period suggests, finding "ways to forgiveness." Chapter Four, "Repairing the Sequence," examines this period and aligns Le Guin with post-feminism. I conclude with a discussion of Le Guin's most recent work: *Changing Planes*, her Western Shore series, and her masterpiece, *Lavinia*. In recent years, Le Guin has turned her attention to the most pressing issues of our time, in particular to the question of why we continue to make war.

CHAPTER ONE

Contrary Instincts

Ursula Le Guin once said that her intention was to "subvert as much as possible without hurting anyone's feelings."[1] As much as any of her words, this statement captures the contradiction that underlies much of this study and in particular of this chapter. Le Guin simultaneously practices good manners and challenges the social order. Her desire to be polite does wax and wane, as later chapters will show. Yet, from her beginnings as a writer through her first period of great success, she attempts to express her individual artistry and still adhere to fictional conventions. That she would be torn in this way seems to be a byproduct of her unusual upbringing, establishing as it did poles of "contrary instincts," Virginia Woolf's phrase for the social forces that pull women in opposite directions.[2] This is evident not only in her personal life, where she balanced homemaking with writing, but in her literary efforts as well. Schooled in a decidedly male, European-oriented literary tradition that favored the realistic over the fantastic, she made a name for herself by writing in the "despised, marginal genres"[3] of science fiction and fantasy, bringing skill and precision to genres not always known for high literary standards. Science fiction and fantasy, while seemingly unconventional, are highly codified, offering on the one hand the possibility of creativity and on the other specific rules of engagement and sometimes hide-bound traditions. At the time of Le Guin's early success, the genres were far less varied than they are now. Even years later she would say that "most science fiction and fantasy is timid and reactionary in its social inventions, fantasy clinging to feudalism, science fiction to military and imperial hierarchy."[4] Despite these comments, Le Guin takes the genres quite seriously. Her early essays, published in *The Language of the Night* (1979), argue for their merit and psychological effectiveness, even their social necessity.

Le Guin's quick ascendancy in science fiction and fantasy brought

31

with it the attention of the academic community, for the most part from specialists who began producing critical essays. Initially, their reaction was generally positive, with critics both unraveling her core themes and motifs and lauding her style and characterization. The eminent critic Robert Scholes, for example, praising her literary skills, described her as "The Good Witch of the West."[5] With time, changes in the academic landscape and bolder attempts on Le Guin's part, the tenor of the attention changed, especially with the publication of her science fiction novels *The Left Hand of Darkness* and *The Dispossessed*. Because they experiment with gender and social structure and probably because they are so popular, they became the center of a storm of negative critical attention, as discussed later in this chapter. Even her much honored fantasy series would undergo scrutiny. Critics argued that Le Guin's work of this period is male-oriented, conservative and reductive.[6] It does show a strong tendency to embrace the traditional: there are few female characters, some of those are stereotypical, and there is an unquestioning embrace of the male quest motif. However, while Le Guin does build on the traditional bases of science fiction and fantasy and later came to disparage her own non-feminist adherence to genre rules, even in this early work she was less in thrall to the masculine forms than is frequently claimed. Even now, she is faulted for what she did not do while her accomplishments are overlooked. An examination of the tradition-bound elements of her fiction and of those that presage and/or predate her avowed feminist conversion shows some reorienting of the conventions, making very masculine literary traditions amenable to her unique sensibility. Le Guin manages, long before the renewal of the women's movement, to find the feminist edges, points of entry into a new paradigm for these genres.

A Good, Germanic Girl

The daughter of author Theodora Kroeber and anthropologist Alfred Kroeber, Le Guin was born October 21, 1929, and was raised in the liberal-intellectual milieu surrounding the University of California, Berkeley campus.[7] Theodora Kroeber's biography of her husband, *Alfred Kroeber: A Personal Configuration*, tells of a rich life marked by the presence of "artists, professors, poets, intellectuals... A Far West sort of Greenwich Village."[8] Le Guin herself recalls the atmosphere as "high powered in a kind of easygoing way."[9] Her father was an originator of the modern study of anthropology; he spent much of his professional life documenting native customs, languages, and stories, particularly those of the California nations. His bibliography includes over five hundred titles, among them the long standard textbook *Anthropology* (1923, 1948) and the *Handbook of the Indians of California* (1925), which remains a fundamental source of information on Native Californians. Kroeber taught at the University of California, Berkeley and was instrumental in building the university's Anthropology department and in establishing its museum. His biography reads like a *Who's Who* of the early twentieth century intelligentsia: he counted among his friends and colleagues Robert Oppenheimer, Franz Boaz, Erik Erikson, Clyde Kluckhohn, Teilhard de Hardin, Carl Jung, and Julian Huxley.[10] Le Guin's mother, Theodora, was equally remarkable, both in her professional accomplishments and in her personal life. Her daughter describes her as a personification of the Victorian "Angel in the House," a self-sacrificing woman who put her family's needs above her own. Her biography seems to confirm this.[11] Kroeber earned her Master's Degree in Psychology at Berkeley in 1920 before entering her first marriage. She returned to Berkeley in 1923, a widow with two young sons, to do further graduate work, this time in anthropology. In 1925 she married Alfred Kroeber, himself a widower, and put off her own writing until her children were grown. In her fifties, she returned to her own work, writing poetry, novels, children's books, and several major works of anthropology and folklore. The first of these, *The Inland Whale* (1959), retells stories of Native Californians. It brought her immediate acclaim and led to her writing the book for which she is best known, *Ishi in Two Worlds* (1961). *Ishi* was a bestseller and has undergone numerous printings and been translated into nine languages. It is a standard text in anthropology, and in a modified format is a children's classic. Kroeber also spent a year as a Regent of the University of California. Like her husband, she continued to write until she died, in 1979.

While it is impossible to know how her remarkable parents specifically affected Le Guin, some of the impressions they made are fairly direct.[12] Her father's habit of writing several hours nearly every day taught her from very early on that writing was something that adults could respectably do. He showed her the value of openness to other cultures and shared with her his interest in the *Tao Te Ching*. Her parents put no restrictions on what she and her brothers read and discussed; most importantly, perhaps, they made no gender distinctions between Le Guin and her male siblings. The Kroebers' high regard for the academic life is manifested in their children's accomplishments: Le Guin's three brothers all received Ph.D.s and Le Guin, like her mother, received a master's degree, did advanced graduate work, and married an academic. Her father's nearly life-long affiliation with the university and her mother's setting aside her work for the sake of her children must have demonstrated to Le Guin a degree of comfort with conventional ideas of family and education. At the same time that they presented the model of middle-class values, Le Guin's parents lived genuinely unconventional lives. Alfred Kroeber, raised in New York, chose the still-wild West over the Eastern establishment, at one point turning down an offer to chair the Department of Anthropology at Columbia. His work as an anthropologist took him into some very unusual circumstances, including long research stints with coastal and desert Native Americans. And Theodora Kroeber was not the typical Angel in the House. As a girl she lived in Telluride, Colorado, a raw mining town, and she seems to have retained throughout her life some of the frontier spirit. While she strongly disapproved of the women's liberation movement of the sixties and seventies, she did not impose upon her daughter a sense of gender-defined limitations.[13] She also made some unconventional life choices. It was in the traditional manner for her to marry Kroeber, twenty years her senior, but far less socially acceptable, even in the late 1960s, for her to marry John Quinn, a man 43 years younger than she.[14] And while the Kroebers associated with some of the major intellectuals of the time, their Native Californian friends were as integral a part of Le Guin's upbringing. The Kroebers tend to be remembered in connection with the Yana Indian known as Ishi, who became a cultural phenomenon in 1911 when he emerged from the California foothills where he had lived in hiding. The so-called "last wild Indian," Ishi was befriended by Alfred Kroeber; until Ishi died of tuberculosis in 1915, they worked to record the Yana language. Despite the power of her biography of Ishi, Theodora Kroeber never met him and neither did Le Guin. Rather, the family's Native Californian friends, the ones Le Guin calls her "honorary uncles," were Juan Dolores, a Papago, and Captain Robert Spott, a Yurok. Their deep influence on Le Guin is evident in much of her work, but most clearly in *Always Coming Home*.[15]

Her parents' leanings into and away from the conventional is a pattern mirrored in Le Guin's own activities. She describes herself as having been "a nice serious little Germanic girl, a good girl" who enjoyed working hard.[16] This is reflected in her distinguished academic career. After graduating Phi Beta Kappa from Radcliffe in 1951, she immediately entered graduate school. Following her father's advice, she chose an academic path so she could support herself while writing, free from the demands of editors. At Columbia University, she studied French and Italian literature, specializations deliberately removed from the writing she was doing. She hoped thus to avoid being influenced by what she read. Despite the calculation this implies, she describes the period as a "long and loving immersion. I found I had an affinity with writers like Ariosto and Tasso, at least to the extent of loving their poetry."[17] Her academic performance was outstanding; in 1952, she received her master's degree and the next year was awarded a Fulbright to study the medieval poet Jehan Le Maire de Belges. On the crossing to France, she met Charles Le Guin, a graduate student in history who was also on a Fulbright scholarship. They married later that year, allowing her to rethink her plans; the Ph.D. was no longer a necessity and Le Guin ended her academic career.

Instead, she wrote and worked while her husband finished his Ph.D. and began his own career. In 1957 the Le Guins had the first of their three children and Ursula combined writing with the work of a housewife and mother. Read superficially, this seems utterly conventional: the woman abandons her academic career, puts her husband through graduate school, and stays home to raise their children. Such a facile interpretation misses both the practicality of Le Guin's decision to leave academia to pursue her writing and the partnership the Le Guins' marriage has clearly been.[18] Moreover, no matter how supportive the partner, taking care of children all day and writing at night could not have been easy. Le Guin was pursuing her career despite the then-prevailing expectation that a married woman should be a full-time mother and housekeeper, not someone who put the children to bed then went to her study to write novels.

The Tradition and Mrs. Le Guin

It is remarkable that Le Guin pursued a writing career at all, given that the academy's accepted works were mostly written by men and that there were few women writers on whom to model a career. Even at Radcliffe, then a women's college, and most certainly at Columbia, Le Guin was schooled in the "Great Books" tradition as defined in literary journals like *Scrutiny* and studies such as F. O. Matthiessen's *American Renaissance*. The standards established by the New Criticism became the basis for judging texts. The "best" fiction, poetry, and drama were kept alive by being anthologized, taught, and written about, while other works faded into obscurity. Le Guin describes the qualities of this canonized writing with some sarcasm in "The Carrier Bag Theory of Fiction," in which she cites the hero, linear narrative, and conflict as the central elements of "great" fiction.[19] In "Text, Silence, Performance," she extends her criticism to academic claims for the superiority of the written text over oral presentation.[20] Men, she argues, have decided how literary greatness is judged, and they have done so according to what their experience tells them is right.[21] That experience is one-sided, and the rules allow for no other points of view or ways of telling stories. If the rules are bent, as they sometimes are, the author or at least the protagonist is usually male. Thus Joyce was accepted as a great author while Woolf was still being dismissed as a minor novelist.[22] But Le Guin's negative assessments of canonical norms would come later in her career. Earlier, Le Guin was less questioning of the male-oriented literary tradition. She read and studied the novelists and poets of Europe and the United States. In 1976 she listed her influences as "Shelley, Keats, Wordsworth, Leopardi, Hugo, Rilke, [Edward] Thomas and Roethke in poetry. Dickens, Tolstoy, Turgenyev, Chekhov, Pasternak, the Brontës, Woolf, E.M. Forster in prose."[23] Elsewhere she adds Yeats to the list.[24]

Though Le Guin is not well known for her poetry, it was to this specific literary form that she began seriously applying herself. And other than an early academic book review, her first publication was in poetry. Her poetry, both as published in collections like *Wild Angels, Hard Words, Wild Oats and Fireweed, In the Red Zone, Going Out with Peacocks* and *Incredible Good Fortune,* and as embedded in her stories, deserves more critical attention than it has received.[25] But, as Le Guin herself stated, it took her a long time to find her voice as a poet.[26] The poems are nonetheless a fascination for the Le Guin scholar, particularly as they are the most personal reflection of the author that we have. While we cannot take them literally, tracking their subject matter does offer insight into Le Guin's personal and professional maturation, almost acting as developmental markers. Early poems, for example, consider the deaths of parents while her recent poems deal with her own aging and mortality. They also offer a record of various historical events, from the eruption of Mt. St. Helens, which she watched from the windows of her home in Portland, to the Tawana Brawley incident and the Iraq War. They are particularly fascinating for the insight they provide into her artistic process. She seems to work out intellectual problems in her poetry, as we shall see in Chapter Two when she hits a stopping point artistically. This is perhaps why her poetry, in particular her early work, does not stand out. Rather than the deft polish of her prose, her poems tend to be rawer, less universalized. That she both reads and writes poetry avidly is clear not only from her lists of influences but from allusions lightly scattered through her fiction. Her references can be fairly overt, as in titles like "Vaster than Empires and More Slow" or in quotations from Henry Vaughan and A. E. Housman. One poem in *Wild Angels* is written to the ghost of Robinson Jeffers. For the most part, though, Le Guin generally alludes more subtly and playfully, allowing the reader a sense of resonance rather than a specific reference. She will, for example, casually nod to Yeats by noting that something must be "changed, changed utterly" or to Marvell: "you can take your galaxies and roll them up into a ball and throw them into a trashcan."[27]

Le Guin first published as a poet in 1959, when "Folksong from the Montayna Province" appeared in *The Prairie Poet*. This poem, set in Orsinia, is an early indication of Le Guin's gift for inventing a cultural history for her imaginary lands. Over the next two years, ten more poems would appear in literary magazines and journals. These poems are fairly conventional in theme, voice, and structure, ignoring both the then current confessional style and Ginsberg's exuberant line. "On Sappho's Theme," published in 1960, is a good example:

> Evening brings home all things,
> Swallow on downward wings.
> Child that comes and clings:
> All things come home from far
> With dusk and evening star.
>
> Twilight in grey and brown
> Passes through fields and town,
> The single star sinks down.
> Only you will not come,
> With dusk or morning, home.[28]

While presaging Le Guin's marriage of concise, rhythmic lines to concrete image and universal theme, the poem misses the power of her fiction, in particular her deft characterization and use of dialogue. In 1975 her first chapbook, *Wild Angels*, appeared though the long poem that opens the book, "Coming of Age," was written in 1961, about the time of her first publications. "Coming of Age" treats the poet's reaction to her father's death, her bereavement and disillusionment with the adult world into which she is thrust. She learns that the world is much smaller than it had seemed to her as a child. The safe towers of her childhood, marking the kingdom of her father, have collapsed. Her brothers, "the young kings," will inherit, but she will not. Ultimately she discovers that she must rebuild the world for herself using what she has learned from her father, in particular the openness or "quantity" of his mind. The poem brings to mind Yeats's blending of images, artifacts, scenes of children, and landscapes of mountains, towers, falcons, and stars. The chapbook's opening invocation to "the wild angels of the open hills" also recalls Ranier Maria Rilke's *Duino Elegies*. His philosophy towards death and his spare, image-rich lines have greatly influenced Le Guin. Like the affirming *Elegies*, "Coming of Age" is about understanding death as the necessary counterpart of life.

When she turned to fiction, Le Guin took a characteristic approach, writing within the stylistic norms of the canonical writers she admired, but making up her own country. Playing on her quasi–European name, she called this place Orsinia, and it became the setting for four unpublished novels and a number of short stories.[29] The step was a liberating one: "as soon as I began work in Orsinia, I realized I didn't have to imitate Tolstoy. I had created a place I could write about in my own terms; I could make up just enough of the rules to free my imagination and my observations."[30] Culturally, historically and geographically, Orsinia seems very much like a Central European country. Le Guin has said that it is probably most like Czechoslovakia, of which she became aware when it was first invaded in 1947.[31] Despite the political concern this indicates, Le Guin's invention was essentially a distancing device. She created Orsinia not to call attention to the plight of a besieged nation, but for purposes of artistic freedom. By locating Orsinia somewhere in Europe, she was able to establish a familiar context for her invented place without being constrained to accuracy.

Even if she was no longer imitating Tolstoy, her Orsinian work clearly bears the influence of the writers she so loved. For example, she describes herself as having grown up in the Tolstoyian school of making the writing transparent, beautiful without distracting the reader.[32] Though Le Guin's prose style was still evolving, even her early work displays her trademark lucidity, so that we follow the story without remarking the technique. From novelists like Dickens and Tolstoy she seems too to have derived her facility for characterization. Thematically, her work also reflects the nineteenth-century novels Le Guin read so avidly. The Orsinian novel *Malafrena*, which she began soon after college but did not finish until much later, is "written like a nineteenth-century novel because that is largely what I was reading, particularly the English and Russians."[33] This book, a historical romance alternating scenes of idealistic political activity in the city with the sleepy, reflective life of a country estate, is in fact very reminiscent of *War and Peace*.

Though she spent much time in Orsinia in her apprentice days, only one story from that period made its way into print before Le Guin had established a reputation for herself.[34] That story, "An die Musik," about the necessity for music in a chaotic world, was Le Guin's first published fiction (in 1961).[35] This and many other of her Orsinian stories begun or substantially written during this period are now collected in *Orsinian Tales* (1976). Though they were revised and published after she had had many more years of experience in her profession, the stories are evidence of Le Guin's relative sophistication and accomplishment in fiction while still in her twenties. Set in an imaginary country, they are nonetheless written in a realistic mode and are fairly conventional in theme. Many turn on the historical possibilities of the setting, from feudalism through the long history of invasions by the Habsburgs, the Nazis, the Communists. However, they are arranged non-chronologically so we do not get a sense of historical change, rather of the sameness of the human condition. As repression, fascism, war, revolt and economic hardship swirl around these characters, they have only each other. In most cases, they hover on the brink of change, the course of their lives hanging on the choices to be made.

Interestingly, a number of strong women inhabit Orsinia. They are generally better able than Le Guin's men to make difficult decisions, to choose the hard road (literally, in several cases). Thus in "Conversations at Night," it is the young woman Lisha who has the strength that her lover, blinded in the First World War, needs. She convinces him to escape the emotional and economic devastation of the slums for a life elsewhere. Similarly, in "A Week in the Country," Bruna shows Stefan the necessity of holding on after her brother, Stefan's friend, is mistaken for a rebel and killed. There are also several mother figures representing home, warmth, comfort. But the stories are still about men. Of eleven, nine are told through a male protagonist; even in "The Lady of Moge," obstensibly about a strong woman who is thwarted by the men in her life, the main character is a man. Moreover, opposite the strong and life-giving women are a number of neurotic females who feed off the strengths of their husbands and sons, draining them of life. In "An die Musik," a gifted composer is unable to work at his art, so weighed down is he by his responsibility for his nervous, sickly wife, bedridden mother, and three children; in "The Road East," a young man dreams of escaping from a mother who lives in a fantasy world, unable to face a blighted reality. Thematically, *Orsinian Tales* offers the traditional fare of the short story: "Ile Forest," framed and plotted like a James story, considers the possibility that a man can be a murderer and not be guilty for it; "The Lady of Moge" leads up to a Joycean moment of devastating epiphany. Despite having been published in 1976, by which time Le Guin had begun to read avidly in feminist theory, they still seem the handiwork of an author well-steeped in a masculine tradition. These are lovely, sometimes haunting pieces, but other than being set in a make-believe country, they take few stylistic or thematic chances.

As Le Guin would discover, following canonical conventions did not ensure publication. Although the work was deeply rooted in the literary tradition, its setting in an invented country may explain why the writing was routinely returned with the comment that it seemed "remote."[36] Neither written in the straight realism of the times, nor fitting into a generic niche, the work probably struck publishers as difficult to market. Despite her publication in literary journals, Le Guin was interested in both a wider readership and a paycheck. She discovered that she had yet to meet one of the two criteria by which publishers judged work: "You must either fit a category, or 'have a name,' to publish a book in America. As the only way I was ever going to achieve Namehood was by writing, I was reduced to fitting a category."[37] It was only when Le Guin wrote in the easily identifiable genre of science fiction that she began to sell books. Her early science fiction novels brought her to the attention of an editor who asked her to write for a young adult audience, thus the classic Earthsea series was born. Having found a way into the market, she quickly hit her stride, setting out on a remarkable writing spree that produced ten books, two short story collections and an essay collection before she took the hiatus described in Chapter Two.

"Despised, Marginalized Genres"

Le Guin would come to disparage the literary world's reliance on genre distinctions, particularly the way that some classifications like science fiction, fantasy, and young adult not only oversimplify but stigmatize the work as not "literature." Yet she has written a number of important essays defining and defending these genres. Understanding how Le Guin works within but still subverts the traditions associated with each type requires some discussion of their ground rules and of how they fit into the broader literary tradition. An initial difficulty, however, is finding any kind of critical agreement not only on what constitutes the genres but also on what to call them.[38] While they are often grouped under the umbrella term "the fantastic," that classification is less encompassing than might be expected; luckily, it is standard practice to break this rather unwieldy term into fantasy and science fiction — as is done in this study. It is then possible to subdivide these nearly endlessly into specific types, for example the paranormal romance, sword and sorcery, steam punk, first contact, utopian, which is not done here.

In the widest sense, "the fantastic" includes many varieties of literature, the common thread being the incorporation of elements that signal a departure from consensus reality. Ironically, critics have sometimes qualified "the fantastic" in a way that excludes most science fiction and fantasy. A major work on the genre, Tzvetan Todorov's *The Fantastic*, defines the fantastic text as incorporating "hesitation."[39] The reader remains unclear, hesitates, about whether events have natural or supernatural explanations, as in the classic James novella *The Turn of the Screw*. Science fiction and fantasy both generally depend on the reader's full embrace of the world the piece depicts; it is not a matter of whether the world exists but of what happens there. Only in a handful of Le Guin's works, such as *Always Coming Home*, "Buffalo Gals Won't You Come Out Tonight?" and *Changing Planes*, does the question linger of whether these events are "really" happening or are only taking place in the mind of the narrator. What we usually call the "fantasies" of Lewis, Tolkien, and Le Guin, Rosemary Jackson would call "faery" or romance literature. Unlike stories set in Middle Earth, Jackson argues, "Fantasy is nothing to do with inventing another non-human world; it is not transcendental. It has to do with inverting elements of this world."[40] For Jackson this inversion is subversive, allowing socially unacceptable notions to find expression. "Faery," conversely, defuses anti-social desire and is thus conservative and nostalgic rather than subversive. Todorov and Jackson base their conceptions of the fantastic on more "literary" works by authors like Gautier, Maupassant and Poe. Fantasy and science fiction, always struggling for academic acceptance, are thus ostracized from what might seem a natural, and somewhat reputable, classification.

Perhaps for this reason, science fiction and fantasy critics have concerned themselves with coining new and more inclusive names for their genres. Robert Scholes uses "fabulation" to mean fiction that presents a world "radically discontinuous with this one, yet which confronts it in some way."[41] Samuel R. Delany prefers "speculative fiction," a term that includes both science fiction and fantasy.[42] In discussing her own work, Le Guin applies the broadest standard, saying her writing is mainly "fantasy." From age twelve, she recalls, "I was writing fantasy, and I never wrote anything else."[43] Le Guin sets no real limits on what the fantastic includes. For example, she clearly sees science fiction as coming under the general heading of fantasy, a category in which she includes Mary Shelley's *Frankenstein or The Modern Prometheus*, routinely cited as the earliest science fiction story. Le Guin calls Frankenstein "the first great modern fantasy."[44] Le Guin also argues passionately for the value of this literature, as she did in her acceptance speech for the National Book Award:

> At this point, realism is perhaps the least adequate means of understanding or portraying the incredible realities of our existence. [...] The fantasist, whether he uses the ancient archetypes of myth and legend, or the younger ones of science and technology, may be talking as seriously as any sociologist — and a good deal more directly — about human life as it is lived, and as it might be lived, and as it ought to be lived.[45]

For Le Guin, fantasy is the only literature that can really speak to our times.[46] She clearly includes both warlocks and spaceships here, though critics tend to separate such elements into different genres. For most critics, fantasy deals with internal landscapes built on myth and archetype, while science fiction helps us cope with what is happening in the physical world. Despite fantastic trappings like faster-than-light spaceships, extraterrestrials, and cloning, science fiction deals with what could conceivably become our reality. Delany offers a classic destinction: science fiction depicts what has not yet happened while fantasy depicts what cannot — due to known physical laws — ever happen.[47] Emphasizing place more than probability, Le Guin's considers fantasy to inhabit "inner lands," while science fiction inhabits "outer lands." For Le Guin, fantasy is about the journey inward, into the psyche and toward self-knowledge. In her essay "The Child and the Shadow," she says that the best fantasies "speak from the unconscious to the unconscious, in the language of the unconscious — symbol and archetype."[48] Unlike science fiction, which should be about characters, fantasy is about archetypes. Science fiction operates by moving outward, extrapolating metaphorically about the human condition. She says, "The original and instinctive movement of fantasy is, of course, inward ... science fiction [is] a modern, intellectualized, extraverted form of fantasy."[49] In her own early work, the short stories and three Hainish novels she published before she became a well-known writer, Le Guin often mixed fantastic elements — feudal lords, elves, winged cats, talking boars — with those of science fiction — faster-than-light starships, time dilation, and leagues of planets. By writing the science fiction novel *The Left Hand of Darkness* and the fantasy novel *A Wizard of Earthsea* back-to-back, she succeeded in separating the two.[50]

Science fiction and fantasy both have long literary roots, particularly in the romance tradition. James Bittner goes so far as to state that the romance is the typical form of most of Le Guin's work, her principle narrative tool for marrying opposites and thus transcending conflict.[51] According to Northrop Frye, "the conventions of prose romance show little change over the course of the centuries, and conservatism of this kind is the mark of a stable genre."[52] These conventions can easily be fitted to Le Guin's fiction of this period. Romance emphasizes the hero's journey, usually the hero's quest for self-knowledge. The struggle or conflict often involves an externalization of an element of the self. Thus Ged in the first Earthsea book must track down and merge with his nemesis or shadow, his own dark side that has taken form. Similarly, Genly Ai of *The Left Hand of Darkness* must come to terms with the feminine part of himself that is externalized in the man/woman Estraven. While the moment of revelation is never again as obvious in Le Guin's fiction as it is in *Rocannon's World*, when Rocannon is given the gift of insight on top of a mountain, it is central to most of her early fiction. These romance conventions epitomize much of what Le Guin would later disparage; they focus on a hero and his conflict, leaving women peripheral. But romances emphasize journey, a typical Le Guin trope. In her introduction to *Rocannon's World*, Le Guin says that circularity is not the natural form of the novel: "the normal, run-of-the-mill novel begins in one 'place' and ends somewhere else, following a pattern — line, zigzag, spiral, hopscotch, trajectory — which has what the circle in its perfection does not have: direction."[53] In Le Guin's fiction, rather than return home, the hero generally learns how to accept an alien place as home. Even when the hero does return to his beginning, as in *The Dispossessed*, Le Guin provides alternating time frames, so that the reader moves back and forth, constructing and reconstructing history. Even while using a long-defined, male-oriented tradition, then, she makes the most of its subversive potential.

In the Perilous Realm

J. R. R. Tolkien uses the term "faerie" in a way that seems clearly to mean what I am here calling "fantasy." In his essay "On Fairy-Stories," he argues that fairy stories are about

> Faerie, the realm or state in which fairies have their being. Faerie contains many things besides elves and fays, and besides dwarfs, witches, trolls, giants, or dragons: it holds the seas, the sun, the moon, the sky; and the earth, and all things that are in it: tree and bird, water and stone, wine and bread, and ourselves, mortal men, when we are enchanted.[54]

Fantasy at its best is "about the adventures of men in the Perilous Realm."[55] Tolkien goes on to say that faerie may most nearly be translated as Magic; later in the essay he also calls this "enchantment." He links faerie to fantasy by stating that "Fantasy, the making or glimpsing of Other-worlds, was the heart of the desire of Faerie."[56] Tolkien's is an early and important study of fantasy; in it he posits both a long history for the genre and an argument for its merit. Against those who would call it suspect or childish, he argues that it is a "natural human activity. It certainly does not destroy or even insult Reason; and it does not either blunt the appetite for, nor obscure the perception of, scientific verity."[57] Instead, fairy stories provide consolation through a happy ending and a revisioning of reality, a lifting of the reader out of a normal sense of the world. As with romance, the reader is transported with the protagonist to that moment of vision from enchanted ground where all contradictions disappear. Fantasy does not offer escape from the real world but a fresh perspective from which to view it.

Beyond its capacity for helping readers cope with their lives, fantasy restores some sense of wonder to a world where reason has triumphed.

Colin Manlove describes fantasy as "evoking wonder and containing a substantial and irreducible element of the supernatural."[58] According to Le Guin's brother, the literary critic Karl Kroeber, fantasy arose from the culture of the Enlightenment, when the fantastic was excluded from civilized life: "Romantic fantasy celebrates the magical in a society for which magic had become only benighted superstition."[59] Nonetheless, many critics see fantasy as politically or aesthetically conservative. Manlove, for example, writes that "fantasy is a profoundly conservative genre. It preserves the status quo, looks to the past to sustain the nature and values of the present."[60] His remarks echo those of Rosemary Jackson about the marvelous suppression of anti-social desires. If the genre is so conservative, could Le Guin write any fantasy that did more than reinforce long prevalent values?

Le Guin's love of fantasy goes back to her childhood when she read freely in her parents' collections of legend, fairy tale and myth. She was partial to Norse myth, which figures sometimes clearly and more often subtly in much of her early work. Her first story, written when she was nine, was fantasy. It was, she says, "about a man persecuted by evil elves."[61] At age twelve, she read Lord Dunsany's *A Dreamer's Tales*, and she remembers the moment of reading the first page as pivotal. Dunsany's unabashed use of the fairy story taught her that people still made up myths, that it was even respectable for an adult to do so. The experience helped her to discover what she calls "her native country," the inner lands of the imagination.[62] Le Guin herself began to write fantasy long before its resurgence of popularity in the seventies. What her early fantasy was like is apparent in *Cobbler's Rune* and *Solomon Leviathan's 931st Trip Around the World*, two early pieces.[63] Written when she was nineteen or twenty, they are somewhat unpolished but nevertheless engaging in their enthusiasm and playful use of language. Written in a style reminiscent of Kipling's *Just So Stories*, they feature talking animals that embark on quests and two common characters, a boa constrictor and her friend, a giraffe. *Rune* is the story of a young horse, Cobbler, who saves his nation from an attack. *Solomon* tells of the snake and giraffe and their quest to find the horizon. The stories take a diversity of elements from the fantasy tradition: odd creatures who seemed inspired by Carroll and Baum, pegasi, runes, Birds of Ill Omen, the Lady of the Unicorns, the whale who swallowed Jonah and Pinnochio. Le Guin obviously did not find fantasy restrictive; in fact, she makes use of the comic inventiveness fantasy allows its lighter subjects. The stories give us a hint of the unbridled Le Guin, the one who had not been inculcated with the "rules" of fantasy. *Solomon*, in particular, seems an early example of the "carrier bag" theory of fiction, mixing an indeterminate quest with a hodge podge of characters.

But Le Guin's reputation in fantasy is built on her superior series set in the archipelago world of Earthsea. The books, ostensibly for young adults but enjoyed by older readers as well, are comparable in quality and likely endurance to the fantasy works of J. R. R. Tolkien and C. S. Lewis. Le Guin says that she did not invent Earthsea but found it: "I am not an engineer, but an explorer. I discovered Earthsea."[64] The discovery came about as Le Guin wrote several short stories, two of which appeared early in her career and a third which she never submitted for publication.[65] In these stories she began exploring the archipelago, working out the rules of the magic so central to the Earthsea way of life. When in 1967 a publisher of children's books asked Le Guin to write a book for young adults, she returned to the archipelago and began to expand what she already knew of it. The resulting novels — *A Wizard of Earthsea* (1968), *The Tombs of Atuan* (1970), and *The Farthest Shore* (1972) — were billed as a trilogy, and follow the central character, Ged, from childhood into old age. For years the series seemed complete; readers had little reason to expect more, although in 1990 Le Guin published *Tehanu: The Last Book of Earthsea*. Given that book's subtitle, the two Earthsea books that appeared in 2001, *The Other Wind* and *Tales from Earthsea*, were a pleasant surprise for Earthsea's many fans. The focus in this chapter is on the original trilogy, in particular on how it fits into the fantasy tradition and where, if at all, Le Guin hints at subversions.

The trilogy draws deeply from the romance tradition. The plots of all three involve quests, and the first and last books revolve around long sea voyages. In *A Wizard of Earthsea* we first meet Ged, the gifted mage who is the spool around which all three novels are wound. This is the story of his youth and his initiation into the world of magic. The book, Le Guin says, is "about coming of age."[66] As a young apprentice, full of promise and pride but not much wisdom, Ged raises up and releases into the world a terrible spirit. When he realizes he cannot escape it, he gathers his courage to chase down and defeat it. When he finally confronts the spirit, he recognizes it as part of himself and rather than defeat it, he merges with it, accepting it as a darker side of himself. The story is remarkably similar to the drama of the self and the shadow that Jung describes, though

Le Guin did not read Jung until after she had written these three Earthsea books.[67]

The Tombs of Atuan is a very different book. Its protagonist is Tenar, who, reminiscent of the Dalai Lama, is identified by her birthdate as the reincarnation of the Priestess of the Tombs of Atuan. Taken from her family at an early age, she is raised in a barren desert enclave, a religious cloister. There she becomes Arha, "the eaten one," ceremonially given to the dark powers that rule that place. While clearly a site of great power, the enclave is neglected by the God-Kings that rule Tenar's country, Karego-At. Though the book is Tenar's story, the early focus on her shifts when she encounters Ged in the underground chamber over which she presides. He is the first man she can remember seeing. In search of half the Ring of Erreth-Akbe, Ged violates the sanctity of the underground cavern, and invites the wrath of the dark powers and their priestess. Despite her fascination with him, Tenar imprisons Ged in the mazes adjoining the cavern; in time, though, her innate compassion leads her to bring him food and water. His magical powers and what he tells her of the world challenge her belief in her way of life. Just as she has saved his life, he restores her true name to her and in this sense helps her to rediscover herself. Having defied the dark powers, she must flee them. With his magic and her knowledge of the labyrinth, they escape the powers that in their wrath bring about an earthquake and the collapse of the tunnels.[68] Le Guin claims that the book's theme is "Sex ... more exactly, you could call it a female coming of age. Birth, rebirth, destruction, freedom, are the themes."[69]

In what was for some time the last Earthsea book, *The Farthest Shore*, we meet Arren, the young man who will become King of Earthsea. The story, according to its author, "is about death," or more precisely about the necessity of accepting death as a part of life. Ged is now middle-aged, and as the Archmage of Earthsea, he is a man of legendary stature. Yet something is amiss in Earthsea; magic goes awry, and people of magical power seem to have lost their sense of morality, of the proper uses of magic. The world is out of balance. When Arren comes to the island of the wizards seeking aid, Ged recognizes in him the man who will fill the long empty throne of Earthsea. He asks Arren to accompany him on a voyage of discovery. What they find, after many days at sea, is that the wizard Cob has learned how to defy death; he has discovered a way to return to life from the dry land, the place of death. Ged and Arren must travel to the dry land, combat Cob, and seal up the doorway of return. Then they must make the harrowing journey over the Mountains of Pain. They are successful, but in combating Cob, Ged spends every bit of his magical power. At the end of *Shore* he is completely without magic, though he has helped to right the balance of Earthsea, both by closing the doorway from death to life and by helping Arren achieve his kingship.

There is a significant amount of scholarship on the trilogy focusing on its Taoism, its depiction of magic, its relationship to Jungian psychology. These are well discussed in Donna White's entertaining *Dancing with Dragons*. Since the focus here is on the specifically feminist, I limit my critical overview to where Le Guin adheres to and breaks free of the traditional view of gender in fantasy writing. It seems almost ungrateful to find fault with the books, for they are truly enjoyable, classic fantasy, but it is important to point out their conservative and generally male-centered orientation.

Like much fantasy, the Earthsea books take us to a quasi-feudal time, with a highly stratified social system based on birth. Wizards, of course, are the exception to this; because they can perform magic, they have some social mobility. Ged, for example, was a goatherd as a boy. But real magic and its associated social power are for men only. Le Guin says of the early books that they "are written totally within the classic Western tradition ... this kind of vaguely medieval, vaguely European context of an unquestioned patriarchal system where only men are wizards, only men have power."[70] As mentioned, the hero is Ged, whose life we follow from his childhood to his advanced middle age. Although *The Tombs of Atuan* and *The Farthest Shore* both feature a young person coming into her or his maturity, Ged's is the unifying presence in all three books. Ged's is also the voice of authority as he instructs and enlightens his younger companions, guiding them along the difficult paths they must follow. As Archmage in a land where magic is power and only men practice real magic, Ged embodies male rule. He is also the ultimate hero: he is a loner yet he inspires great loyalty; he is a very great wizard, legendary even among dragons; he has conquered personal and universal demons, giving up his own power to heal the world and bring a king once again to the throne of Earthsea. As Manlove points out, the magic that is the heart of Earthsea is itself a highly conservative art. In Earthsea, magic is an intricate part of the world's balance; no magic act, however small, can be performed without consideration of its impact.

Women, when they infrequently appear in Earthsea, misuse what magic they possess. "Weak as women's magic" and "wicked as women's magic" are Earthsea commonplaces. The village witches are portrayed as petty and are for the most part women of little real power. In *Wizard*, a beautiful young sorceress entraps Ged; in *Shore*, a witch has succumbed to the temptation of immortality and gone mad. Even Tenar, who is described by Ged as having great power, never does anything overtly magical; what her power is and how it might be used is never made clear. For the most part, women do not have a significant place in the first and third books at all. The books deal with the things and the world of men; even *Tombs*, set though it is in a women-and-eunuchs-only religious enclave, is about women who deny life in order to serve a patriarchal deity. In *Coyote's Song*, Erlich relates Le Guin's own sense that Tenar's compound is "*totally controlled by men*— a subservient element in the totally male-dominant regime of the godkings."[71] While *Tombs* features a world populated almost entirely by women and abounds with images of the female, that female world is overwhelmingly negative. The women in power are unsexed; they collude with the male-dominated religious state to deny Tenar her youth and freedom. They live in a desert world, a place where human life does not flourish, leading cloistered, celibate lives and perpetuating dark rituals. The powers that seem to inhabit the place are clearly linked to the female. In particular, the labyrinth where much of the action takes place is decidedly symbolic; it is a place where light never enters, described as a large central vault with winding passageways and a single door to the outside world. The finale of the book, as the tunnels collapse, is ironically orgasmic. The dark powers are impersonally malicious, though they attempt to kill Tenar and Ged for violating their sanctuary and taking their treasure. There is no hint here, as there will be in the later Earthsea books and in *Always Coming Home*, that these female-associated dark powers are to be treated with reverent fear and respect.

Le Guin's critics and in fact the author herself have spent a fair amount of time and energy taking these books to task for their male orientation, their neglect of female characters, and their sometimes misogynistic portrayal of women. While there is truth to these critiques, it is still important to recognize what Le Guin does here to break open the genre. For one thing, the emphasis on Taoist balance was unusual in Western fantasy up until that time. Unlike C. S. Lewis' insistent Christian message, or Tolkien's diametrical opposition of good and evil, Le Guin considers it necessary to accept the good with the evil, the light with the dark. Moreover, Ged is less sterotypically heroic than a character like Aragorn, who though flawed is still masterful, or from Gandalf, who like Ged expends himself saving his companions but who returns stronger than before. Tenar herself is a gem of a character, an early demonstration of Le Guin's ability to write about girlhood, particularly capturing the complex internal life of an introvert. Tenar is capable of wrongdoing, but also of tenderness toward the eunuch who attends her and toward the girl, Penthe, who plants the suggestion that there is more to life than virginity. She is also brave, both in approaching Ged and in defying the forces she has spent years worshiping. That Le Guin was able to build on this early scaffold to create the Tenar of *Tehanu* and *The Other Wind*, one of her most vibrant characters, is testament to the characterization established here.

Fettered Thought Experiments

Like fantasy, science fiction is difficult to define, though most critics agree that it arises from the manner in which our scientific and technological innovations have outpaced our ability to make ethical and etiological sense of them.[72] Brian Aldiss and David Wingrove suggest this in their sprawling history of the genre, *Trillion Year Spree*. They define science fiction as "the search for a definition of mankind and his status in the universe which will stand in our advanced but confused state of knowledge."[73] In his hallmark study *Metamorphoses of Science Fiction*, Darko Suvin calls science fiction the "literature of cognitive estrangement."[74] The reader is both distanced from the text and asked to make sense of it. Le Guin, who has in several places registered her respect for Suvin's criticism, agrees that the remove inherent in Suvin's definition is crucial. She says that the "pulling back from 'reality' in order to see it better, is perhaps the essential gesture of science fiction. It is by distancing that science fiction achieves aesthetic joy, tragic tension, and moral cogency."[75]

Extrapolation is the key to achieving the distance or estrangement necessary for science fiction. This extrapolation, however, should be rationally derived from the world as we know it; it should not break the laws of physics. Joanna Russ, both a writer and a critic of science fiction, calls the genre "what if" literature. Science fiction "shows things not as they are but as they might be, and for this 'might be' the author must develop a rational, serious, consistent explanation, one that does not (in Samuel Delany's phrase) offend against what is known to be known."[76] Much of this "what if" is a matter of extrapolating on human problems brought about by technological change. This is evident in the common themes of science fiction. Hoda Zaki identifies these as nuclear war and its impact on Earth, aliens, parallel universes and time travel, the interactions of people and machines, the colonization of space, and interpersonal and family relationships in space.[77]

Despite the revolutionary potential of science fiction, the chance it offers to envision new possibilities, it often reflects some of our most basic impulses and traditions. Le Guin says,

> In most science fiction until quite recently, women either didn't exist, or if they existed, they were these little stereotyped figures that squeaked.... The society usually presented in stock classic science fiction is an extrapolation of great enterprise capitalism, or an extrapolation of the British Empire of the 1880s, and nothing further. There's no Marxism; often there's not even any democracy. This is American science fiction I'm talking about ... American imagination thinking about getting to another world. When they get there, they find a feudal society, they find an intergalactic empire exactly like the British Empire, or they find the Rotary Club.[78]

Though science fiction in the last forty years has changed considerably, it has a long tradition of reinforcing its tropes.

A key atavism is the treatment of women in science fiction that had been, and in some quarters continues to be remarkably sexist.[79] Until the innovations of the sixties and seventies, science fiction had very little room for women. Not only were very few women writing science fiction (and most of those under gender-disguising names), in their infrequent appearance women were depicted as hapless victims, bimboids, wives patiently awaiting their husbands, breeders, or witless crewmembers who caused disastrous problems. Mostly they were not depicted at all; the beauty of space for many writers seemed to be that they could, like scouts on a camping trip, avoid women altogether. Pamela Sargent remarks upon this history:

> One can wonder why a literature that prides itself on exploring alternatives or assumptions counter to what we normally believe has not been more concerned with the roles of women in the future.... Either science fiction is not as daring or original as some of its practitioners would like to believe ... or this literature, designed to question our assumptions, cannot help reflecting how very deeply certain prejudices are engrained.[80]

In part, this lack of awareness may be due to the largely male readership of pre-feminist science fiction; there were few readers whose sensitivities were attuned its inequities. But women came to write and subsequently to read science fiction more and more by the sixties. Philippa Maddern, writing about the poverty of much science fiction until the sixties and seventies, credits women writers — Le Guin in particular — with revitalizing the field.[81] This is high praise, though it leaves out other innovative female writers, like Joanna Russ, Marge Piercy and James Tiptree, Jr., (the pseudonym of Alice Sheldon) among others.

Le Guin was herself drawn to science fiction in the sixties because it seemed a genre in which her writing — routinely rejected by mainstream publishers — might finally be accepted. Although this possibility did not occur to the adult Le Guin until then, she was familiar with science fiction from reading pulp novels and magazines as a child. In the early forties, she read *Thrilling Wonder, Astounding* and the other science fiction magazines popular at the time. Perhaps sensing her affinity for the medium, she chose a science fiction magazine for her first attempt at publication. At ten or eleven she submitted the story mentioned in the Introduction, involving time travel and the origin of life on Earth, to *Amazing Stories*, the editors of which promptly returned it despite its being, as she describes it, "very breezy in style."[82] Le Guin's appetite for science fiction waned by the late forties, when it seemed "to be all about hardware and soldiers."[83] As mentioned she would not return to science fiction until the early sixties, when she found, by reading Cordwainer Smith's "Alpha Ralpha Boulevard," that science fiction had broadened. Smith reworks "Paul et Virginie," Bernardin de Saint-Pierre's 1788 story of doomed lovers. In Smith's allusive style and playful use of science fiction conventions, Le Guin immediately recognized the genre's potential for sophisticated and meaningful fiction, and the turned her attention to writing science fiction and fantasy. Between 1962 and 1964 she published seven short stories in the magazines *Amazing* and *Fantastic*.[84] Her first efforts to write science fiction were motivated by a desire to get published, and the stories reflect this. Yet, while not nearly as profound or textually complex as her later work, they are indicative of the Le Guin to come. "April in Paris" (1962), for example, is about four people whose only link is their loneliness, yet who unite as lovers and friends. "The Masters" (1963) is set in a post-holocaust society where all but the most parochial knowledge is proscribed; the story's protagonist is drawn into an intellectual underground through which he learns both the cost and the necessity of intellectual pursuit. "Darkness Box" (1963) plays on the futility of war and the repetitions of history. These ideas all find some expression in Le Guin's later work, serving even as the seeds of later novels. "Dowry of the Angyar" (1964), certainly the best of Le Guin's early stories, would become the prologue of Le Guin's first science fiction novel *Rocannon's World*. "April in Paris" presages the quad relationship groups and the time travel of her recent science fiction.

"Dowry of the Angyar," discussed in some detail in the Introduction, bridges the gaps between science fiction, fantasy, and traditional fiction. Le Guin retells an old story, the Norse myth of the necklace *Brisingamen*. In Le Guin's version, the story is tragic and romantic, involving a young woman's quest for her inheritance, a priceless necklace. She is Semley, a beautiful noble woman whose people have fallen on hard times; in her youthful insecurity, she believes that regaining the necklace will ensure her husband's love and improve her social standing. She regains the necklace but loses everything else. The story has the elves and dwarves, the flying steeds and hero-oriented feudal society of standard sword-and-sorcery fantasy. To this Le Guin adds science fiction elements including spaceships, time dilation, and intergalactic warfare. The mix is both charming and ironically played upon. *Rocannon's World* (1966), the book that grew out of this short story, continues in the style of "Dowry." Here the short story becomes "Prologue: The Necklace" and serves to introduce the character Rocannon. An ethnologist from the League of All Worlds, he meets Semley when she comes to retrieve her necklace. Drawn by her beauty and the mystery of her unstudied race, he goes to her planet on an ethnological survey. Semley is long dead by the time he arrives while, due to time dilation, he has aged very little. He alone survives an attack on his survey team by an unknown enemy using the planet as a base for an intergalactic revolt. Rocannon is compelled to revenge his friends and protect the planet. With the help of Semley's grandson, the noble Mogien, he finds and destroys his enemy. His quest is told in loosely related episodes involving a rather wide variety of peoples and creatures, including angelic-looking insectoids and the furry, talking Kiemhrir.

Rocannon's World combines many elements from Norse myth, science fiction, and fantasy, not always seamlessly. If Le Guin based Semley on Freya, Rocannon is based on Odin, the chief god of Norse mythology. As Rocannon's reputation grows, he is called the Wanderer (one of Odin's names) and even "god." Like Odin, he survives when an attempt is made to burn him alive, and like Odin, he receives a gift of wisdom for which he must pay dearly, in Rocannon's case with the life of his friend Mogien. At the end of his successful quest, he marries a native woman and settles down, content to live out his time on this foreign planet. The League of All Worlds (later called the Ekumen) even names the planet after him. In Rocannon we see the alien anthropologist so ubiquitous in Le Guin's later work. He continually questions his own objectivity and desires to establish real communication and bonds of affection with the people he is ostensibly studying. Yet, his most important discoveries are about himself.

In 1966 Le Guin published *Planet of Exile*, which like *Rocannon's World* tells its story through the voices of several people. This slim volume is better crafted than *Rocannon's World*, more cogent and compelling. It is the story of two cultures, one native to a planet, and the other exiled there, brought together by a crisis that forces them to cooperate or face mutual annihilation. Their cooperation is grudging — they have over the years built up considerable misunderstanding and prejudice. The story of their union is epitomized in the lovers Rolery, a native, and Jakob Agat, leader of the technologically advanced exile culture. Like Rolery and Jakob, whose love necessitates putting aside cultural differences, the two peoples are forced to cooperate in order to survive. Eventually, the exile culture discovers that it has begun to adapt physiologically to the planet, and through Rolery and Agat it is learned that the groups can interbreed. As does *Rocannon's World*, *Planet of Exile* ends with the protagonist's marriage to a native woman and his newfound sense of being at home on an alien planet.

We learn of the fate of Jakob and Rolery's people in *City of Illusions*, the last of Le Guin's early science fiction novels. *City of Illusions* is not always well written. Le Guin herself says that the book is only half thought out and that she should not have published it as it stands. She identifies the book's primary fault as its unconvincing villains.[85] These are the Shing, humanoids who have used their capacity for lying telepathically to take over an unspecified number of planets from the League of All Worlds. The book's protagonist, Falk, is literally a man in search of himself. We first see him naked and nameless, his mind completely empty, in what may as well be the forest primeval but is an America of the far distant future. There are very few people left, and because of the fear of the Shing, they live in small groups or tribes. They practice sustainability, combining judicious use of technology with a communal-minimalist sensibility. When

Falk is found by one such group, he is taken in and taught life skills and Taoist values, but because he must discover who he really is and how he came to be exiled, he undertakes a quest for self-discovery. Convinced that he can learn his identity from the Shing, he walks from somewhere on the eastern seaboard to the Black Canyon of the Gunnison, an epic journey across an empty, wilderness America. When he arrives at the Shing city, the enemy offers to restore his mind with the ulterior motive of gaining the coordinates to Falk's homeworld, which they plan to subdue. Falk fairly easily overcomes their influence with some stock science fiction mind games, discovering in the meantime that he is Ramarren, his ship's navigator. By mind-wrestling a Shing, he defeats the enemies' attempts to learn the location of his planet. He then steals a spaceship and returns home.

Despite structural flaws of pacing and of course its "villain trouble," *City of Illusions* is in some ways Le Guin's most interesting early work. It is especially fascinating for its setting in a wild-again American continent, a place Le Guin would once more explore, much more fully and more site-specifically, in *Always Coming Home*. In both works, Le Guin gives us the opportunity to visualize America as it once was and challenges us to reinvent an inhibitory ethic for it. Her Falk is the very type of the American Adam that R. W. B. Lewis identifies as the great American literary hero.[86] Only, whereas that Adam wanted to forget his past, Le Guin's goes out in search of it. The book reflects the American Literary Renaissance in other ways — next to Lao Tsu's *Tao Te Ching*, Thoreau's *Walden* is the great text of the peaceful people who befriend Falk.

With these three books, Le Guin honed the skills she would soon exhibit in her renowned books, *The Left Hand of Darkness* and *The Dispossessed*. In the meantime, she was helping to reshape the conventions of science fiction. She calls into question the nature of storytelling, the relativity of truth. In *Rocannon's World*, Le Guin considers the experience of writer and reader in words that will closely echo the opening passages of *Always Coming Home*:

> one feels like an archeologist amid millennial ruins, now struggling through choked tangles of leaf, flower, branch and vine to the sudden bright geometry of a wheel or a polished cornerstone, and now entering some commonplace, sunlit doorway to find inside it the darkness, the impossible flicker of a flame, the glitter of a jewel, the half-glimpsed movement of a woman's arm. How can you tell fact from legend, truth from truth?[87]

As she frequently will in her later fiction, in this early s cience fiction Le Guin attempts to tell "truth from truth" by using multiple voices. These voices come in the form of field reports, the legend of Semley and her necklace, and the story of Rocannon; given the variety of texts, none privileged over the other, the reader must help construct a "truth" relative to his or her own biases. She also brings to her science fiction special attention to characterization. This legacy of her long apprenticeship in traditional literature is not new to science fiction, but appears surprisingly like an innovation in relation to the writing of such well-respected writers as Isaac Asimov and Arthur C. Clarke, who focus more on story than characterization. In science fiction — sometimes called a literature of ideas rather than of people — Le Guin's insistence on characterization has surprisingly been a matter of debate.[88] In "Science Fiction and Mrs. Brown," an essay that builds on Virginia Woolf's piece "Mr. Bennett and Mrs. Brown," Le Guin argues that even in science fiction meaning is relayed through character.[89] Le Guin's own fiction does tend to falter when ideas become more important than people — as they do in parts of *The Dispossessed* or *The Word for World Is Forest*.

In her early science fiction novels, Le Guin begins to use the "future history" sometimes called the Hainish Cycle. The future history is a significant science fiction convention used by authors like Robert Heinlein, Isaac Asimov, Cordwainer Smith and Samuel R. Delany. Future histories are usually worked out over the course of several novels and can span generations. The earliest future histories tended toward the grandiose, the imperialistic, and the unsophisticated. All-American heroes, militarism and good versus evil ideology were standard fare. Le Guin's early stories reflect these conventions. For example, the League of All Worlds in *Rocannon's World* is cruel in its extraction of war taxes from impoverished peoples. But Le Guin's league is never neo–Nazi or English-colonial, and she softens her future history as she goes along. The League, with its emphasis on a Reaganesque "peace-keeping" military force, eventually becomes an Ekumen devoted to the cooperative exchange of information. In Le Guin's loosely linked history, all humanoids are descendants of a single people, the Hain, who in the distant past seeded a large number of planets. Racial differences can be great: some of the Hain's descendants are clearly related, others resemble green monkeys, while some are androgynes. These differences seem to be the result both of adaptation and of sometimes-perverse experimentation on the part of the Hain, but the single origin is key, another instance of the unity underlying difference that is so much a part of Le Guin's body of work. Phillipa Maddern cites Le Guin's true embrace of the alien as the hallmark of her fiction — from the alien-fearing science fiction that went before her. Yet there are no real "aliens" in Le Guin's science fiction since they are all offspring of a single humanoid species. The union of aliens in Le Guin's novels is more properly a reunion of related peoples. Her future history thus comes under fire from critics who find it too easy; that all humanoids come from a single stock avoids the issue of truly confronting an alien other.[90]

As with the Earthsea books, Le Guin's unconscious use of conventions is indicated by the relative lack of female characters in these three hero-oriented stories. In *City of Illusions*, Falk/Ramarren leaves behind two lovers, both of whom apparently don the widow's veil when he departs. A third female, the villainous Estrel, stands in stark contrast, using her wiles to lead Falk to the Shing. Semley of *Rocannon's World* and Rolery of *Planet of Exile* are both intriguing characters, with a deep core of courage, but both are naïve, impetuous, and in Semley's case, vain. Rolery, in particular, has a strong, independent sense of self. She is willing to take significant risks and to incur the ill will of Jakob Agat's people. Le Guin defends herself against charges that she never wrote about women during these early years by pointing to Rolery. She sees Rolery "as the central mover of the events of the book, the one who chooses." Yet, Le Guin admits, "[t]he men take over."[91]

These three early science fiction novels, sometimes called the Hainish trilogy, marked Le Guin's apprenticeship in science fiction. Between 1968 and 1974, she published four more science fiction novels: *The Left Hand of Darkness*, *The Lathe of Heaven*, *The Word for World Is Forest* and *The Dispossessed*. The first of these, *The Left Hand of Darkness*, indicated her mastery of the genre. The book won both the Hugo and Nebula award and brought Le Guin considerable fame as a science fiction writer. The last of the novels from this period of very considerable success, *The Dispossessed*, also won Hugo and Nebula awards. *The Left Hand of Darkness* and *The Dispossessed* will be discussed at length, for the debate they inspired had much to do with Le Guin's increasing involvement in feminism. But all four novels show Le Guin using fiction as a means of thinking through social crises, using science fiction to conduct "thought experiments." Each novel tests an idea: What if dreams could change reality? What would a planet without war be like? What would an anarchic planet really be like? Seen as thought-experiments, these novels rather neatly fit Joanna Russ' definition of science fiction as "what if..." literature.[92] This literature is not, according to Le Guin, predictive but rather descriptive: "The purpose of a thought experiment ... [is] to describe reality, the present world."[93] A brief discussion here of *The Lathe of Heaven* and *The Word for World Is Forest* should indicate the consistency with which Le Guin was using fiction as a means of thinking through and protesting the then current crises of environmental devastation and war.

The Lathe of Heaven owes much to the writing of Philip K. Dick, a truly original science fiction writer much admired by Le Guin. *Lathe* postulates that reality can be changed by dreams, the dreams of one man, George Orr. It is set in a Portland of the not-too-distant future, a time made dismal by global warming and overpopulation. The protagonist is guilt-ridden over his ability to change reality to match his dreams, as when he dreams a sexually aggressive aunt out of existence. He seeks help from the overbearing Dr. Haber, who sees in George the potential to change the world. Haber takes control, forcing George to dream different realities. His suggestions are far too broad, and neither George nor Haber have any real control over them. For example, when Haber suggests that he dream of ending hunger, George dreams of a plague that radically depletes the world's population and thus ends the food shortages. His dreams work, but not in the way Haber intends. George is upset by the disastrous results of Haber's machinations, but much more so that Haber feels it right to meddle in the world's equilibrium; what right has he to play God? The novel takes on science fiction's trope of "white man makes right," positing instead a Taoist philosophy that we must use the utmost care in every action we perform. George epitomizes the wisdom of *wu wei* (action through stillness) while Haber exemplifies the Western idolization of progress.

The Word for World Is Forest was written in 1968 in England, where the Le Guins spent a sabbatical year. Le Guin was frustrated at being unable to participate in anti-war activities while in England, so she wrote out her anger over the Vietnam War in *Word*. The result is a sometimes didactic but deeply tragic novel. Le Guin uses science fiction conventions as distancing devices to comment on the war. At the same time, she turns Golden-Age science fiction inside out, to show how weaponry and bigotry in the wrong hands can forever change people. The story involves a wooded planet inhabited by small, peaceful forest dwellers who seem clearly to represent the Vietnamese; the imperialistic "colonists" who come

to export the planet's forests back to wood-poor Earth are the United
States forces. The story follows the native Selver, whose wife has been bru-
tally murdered. Once a peaceful man, he now wants revenge. Selver's people are used as slave labor by the colonists, who routinely rape, torture
and murder them. The colonists do not see the natives as human and have
little trouble abusing and destroying them. In actuality, the native race,
from the same Hainish stock as the colonists, have a well-developed civilization based on dream interpretation. Selver is a great dreamer and hence
a god to them. What he dreams is that these peaceful people must rise up
against the colonists in order to save themselves. After a number of lethal
raids, they negotiate an end to their enslavement with the colonists, regaining their freedom but losing their former peacefulness. They are utterly
changed.

Thinking about how a world might avoid war had earlier led Le Guin
to begin a novel based on the "what if" question, "what if a planet had
never had a major war?" What would explain that? Searching for an answer,
she considered the connection between war and gender. Could war be a
by-product of the sexual and social differences between men and women?
Would the impulse and rationale for war still exist if there were no gender differences? Could a race of androgynes avoid war?[94] The novel that
resulted, *The Left Hand of Darkness*, shows that Le Guin had begun to
think seriously about feminist issues by 1967–68, even if it would be some
time before she aligned herself with the women's movement. It was, she
has said, her attempt to think through issues of gender oppression. Though
she read Mary Wollstonecraft, Margaret Mead, and Ashley Montagu in
preparation for her novel, the texts of the contemporary feminist movement were for the most part yet to be written or, like Simone de Beauvoir's *The Second Sex*, had not yet come to her attention. When it occurred
to her that the inhabitants of her peaceful planet were androgynous, the
lack of war on the planet became secondary. Her interest shifted instead
to the interpersonal dynamics of a race of people who did not identify one
another as male or female. While this thought-experiment may seem
remote from our experience, it describes our situation by contrast. These
androgynes do have small-scale aggressions: border disputes, skirmishes
and the like. But in depicting what they do not have — war, sexual aggression or discrimination, ecological devastation — Le Guin implies that there
is a link between gender and the breakdown of interpersonal relations that
such social ills indicate. She thus tacitly comments on the link between

many of our pervasive problems and the emphasis we place on sexual difference.[95]

Our sense of gender roles is represented in the novel by the heterosexual narrator, Genly Ai. Genly, the envoy sent to bring the planet Gethen into the Ekumen, is a conservative young man. Though he has trouble admitting it, he is made uncomfortable by the androgyny of the Gethenians. For much of the novel, his unease colors his relationship with Tharem Harth rem ir Estraven, the prime minister who is Genly's only real ally. When Genly is arrested and sent to a gulag, Estraven feels responsible and rescues him in an epic escape across hundreds of miles of glacial wilderness. During this perilous journey they learn to love each other, and Genly comes to understand the root of his wariness toward Estraven:

> And I saw again, and for good, what I had always been afraid to see, and had pretended not to see in him: that he was a woman as well as a man ... he was the only one who had entirely accepted me as a human being: who had liked me personally and given me entire personal loyalty: and who therefore had demanded of me an equal degree of recognition, of acceptance. I had not been willing to give it. I had been afraid to give it. I had not wanted to give my trust, my friendship to a man who was a woman, a woman who was a man.[96]

Though they survive the journey across the ice, Estraven is later killed. While Genly's mission is a success, he has lost his friend.

The Left Hand of Darkness was and is a very popular book, a genuine innovation in science fiction as well as a well-written and compelling story.[97] Its topicality — it broached the idea of androgyny just about the time it was becoming current within the feminist movement — brought it to the attention of critics who still occasionally argue its feminist merits. Le Guin has claimed that the book is not really about gender at all — that it is a book about betrayal and fidelity. Whether or not this is true, critics have tended to focus on the issue of androgyny, and particularly on how well Le Guin did or did not depict this androgynous culture. Among the points of contention are the author's use of "he" as the generic pronoun, her arguable failure to depict Gethenians as women as well as men, her use of a male protagonist, her perceived heterosexism, and especially her use of the myth of androgyny.[98]

Le Guin's decision to use "he" and "him" as the grammatically appropriate pronouns for a race of persons who are both he and she seems glaringly inappropriate to readers made sensitive to language by feminist awareness.[99] The male pronoun is joined throughout *Hand* by male-specific monikers, like "king," "lord," "brother," "son." When Le Guin revised the short story "Winter's King," substituting the female pronoun for the male/generic, she showed by reversal how we tend to then read the story as if it were about women — albeit somewhat masculine women — rather than as if it were about androgynes.[100] Critics have argued that not only the language, but also the details of the text conspire to make the Gethenians seem more like men than menwomen. These critics see the androgynes as nearly always depicted in what we have traditionally considered male spheres, for example politics and physical adventure. The Polish writer Stanislaw Lem, for example, argued that in manner of dress, speech and behavior, Le Guin had depicted only men.[101] Joanna Russ, like Lem a top science fiction writer and outspoken critic, adds that we imagine the Gethenians as men in part due to Le Guin's failure to depict family structure and child-rearing practices. The pervasive maleness of the novel is highlighted by Le Guin's use of a male protagonist as the only non-androgynous character given any extended treatment.[102] It is difficult to test how androcentric Le Guin is being in *Hand*, since the only sustained non-androgynous view we have in the novel is from a biased human male. When Genly Ai, who is intended to seem sexist, makes what can be read as a negative statement about a Gethenian's womanliness, it could be attributable to his male bias. Jewell Parker Rhodes compellingly argues, however, that his remarks to some degree reflect Le Guin's own views. The book is meant to chronicle Genly's realization of and evolution away from a fear of and prejudice toward women. Yet after his conversion, he identifies a Gethenian adolescent as a boy, saying, "he had a girl's quick delicacy in his looks and movements, but no girl could keep so grim a silence as he did."[103] Had he, and the author, truly been enlightened, Rhodes argues, Genly would not have made such a comment.

The issue at the heart of the debate is less Le Guin's androcentrism than her use of androgyny itself. The myth of androgyny and its possible implications for feminism have long polarized the feminist community.[104] At its simplest and most popularly relevant, the concept of androgyny is that all humans have both male and female qualities. Given the chance to develop without a sense of gender-specific behavior, people would see no gender-linked limitations on what they could achieve. Carolyn Heilbrun defines androgyny as "a condition under which the characteristics of the sexes, and the human impulses expressed by men and women, are not rigidly assigned."[105] The most obvious significance of such a belief is that gender-based discrimination could eventually be eliminated by raising children to believe there is no inherent difference in male and female capability. Although some criticism of Le Guin's use of the myth of androgyny came from those who believed that it was not explored fully or was not thematically integral to the text, most criticism came from feminist scholars concerned about the implications of the myth itself.[106] Rhodes argues that the myth is both androcentric and essentialist. It positions men and women as different, and upholds stereotypes of women as weak and emotional, men as strong and logical. Moreover, historically the man is depicted as questing for and discovering his female identity.[107] This is true in literature as well as in such areas as psychology. Androgyny is a crucial aspect of Jung's theories, for example. Jung believed that men should uncover their *anima* or female nature but that women should not attempt to discover their *animus* or male nature, primarily because it would threaten men and defeminize women. He says in "Woman in Europe," "The mental masculinization of the woman has unwelcome results.... She may even become frigid."[108]

Critics have also complained about what they perceive as Le Guin's homophobia.[109] Gethenians are more hermaphrodites than androgynes, capable of becoming either male or female during the short fertile period they undergo monthly. In their sexually active phase, called kemmer, Gethenians have a very strong need to find a partner. When they do, they couple for the duration of the kemmer period, one taking on the male and the other the female role. They have no choice in this differentiation, and do not know from month to month which sex they will become. Of the possibility of a homosexual couple occurring at this time, Le Guin says, "If there are exceptions, resulting in kemmer-partners of the same sex, they are so rare as to be ignored."[110] This dismissal of homosexual relations has angered some readers who see in it Le Guin's heterosexual and even homophobic biases.[111]

Much of the criticism that Le Guin received for *Hand* was repeated about her novel *The Dispossessed: An Ambiguous Utopia. Dispossessed* tells the story of the physicist Shevek, a native of Anarres, a planet with a social structure based on anarchy. Shevek has developed a theory that would allow for the instantaneous transmission of communications across vast distances of space. While he is deeply loyal to his anarchist society, he feels intellectually stymied by its provincial resistance to change and challenge. He decides to take his ideas to Urras, the planet from which the Anarresti were exiled six hundred years before. Urras starkly contrasts with his home world, and Shevek becomes deeply disturbed by its political repression and conspicuous consumption. His presence on Urras sparks a revolution there that is violently suppressed, and he eventually decides that no one should have ownership of his theory. Instead, he turns it over to the neutral Ekumenical ambassador and returns home.

Critics have paid sustained attention to *Dispossessed*— two collections of essays on politics in the novel came out in the late 2000s alone. The book has been praised as well as quite thoroughly taken to task for its perceived shortcomings. Some critics cite structural problems, claiming that the story or foreground does not fit well upon the novel's background, in particular that Shevek's beliefs do not fit the anarchist society in which he was raised. Annares is nominally androgynous, in a social or cultural sense, and many of its tenets work to disrupt the materialism of marital relationships and private ownership. Yet, as critics point out, much of the text contradicts what the society seems to stand for. Tom Moylan, for example, says that while the novel "expresses a libertarian and feminist value system, the gaps and contradictions in [Le Guin's] text betray a privileging of male and heterosexual superiority and of the nuclear, monogamous family."[112]

Semantics, another area of contention, is as important in *Dispossessed* as in *Hand*; again, we expect the language to reflect the socially androgynous society at the heart of the novel. Although all people on Anarres are supposedly equal, regardless of gender, the language of the text does not help create this impression. The new society invents a new language and uses computer-generated names to avoid ties with the past. But the reader does not feel the impact of this because all the names in the book, whether Anarresti or Urrasti, are foreign. And because the book is "translated" into English, we lose the impact of the differences between the two languages supposedly being spoken. We also run into much the same problem of gender-specific language here as in *Hand*. For instance, the word *ammar*, like "comrade," expresses communality, but is translated as "brother." And rather than find an English word that would convey the sense of "foreman" without the gender specificity, which the Anarresti surely would do, Le Guin opts to use the male-based word and then to identify the person as female. Sometimes she seems to make such choices to catch the reader off guard, to point out the reader's own preconceptions, but this only draws attention to the gender dichotomy. As in *Hand*, the maleness of the language is underscored by the use of a male protagonist.

Although Le Guin seems to be striving toward the ideal of androgyny, essentialist notions appear throughout *Dispossessed*. It is no surprise that on Urras men and women interact as aliens. On that high-capitalist, socially and sexually-stratified world, women are almost purely sexual objects, possessions of men, excluded from education, politics, the arts — indeed from all sources of public power. On sexually equal Anarres, however, Shevek has a conversation with a male coworker, Vokep, that echoes the Urrasti conviction that women are different from and probably inferior to men. Vokep, brought up under the same anarchist social conditions as all Anarresti, argues that, "Women think they own you. No woman can really be an Odonian.... What a man wants is freedom. What a woman wants is property. She'll only let you go if she can trade you for something else. All women are propertarians."[113] Shevek rejects this essentialist notion with its deep insult. For an Anarresti, to be called a propertarian is a significant personal attack. Remembering a lover with whom he had his first real sexual experience, he realizes that it was her freedom, her willingness to surrender herself sexually, that allowed him to experience his own sexual freedom. He thus disagrees with Vokep, but replaces his companion's sexist comment with his own essentialist notion: "I think men mostly have to learn to be anarchists. Women don't have to learn."[114] Women and men are thus, in Shevek's mind, born different. Of the above-mentioned sexual encounter, he also thinks, "Defeat, surrender, had its raptures. Beshun [the former lover] herself might never want any joy beyond them."[115] The notion that a woman might seek nothing more from sexual relationship than defeat and surrender reinforces stereotypes of women as passive and selfless.

Vokep's further comment that having babies makes women propertarians is borne out by Shevek's partner, Takver. Though a sensible and intelligent woman, she gives way under stress to impulses over which she seems to have little control. Deprived for a long time of Shevek's company, she makes a fetish of their daughter, going against social custom by keeping her at home and breastfeeding her for three years.[116] Her common sense is "obscured by maternal ambitions and anxieties."[117] That bearing children is the decisive line between men and women — in the social and biological senses — is further illustrated in her convincing Shevek to set aside his principles in order to become published. She later regrets this. If she had not been pregnant at the time, she says, she would have behaved differently:

> Pregnant women have no ethics. Only the most primitive kind of sacrifice impulse.... It's a racial preservation drive, but it can work right against the community; it's biological, not social. A man can be grateful he never gets into the grip of it. But he'd better realize that a woman can, and watch out for it.[118]

Though the biological aspect of gender difference is indisputable, the social aspect is more difficult to ascertain. Yet Le Guin seems to be arguing here that true androgyny is not possible. Even in a society dedicated to total equality of all peoples, biological imperatives draw a line between the sexes. Androgyny is mitigated by essential difference.

Some critics argue that Le Guin, particularly in the depiction of female characters, unintentionally reinforces stereotypes of men and women. Shevek embodies the artist/scientist as hero. He is a charismatic figure who leaves home and family to go off on a voyage of discovery.[119] Le Guin takes pains to indicate that both men and women can be gripped by the creator spirit, can equally be caught up in the difficult work of intellectual/artistic production. Yet the descriptions of Shevek deep in the effort of writing his *Theories of Simultaneity*—needing both solitude to work and someone to look after him—sound very much like those of the male artist in "The Fisherwoman's Daughter." Shevek is also larger than life, equivalent to the iconic Odo, the anarchist who led the revolution on Urras 600 years earlier that resulted in the exile of Shevek's ancestors. Not only does he make a very great scientific discovery, Shevek also becomes the inspiration for social change on the planet he visits. But, as with Le Guin's best characters, heroic or not, he is engaging, complex, capable of error, and ultimately true to his noble intentions.

The women are less well-rounded and seem more like foils to one another and to Shevek than like independent people. Shevek's mother, Rulag, who like him is a gifted scientist, is depicted as selfish and cold. She left her partner and young son Shevek to pursue her work, a completely accepted and encouraged life choice on Anarres, yet she seems to Shevek like a deserter. When she comes to see him twenty years later, she is lonely, left so it seems by her choice of work over family. She offers her son friendship, but Shevek rejects her, unable as he is to get over the old hurt. Rulag later acts vindictively towards him, patently in revenge for his spurning her. She is thus not only selfishly ambitious (in his eyes) but made to seem irrational as well. Her lack of maternal feeling is more than made up for by Takver, is the quintessence of woman as natural being. A biologist, she is passionately connected with the natural world. Shevek thinks that she is one of those "whose umbilicus has never been cut. [She] never got weaned from the universe."[120] She is the sensualist to Shevek's intellectual. When we first meet her, she is eating and has grease and crumbs on her face. She is at that moment listening to Shevek speak movingly about suffering. Immediately she recognizes in him the man with whom she will eventually partner, while he fails even to register her name. She is a strong character, accustomed to hard work, rather contemptuous of those who are not, and hot tempered. Yet she seems passive in her inability to resist biological imperative and particularly in her role as the wife and mother who waits for her man to return. Vea, the Urrasti woman to whom Shevek is sexually attracted, is the final member of this triptych of female characters. She epitomizes the woman as seductress-tease who uses her considerable sexual wiles to arouse Shevek. Physically contrasted with Takver, Vea eats very little, gets no exercise, sleeps late, and in the Urrasti fashion is completely shaven and dusted with glittering powder. She wears jewels at throat and navel that are attached by magnets implanted under her skin. Takver would call Vea a body profiteer, someone who uses her body in a power struggle with men. Her social demeanor is as contrived as her appearance, and in fact she seems to be working as an agent for the Urrasti government which wants Shevek's theory. What power she has is coercive and covert; she flatters, cajoles, and threatens all at once. The women of *Dispossessed* all seem trapped in stereotype.

The charges of homophobia made against *The Left Hand of Darkness* are repeated in criticism of *Dispossessed*, particularly by Samuel R. Delany. Delany sees in Bedap, the novel's only declared homosexual, the insinuation that homosexuality is somehow unnatural.[121] Though Le Guin does provide in *Dispossessed* for both occasional homosexual pairings and for long-term homosexual partnerships, these are only cursorily depicted. Bedap and Shevek do copulate (to use the Anarresti word) but more out of friendship than real desire; it seems, in fact, something that Shevek does for Bedap's sake rather than his own. Our sense of Shevek's heterosexuality is thus never really challenged. In fact, according to Tom Moylan Shevek's periods of great creativity always come after sexual encounters, thus depicting him as the great white male progenitor.[122]

If there is anything really revolutionary in *The Dispossessed*, it is that the anarchy in which Shevek lives was founded by a woman, Odo. Her story is told in "The Day Before the Revolution" (1972), a kind of prequel to the novel. "The Day Before the Revolution" is about Odo's life when she is a relatively old woman. Mostly told in retrospect, it is made up of her ruminations on her long-dead husband, her childhood, her many years in prison, and her life's work as the architect of a social revolution. As the title indicates, the story is set on the day before the world revolution that she has brought about. It is also the day she dies. Le Guin quickly captures the ambiguities of Odo's personality: she is the founder of Odonianism who is not a good Odonian, the crippled old woman uninterested in the events she has helped to create, her mind now sharp and biting now blurred and imprecise. Odo is easily one of Le Guin's most completely drawn female characters up to that time. Critics might argue that in her portrayal of Odo, Le Guin has fallen back on stereotypes of women as vain, physically frail and intellectually feeble. What she has not done is simply make Odo a female version of the charismatic male leader. The weight of her accomplishments is palpable, both to the reader of *Dispossessed* who knows what her revolution will bring about and through the details subtly inserted into the story, including the references to her writings, her imprisonment, and her leadership. "The Day Before the Revolution" humanizes this iconic social revolutionary, while reminding us that Odo, a great social philosopher and the founder of a new society, is also a woman. At the same time, Le Guin gives us one of the few stories of any length that treat an old woman as a viable literary character, one still intelligent, self-deprecatingly witty, and sexually interested despite her diminished physical capacity.

In her defense of *The Left Hand of Darkness*, Le Guin says,

> [t]o me the "female" principle is, or at least historically has been, basically anarchic. It values order without constraint, rule by custom, not by force. It has been the male who enforces order, who constructs power structures, who makes, enforces, and breaks laws.[123]

It is not therefore really surprising that in *Dispossessed* she should make a woman the creator of an anarchist society. Odo, who seems clearly to be modeled on the American anarchist Emma Goldman, doesn't live to see the revolution her ideas started and she dies not on Anarres — the planet the anarchists make their own — but on Urras, the "home" planet. Interestingly, like Shevek, Odo was partnered and thinks often of her lover, who was killed years before in a failed uprising. Though she has looked at other men with desire (a major element of Odonianism is sexual freedom), there has never been anyone for her but him. Odonianism does not forbid partnering, but it does not make much room for this materialist practice. Though Odo recognizes the inconsistency of her relationship, she shrugs off the ambiguity of her actions and refers to the man as her "husband" although the proper Odonianism is "partner."

In both *Hand* and *Dispossessed* Le Guin was attempting genuine thought experiments, trying out scenarios for improving the human condition. While she was successful on some levels — at least for some readers — the criticisms described here do have validity. Given her intentions, the question remains not just for Le Guin but for all writers working within a specific genre: how much do conventions unconsciously constrain the writing? How much was Le Guin steered by science fiction conventions that, for example, tacitly allow only for a male protagonist? Bittner, discussing Genly Ai, argues both that Le Guin quite deliberately chose a male protagonist and that "the dialectic of the romance (and science fiction estrangement) almost [makes the male protagonist] imperative."[124] Given science fiction conventions, Le Guin had no real choice but to use a male protagonist. Joanna Russ says of the lack of women characters in science fiction: "It's the whole difficulty of science fiction, of genuine speculation: how to get away from traditional assumptions which are nothing more than traditional straightjackets."[125] Sarah Lefanu blames not science fiction, but the conventions of the traditional novel for what she sees as Le Guin's lack of radical imagination. She says that Le Guin's "Conception of her beloved outer space and inner lands is too closely related to parameters set by mainstream narrative modes to explore to the full the explosive potential of science fiction. Le Guin speaks with the voice of authority ... rather than against it."[126] Lefanu sees Le Guin as too dedicated to the notion of character — male character. *The Left Hand of Darkness* and *The Dispossessed* belong in her mind to the tradition of the bourgeois novel that constructs rather than deconstructs the subject as hero. Le Guin is by both these critics' accounts fettered by the weight of literary tradition. Many of her critics seem personally disappointed in Le Guin. Both Russ and Delany remark positively on some aspects of her work only to express the feeling that she should have been radically aware, more overtly political, even politically correct. Some, like Natalie Rosinsky and

Lefanu, somewhat unfairly use Le Guin to make a point about how much more can be done with science fiction. These critics give only a diluted recognition of the originality of Le Guin's novels. If *Hand* and *Dispossessed* were not the first of their kind, they did bring much greater attention to both the issue of androgyny and the possibilities of the utopian tradition.

Craig Barrows and Diana Barrows are among those who disagree with critics like Lefanu, Russ, Delany, and Rosinsky. They argue that Le Guin uses a naïve and rather sexist male protagonist in *Hand* because her intended audience is not feminists or women, but "typically biased heterosexual males."[127] She is trying through Genly Ai to convert them. "The role of Genly Ai ... is not to reinforce stereotypical male attitudes but to expose them; he is the means whereby men can confront their own ambiguous responses to women."[128] The Barrows' argument is supported by a statement Le Guin made in a 1974 interview about why she chose a male protagonist:

> I thought men would loathe the book, would be unsettled and unnerved by it.... Since the larger percentage of science fiction readers are male.... I thought it would be easier for them if they had a man — and a rather stupid and bigoted man actually — to work with and sort of be changed with.[129]

This reminds us, again, of Le Guin's stated desire to subvert without hurting feelings. On the other hand, if this account is true, it is an overtly political move on the author's part. Rather than reach the few already converted, she set out to convert some of those not then sympathetic to feminism. The desire not to alienate a male readership does, in fact, alienate some feminist readers who might otherwise find in Le Guin an ally. Her tactics were, as Lefanu and Rosinsky have pointed out, ultimately too conservative for some. Le Guin may have been apologizing indirectly to these readers when she told an interviewer that a woman protagonist simply would not have worked: "I knew a woman would just love it. There wouldn't be any dramatic scenes.... She would have just run around saying, 'Oooh, this is wonderful.'"[130]

That Le Guin could have been more inventive in her depictions of these alternative societies, and in choosing pronouns and protagonists, seems evident in view of the success some writers of feminist utopias have had. An interesting contrast can be made with Joanna Russ' *The Female Man*, for example, where a woman from an all-female planet (thus in a sense a genderless one) visits 1960s Earth. Her "androgynous" behavior stands in hilarious and sometimes painful contrast to the gendered interactions of men and women. Marge Piercy and Dorothy Bryant, among others, have created pronouns that do not carry the weight of gender.[131] Many writers, including these three, have envisioned alternative societies that depict women and men in roles outside the gender associations that still underlie our conceptions of male and female. But for the most part these writers followed Le Guin and benefited not only from her example—both positive and negative—but from the increasingly influential and dynamic women's movement. While Le Guin is often used in studies of feminist utopias as an example of what the others had to rise above, she is less frequently given credit for what she herself accomplished.

Feminist discourse's impact on Le Guin is evident in her change of mind about the male pronoun. She defended her use of he/him/his as late as 1976: in "Is Gender Necessary," she said she refused "to mangle English by inventing a pronoun for he/she. 'He' is the generic pronoun, damn it.... But I do not consider this really important."[132] By 1986 she told an interviewer, "I realize that he doesn't mean he-and-she. We're told that it does, but it doesn't. People don't take it as such ... it does reduce the world to the male."[133] In 1987 she put some closure on the issue by publishing a revision of "Is Gender Necessary" in which she stated that she now took the matter more seriously; she was unaware at the time, "how the pronouns I used shaped, directed, controlled my own thinking."[134] She has also written a screenplay of *Hand* which uses the pronouns "a," "un," and "a's."

As to criticisms that her androgynes seem more like men than women, Le Guin has conceded that she left out too much by not putting the androgynous characters—like Estraven—in roles we would perceive as female. We would, she believes, be more willing to accept Estraven as a man and a woman if, for example, we had seen "him" mothering "his" children.[135] Yet, she goes on to say that male readers were more willing than female readers to fill in these omissions, perhaps because they identify with the male protagonist. A female reader, looking for herself in the text, is likely to find little here to hook onto. Le Guin's revised opinion is that:

> Men were inclined to be satisfied with the book, which allowed them a safe trip into androgyny and back, from a conventionally male viewpoint. But many women wanted it to go further, to dare more, to

explore androgyny from a woman's point of view as well as a man's.... I think women were justified in asking more courage of me and a more rigorous thinking-through of implications.[136]

This thinking-through, and Le Guin's subsequent escape from at least some of her internalized assumptions, was soon to come.

CHAPTER TWO

The Voyage Out

By 1974, when *The Dispossessed* appeared, Le Guin was exhausted. In nine years she had published seven science fiction novels, the Earthsea trilogy, a book of poetry and a number of articles on science fiction and fantasy. She had won Hugo and Nebula awards as well as the National Book Award. She had also begun the draining task of being a public figure: along with a name made came interviews, award ceremonies, speaking and teaching engagements, and criticism to respond to or ignore. "I sat around and was sure I never would write again," she recalls of this period. "I read Jung and I consulted the *I Ching*. For 18 months, it gave me the same answer: the wise fox sits still or something."[1]

"Danae 46" appears to be about this period of time, when Le Guin was sure she would "never write again."[2] The poem takes its name from the story of Danae, whose father, heeding a prophecy that he would be slain by his grandchild, locks her in a tower to prevent her from contact with men. She is visited there by Jupiter who enters in the form of a golden shower; she conceives and the child of their union does eventually kill Danae's father. Read as a play on the artist locked in her writing room, waiting for inspiration in the form of the god Jupiter, the poem takes on interesting connotations:

> God of the gold rain,
> the room is cold;
> will you not come again
> To me old?
>
> God in the bright shower,
> it grows late
> in the room in the tower
> where I wait.

O the shining terror
of the first embrace,
the eyes, the arrows
of your eyes, your face!

The window is open.
I have set the board.
One spark, one token!
I am mortal, Lord.

Danae/the poet worries that her lover/inspiration will not return to her, has perhaps lost interest in her due to her age. The god is immortal, but she is not, and she fears that her time is running out. She waits in a kind of ecstasy of anxiety for his coming and the infusion of creative inspiration that he represents. If Le Guin has written herself into this poem, we can be sure that Jupiter eventually returned; Le Guin has done much fine writing since *The Dispossessed*. We can add a fanciful twist to our reading of the poem. If we cast Le Guin as Danae, and her later literature as the child born of her union with the muse/Jupiter, we must wonder if that "child" reaches back to slay its "grandfather." The grandfather might be the literary tradition that has constrained women writers for so long, keeping them from delivering books that might threaten the status quo. Or he might be Le Guin's own literary production, her pre-feminist work. In either case, her writings of the next two decades depart from what she had written earlier and from the literary traditions that influenced her.

The *I Ching's* advice to Le Guin was well taken. Her combined lack of inspiration and the consequences of fame were not the only factors with which she had to contend. She had to deal with the scrutiny of the science fiction community of writers and critics, where she was in some corners praised and in others brought to task for her perceived failures of feminist vision. While she defended herself, she also opened to feminist theory. She began seriously to question her relation to gender issues and the literary tradition, to consider her art through a feminist prism. The implications of this for Le Guin's writing were enormous, likely amplified by her new public role and the responsibility inherent in fame. Clearly she had influence: how would she use it? That this paradigm shift was challenging is evident in the art she produced over the next decade. It is sometimes cautious, lacking the fluidity of her early work. In comparison with her very productive earlier period, there is much less original work. Instead she used the time to put together collections, one of essays and three of short stories. One collection, *Orsinian Tales*, indicated that Le Guin had made a strong enough name in genre fiction that she could now publish these more mainstream stories, some of which had been previously rejected. At the same time that she was publishing less new work, what she was writing shows feminism rising to the surface of her artistic consciousness, as metaphorically played out in the story "The New Atlantis." She also worked out a feminist poetics. For example, in *The Eye of the Heron*, she "breaks the sequence" of traditional narrative by replacing the male hero with a female who is not "heroic" but is nonetheless a leader. Finding science fiction and fantasy too confining and conventional, she breaks with these as well, in the short story "Pathways of Desire" and the young adult novel *The Beginning Place*. From breaking with the narrative sequence and the generic frame, Le Guin moved on to sketching out the woman's story, creating tightly condensed narratives of key moments in a woman's life or, as in the impeccable "Gwilan's Harp," a whole life in miniature. The question of language, in particular of the "mother tongue," arises frequently in these stories, as Le Guin struggles, along with other feminist writers, to determine if women's writing — from the naming of objects to the construction of sentences — is inherently different from men's. Out of this work a feminist narrative begins to emerge, iterations of a new thought experiment: what if the writer wrote like a woman? At the same time, Le Guin's tone shifts. Having undergone an "awakening" or consciousness raising to use the old-fashioned term, Le Guin begins to sound less and less in this period like someone who "doesn't want to hurt feelings." The work is sharper, darker and sadder than in the previous decade. As discussed below, it is not always her best work, having something of the quality of a second apprenticeship. Toward the end of this period, which ends in the bright Antarctic sunlight of 1982's "Sur," the writing grows more hopeful but also more separatist and essentialist.

When We Dead Awaken

In 1975, Le Guin published a short story, "The New Atlantis," about a literal sea change, the rising of a long submerged continent and the return of its dormant culture. Like *The Lathe of Heaven*, "The New Atlantis" is set in a grossly polluted, overpopulated, commoditized and bureaucratized twenty-first century Portland, Oregon. Marriage is illegal, as is any kind of privately controlled enterprise, including intellectual enterprise. Belle, the primary character, is minimally employed in a factory that manufactures paper bags, but the viola is her passion. She is secretly married to Simon, a scientist who has just returned from eighteen months in a forced labor camp. His "crime" is to have developed a solar-powered energy cell that if brought to completion would endanger the government monopoly on energy. At the time of these events, a curious geologic phenomenon is occurring: a new continent, or perhaps the long-submerged continent of Atlantis, is rising from the sea, drowning the American mainland. Belle's first person singular narrative is interpolated with a narrative in the first person plural. This is the voice of the inhabitants of the old continent who have been physically and psychically frozen for centuries or millennia at the bottom of the sea. They are the dead reawakening, inching towards self-awareness as they rise up out of the depths. As they regain consciousness, they remember what they had long forgotten, that they had built a civilization, had lived lives, had existed and still do.

This curious and unexplained event is linked to Belle, her music, Simon's return, and his invention of a cheap, nonpolluting source of energy. Consciously she is only half-aware of the threatening reality of the rising continent; she is preoccupied with Simon, his injuries sustained in the labor camp, and the threat of the FBI, who have bugged their apartment. Yet she is linked with the inhabitants of Atlantis. In her music she seems simultaneously to translate their voices and to reach out to them, as they listen to her playing. They begin to see real light just as Simon and his friends perfect the solar-powered energy cell that would in another political reality give power to the people; in Belle's reality it will be Simon's undoing. Belle is linked to the Atlanteans when Simon jokingly tells her not to cry or she will submerge the whole continent. At about the time that the continent finally reemerges and life begins again for the Atlanteans, Simon is rearrested — certainly for good this time — ending his and Belle's life together.

Darko Suvin calls "The New Atlantis" a parable of de-alienation.[3] He sees the rising continent as a foil to the failing American continent. The ascending culture represents a Golden Age of communality and harmony; it is juxtaposed with America as a corporate state in the advanced stages of destroying itself. In "The New Atlantis" the forces of de-alienation that the rising continent stands for are coming to the forefront: "These forces of a new and better creation are now ready to rise in full stature to the surface of our Earth."[4] What would seem the open optimism of this new coming is mitigated by the fact that with its advent passes the old world and the good people, like Belle and Simon, who are innocent victims. Suvin, a Marxist, sees in the text suggestions of the sweep of historic currents, including the "revolutionary political and ideological movements of the last century or two, say since 1789 and 1917."[5] But the rising continent also suggests a feminist upswell, the rediscovery of female solidarity, Adrienne Rich's dead awakening, the forgotten or submerged cultural heritage of women again seeing the light of day after centuries of burial. Certainly the Atlanteans' descriptions of their confinement echo those of women over the ages who have felt culturally constrained.

> It was dark for so long, so very long. We were all blind.... We could not move at all. We did not move. We did not speak. Our mouths were closed.... Our eyes were pressed shut. Our limbs were held still. Our minds were held still ... if we had ever been alive, we had forgotten it.[6]

The suggestion that this rising continent parallels the rising women's movement is supported by the narrative's critique of gender roles. In this politically and socially repressive society, women are not, for example, allowed into medical schools. The question of essentialism arises as well. Belle believes that women are natural anarchists, claiming, "It's men who make laws, and enforce them, and break them, and think that the whole performance is just wonderful. Most women would rather just ignore them."[7] She makes this observation in relation to a female black market woman doctor who delights in Belle and Simon's illegal marriage. The woman's love of illegality for its own sake makes her, in Belle's opinion, "like a man."[8]

In fact, the totalitarian regimes that Le Guin writes about with growing frequency in the 1970s cannot simply be described as males ruling and females submitting. "The Diary of the Rose" examines the process of disaffection brought about in a naïve and idealistic doctor by her exposure to a male political prisoner. Rosa Sobel, the "rose" of the story, operates a psychoscope, a machine that turns neural impulses into pictures. This tool of psychotherapy allows a doctor to "see" into a patient's mind and thus helps the doctor in diagnosis and treatment. Rosa is unaware of the political realities of the totalitarian regime of which she is a part. She is given charge of a patient, Flores Sorde, who is said to have had a psychotic episode but who is actually a political prisoner. Though Rosa believes she is meant to cure him, the treatment is a ruse; Sorde knows he will inevitably be labeled psychotic and be given electroshock therapy. Rosa's exposure to the imaginative and intelligent Flores changes her and she eventually sees the truth about her work and her society. She is unable to save Flores from the inevitable, but he has left his mark on her. Once unquestioningly loyal, she becomes both more self-aware and self-defining. The ironically named Flores has helped her to blossom, but has also given her a taste of the bitterness of reality: "I am Rosa. I am the rose. The rose with no flower, the rose all thorns, the mind he made, the hand he touched, the winter rose."[9]

Sorde, like Simon of "The New Atlantis," exemplifies how Le Guin's male characters become increasingly less heroic in the second half of the 1970s. Some are injured or otherwise debilitated, as in "The New Atlantis," "The Phoenix," and "The Eye Altering."[10] Others are at a moment of emotional or psychological crisis. "The Water Is Wide" tells of a man whose grief over the death of his wife nearly sends him into insanity. "Two Delays on the Northern Line," set in Orsinia, presents men working through the deaths of a mother and, again, a wife. In these stories Le Guin explores how men deal with overwhelming emotions. "The Water Is Wide" is especially interesting in that Gideon is saved by his sister Anna, who is also widowed. United by blood, love and their common losses, they merge into Gideanna, an inseparable unit. Anna, who is stronger than her brother, helps him to accept mortality.

Here Le Guin turns our attention to one of the many tasks that tend to fall to women: helping others die. While she does not examine this idea again for some time, it heralds her attention to particularly female experiences.[11] "The White Donkey" describes a young girl whose meetings with a unicorn end when she enters a premature, arranged marriage. "Gwilan's Harp" follows the life of a gifted musician who discovers in old age that she is her own greatest instrument. "Malheur County" is about a widow living with her also widowed son-in-law and his young child. These last two stories, in particular, are compelling individual portraits of women. They live typical women's lives — marrying, bearing children, keeping house, growing old.

Running for the Hills

These stories show a marked change in Le Guin's writing, a genuine concentration on female characters. It would take some time, however, to work out a novel that fully concentrated on a female character.[12] A turning point came with *The Eye of the Heron*.[13] She tells how she was stalled while writing the book because the young hero, Lev, seemed to insist on getting killed.

> What I didn't know when I planned out the book was that the hero was going to have to be killed by the middle of the book, and that he wasn't the hero, that the hero was actually a girl from the aggressive culture, only she isn't really a hero either.[14]

Like "The New Atlantis," *The Eye of the Heron* is about a totalitarian regime and the counterculture at odds with it. These stories also feature a male character who is important in the woman's life, but who will by the story's end be effectively silenced by the controlling powers. Here we can see Le Guin acting out in her fiction a process that was happening in her subconscious — the male ushering in the female, then bowing out as the female takes control. *Eye* is, Le Guin has said, the book in which she stopped writing about men and started writing about women.[15] As discussed in the preceding chapter, contrary to the frequent criticism that Le Guin never writes about women, at least three of her novels prior to *The Eye of the Heron* featured complex female characters: Rolery from *Planet of Exile*, Heather LeLache of *The Lathe of Heaven*, and Tenar of *The Tombs of Atuan*. But in none of these does the female control the entire narrative. Even in Tenar's story, easily the most female-centric, Ged is central to the plot development. In *The Eye of the Heron*, on the other hand, the female lead outlasts the male, taking pride of place by the end of the novel. *The Eye of the Heron*, in fact, begins Le Guin's process of shaping a truly feminist work, bearing as it does many elements (not all fully worked out) of the feminist project.

The Eye of the Heron tells the story of two radically different peoples forced to coexist on an extra-planetary penal colony. Their cultures, one dominant/sadistic and the other pacifist, are personified in the two male leads. Don Falco is a political leader or Boss of Victoria City. His people are deeply steeped in machismo and have organized their society into a sexual and cultural hierarchy. Lev is the young idealist, the natural leader of the pacifist group exiled on Victoria. His people live in a smaller settlement they call Shantih. City and town must cooperate in order to survive on this otherwise unexplored and uninhabited planet. Yet over the years the city has abused the relationship and now effectively controls the pacifists. Despite, or because of, their belief in nonviolent resistance, the

People of the Peace (as they call themselves) are essentially defenseless against the arrogant brutality of the Bosses. Balancing the similarly self-assured leaders is Luz, Don Falco's daughter.

Luz initially resembles the stubborn, beautiful, and feisty rich girl so common to romance novels, but this image is undermined by the suggestion of her imprisonment. We are introduced to her in a scene reminiscent of the opening of *Jane Eyre*, which so clearly establishes Jane's marginalization and confinement. It is raining outside, and Luz sits in a deep window seat, looking through a book. She has never seen a book before and if caught would probably be punished. Clearly Luz has become adept at stealing for herself what small liberties she can, but she is a virtual captive of her father's house. She can either marry the brutal son of a Boss or be a scorned spinster acting the role of aunt to another woman's children. When she overhears her suitor's plot to raid Shantih and rape the women, thereby inciting the pacifists to violence, she escapes her father's house to warn Lev, an action that ensures her permanent exile. While Lev acts as her guardian and mentor, she quickly learns to think for herself and even to challenge his ideals, deftly cutting to the heart of the People of the Peace's dilemma. As with Rolery in *Planet of Exile*, her liminal position gives her insight into the problems of this culture.[16] She realizes the danger of nostalgia for the Old World and the old ways, both for her father's society and for Lev's. When Lev is killed in a confrontation with the city guard, Luz quietly becomes the leader of a faction within Shantih. Rather than stay in servitude to the city — albeit remaining true to the tenets of peaceful resistance — Luz opts for simply running away. With a small group from Shantih, she leaves the town and Victoria City behind, departing in the dark and leaving no path. The way to freedom is not, as she sees it, compromise, but rather beginning again, leaving the old order behind rather than attempting to accommodate it and risk being diluted by it.

Clearly here Le Guin has broken with the narrative flow of the traditional novel, essentially killing off the main male character and replacing him with the female. Unlike Rolery and Jakob, whose coupling represents the joining of cultures, Luz and Lev never meet sexually and he is killed before their relationship can get that far. And while they are attracted to one another, their philosophies clearly are at odds. The missed connection underlines a shifting sense of gender in Le Guin's work, and indeed a shift from admiring and adopting the "male" way of doing things.

Vera, an older pacifist who acts as a mentor to Luz, ruminates on the differences between men and women:

> It seems to me that where men are weak and dangerous is in their vanity. A woman has a center, is a center. But a man isn't, he's a reaching out. So he reaches out and grabs things and piles them up around him and says, I'm this, I'm that, this is me, that's me, I'll prove that I am me! And he can wreck a lot of things, trying to prove it.[17]

These are Vera's ideas of course, and not descriptive of all the men in the book. Lev's father, Sasha, for example, does not fit this model. But Don Falco and Lev, both leaders among their people, certainly do.[18] Women and men are also depicted as thinking and reacting differently. Luz's disregard for both her father's sense of social order and Lev's reflects Lillian Smith's quip that "What Freud mistook for her lack of civilization is woman's lack of loyalty to civilization."[19] Whether this is an essentialist notion or one illustrative of the kind of socialized differences in men and women that Carol Gilligan argues for is not clear here. Luz sees no reason to play by the rules of the game. It is not, after all, her game. She suggests that rather than continue to fight with the Bosses, the People of the Peace simply leave and begin their own colony.

Lev had been appalled at Luz's suggestion that they give up their ideals. To him there was no greater good than holding onto the belief system his people brought with them from Earth. And though Lev believed he had a center, his self-worth was caught up in being a leader to the People of the Peace. His repeated insistence on holding fast to the ideals of nonviolent resistance betrayed a reluctance to part from the known and to improvise from his own sense of truth. Luz, on the other hand, grows into a strong, self-validating person, her own center. The image of a center is emphasized in the novel by a number of repeated images. The eye of the heron, for example, represents the serene center of a being wholly at peace. The herons themselves frequent the quiet pool at the center of a ring of trees formed, as in a redwood forest, around the spot where a single, huge parent tree once stood.[20] Lev is often seen sitting in such a ring, contemplating the center and watching the herons dance. But Luz herself is more like the parent tree; around her a new colony will grow.

Woman is also here equated with the natural wilderness, that vast fearful unknown that has until now effectively imprisoned the colonists in their small enclaves. Talking with Luz about the wilderness, Lev imagines her there, a woman standing alone in a place without help or shelter, a woman in the wilderness; and pity was lost in admiration and in fear. He was afraid of her. There was a strength in her that was not drawn from love or trust or community, did not rise from any source that should give strength, any source he recognized. He feared that strength, and craved it.[21]

Immediately, though, he begins to think that she must be subsumed in his community, "she must be one of them, acting with him, supporting him, not filling and confusing his thoughts like this."[22] Lev, for all his pacifist idealism, needs to be the leader, and he is threatened by the wildness in Luz that he can never control. Though he helped originate the plan to start a new colony, Lev is not the kind of person likely to succeed there. His fear of the wildness in Luz and his need to control it suggest that he would treat the actual wild in the same way, be unable to accept its radical otherness. Later, Luz contemplates the idea of God and concludes that God belonged to the city and had nothing to do with the wilderness. In many ways, the city and Shantih represent the old way, the order and rule of men. In striking out into the wilderness, Luz and the others are heading into the territory of women, exploring unknown and fearsome terrain.

When she sat down to write *The Eye of the Heron*, Le Guin was, according to her own description, still not consciously wary about how conventions tended to steer her toward the male. The book was to have been rather conventional in both plot and theme. It is in fact conventional in terms of structure and development, using the same multiple points of view and straightforward exposition of many of her earlier books. But Lev's insistence from her subconscious that he had to die midway through the narrative indicates that feminism had made an impact. The male character that would otherwise have taken over gives way to a vital female character. And while her earliest books depicted skirmishes, acts of guerilla warfare, and an all-out battle in defense of a fortified city, there is only one brief, bloody and unglamorous confrontation in *The Eye of the Heron*. This is a narrative not of action, but of choosing not to take action. Luz is the true driving force of *The Eye of the Heron*, first in following her impulse to warn Lev of the impending attack and later in quietly asserting the wisdom of simply running away from both Victoria City and Shantih. There is, she instinctively knows, no sense in loyalty to a lost cause. In this she follows the Taoist concept of *wu wei*; she recognizes the uselessness of continuing to submit to a system locked in an oppressive stale-mate. Many in Shantih castigate Luz and the other new colonists for "run-ning away," for rejecting Shantih's commitment to steadfast unity even if it means that some must be sacrificed. Luz sees dying as a dubious honor, and because she knows first-hand the power and cruelty of the Bosses, she understands better than the People of the Peace the absolute intractabil-ity of their situation. Her running away is in essence a choice to remove herself from an impossible situation, to find a more natural way to live. But while Le Guin is clearly aligning the old order with the male — with men, in fact — and the emerging new world with the female, she does not exclude men from the new world. Both women and men leave Shantih to establish the new colony. Lev's father, who is of a very different tempera-ment than his son, is one of the new colonists. There is also the sugges-tion of a relationship between Luz and one of the men who makes the journey with her. There will have to be male-female relationships, of course, if the colony is to survive. *The Eye of the Heron* is not a novel of female separatism. Anyone able to accept the danger of the wilderness and to break with the past is welcome in the new colony.

This solution, like those posed in *The Left Hand of Darkness* and *The Dispossessed*, does not satisfy all readers. As Le Guin made clear in 1978, she is not a radical feminist. That is, in her implied definition, she does not advocate separatism or ascribe all injustice to sexual discrimination. As a statement of her beliefs at this time, the following passage is worth quoting at length:

> I am often angry, as a woman. But my feminist anger is only an element in, a part of, the rage and fear that possess me when I face what we are all doing to each other, to the earth, and to the hope of liberty and life. I still "don't care" whether people are male or female.... One soul unjustly imprisoned, am I to ask which sex it is?... The answer of some radical feminists is, Yes. Granted the premise that the root of all injus-tice, exploitation, and blind aggression is sexual injustice, this position is sound. I cannot accept the premise...[23]

She does not accept the premise and cannot therefore write from the view-point of radical feminism. A later story, "Sur," where a group of women are the first to reach the South Pole, does suggest that in certain circum-stances women can achieve more when not in male company. Le Guin does, however, go on to praise radical feminists who take on the painful task of upholding their ideology no matter what the cost in ingratitude and obloquy.[24] She is personally grateful that feminist ideology has forced her to really examine her beliefs. This self-evaluation has not come easily to her because she has always considered herself well aware of her "being-as-woman." But she has used the tools of feminism, she says, "to try to figure out what makes me work and how I work, so that I will no longer work in ignorance or irresponsibility."[25]

One thing this soul searching made clear to her was that

> The "person" I tend to write about is often not exactly, or not totally, either a man or a woman. On the superficial level this means there is little sexual stereotyping — the men aren't lustful and the women aren't gorgeous — and the sex itself is seen as a relationship rather than an act. Sex serves mainly to define gender, and the gender of the person is not exhausted, or even very nearly approached, by the label "man" or "woman." Indeed both sex and gender seem to be used mainly to define the meaning of "person," or of "self." Once, as I began to be awakened, I closed the relationship into one person, an androgyne. But more often it appears conventionally and overtly, as a couple. Both in one: or two making a whole. Yin does not appear without yang, nor yang without yin. Once I was asked what I thought the central, constant theme of my work was, and I said spontaneously, "Marriage."[26]

It can be said of Le Guin's male characters, even from the beginning, that they are not the typical one-dimensional space opera heroes. Though they tended before 1975 to be larger than life, they did have vulnerabilities that softened them and made them more human. Gavarel Rocannon, for example, is graying; Jakob Agat is helpless against his desire for Rolery; Genly Ai makes some rather serious errors in judgment.

When she wrote *The Eye of the Heron*, Le Guin also turned specific attention to the issue of language — by the mid-seventies, a significant concern of feminist scholars. She had in *The Dispossessed* recognized that language held over from an oppressive culture carries with it harmful baggage. The Odonians realized the impossibility of separating words from their connotations. Yet we have seen that even in *The Dispossessed* Le Guin's use of language was problematic. Her 1976 defense of *The Left Hand of Darkness*, moreover, still denies the power of connotation and seems to argue that the writer does not have the right to change the rules of grammar to pursue an idea. Susan Bernardo and Graham Murphy point out that *Eye* can be read in the context of post-colonial theory about the imposition of language. Using a non-native language to describe an alien object results in a cognitive gap between signifier and signified.[27] An invented language, made to fit the new world, is the remedy. In *The Eye of the Heron*, Le Guin does not experiment with language, but she does call attention to its power and for the first time seems to argue that we can, indeed must, change language. Luz recognizes early on the need to give the colony new names. The old names carry with them old attitudes. The name Victoria, for example, is an Earth word. Luz says that they should give the planet a new name, "One that doesn't mean anything. Ooboo, or Baba."[28] These sound like baby words because the colonists are starting from the beginning, constructing a new language for a new order. When the colonists leave Shantih, they realize that they must be silent until they have learned or intuited the language appropriate to the wilderness. Here Le Guin begins to tackle the question of whether writing in the traditional language of fiction automatically and unconsciously draws women into writing the way men do. She says, "English prose is unsuited to the description of feminine being and doing, unless one to some extent remakes it from scratch. It is hard to break from tradition; hard to invent; hard to remake one's mother tongue."[29] Luz, the natural anarchist, recognizes that for the new colony to work, it must give up the language as well as the social forms carried over from Earth. The new planet, a vast wilderness, is unsuited to those structures. The colonists must unlearn the old ways and the language of power, and learn a language that fits the wilderness.

If the language to be unlearned is the father tongue, that which we must learn or relearn is the mother tongue. Le Guin's conception of the mother tongue will be explored in more detail in the following chapter, but it is important to establish here that she had already begun to incorporate this idea into her artistic remaking as early as *The Eye of the Heron*. In the poem "Invocation," published in 1981, the persona entreats the muse to give her back her mother tongue. This tongue, linked to the wilderness, is a language of unmaking:

> Give me back my language,
> let me speak the tongue you taught me.
> I will lie the great lies in your honor,
> praise you without naming you,
> obey the laws of darkness and of metrics.
> Only let me speak my language
> in your praise, silence of the valleys,
> north side of the rivers,

third face averted,
emptiness!
Let me speak the mother tongue
and I will sing so loudly
newlyweds and old women
will dance to my singing
and sheep will cease from cropping and machines
will gather round to listen
in cities fallen silent
as a ring of standing stones:
O let me sing the walls down, Mother![30]

Hard Words, the collection in which "Invocation" appears, also includes the exuberant series of poems "The Dancing at Tillai," which explores the interrelations of creativity, sexuality and death. These poems originally appeared in *Tillai and Tylissos*, which included responsive poems by Le Guin's mother, by now married to John Quinn. Theodora Kroeber Quinn answers her daughter's calls for comfort, particularly comfort from the fear of death. The chapbook was published in 1979, the year of her mother's death and the year Le Guin turned fifty. Despite the mingled anticipation and exhilaration of many of Le Guin's poems, we can see in them the daughter's fear of her mother's death and in that the reminder of her own advancing age. Kroeber's poems invite the daughter/persona to join the dancing at Tylissos, to consider the Old Queen embowered with her young husband, still dancing the dance of sexual joy and creativity. These poems and others in *Hard Words*, like "Simple Hill," "The Child on the Shore," and "The Indian Rugs," explore the relationships among generations of women that will become a major focus of Le Guin's later writing.

Breaking with Tradition

In 1979, Le Guin published three works that are attempts to distance herself from the genres she had long loved, studied and practiced. *Malafrena*, "The Pathways of Desire," and *The Beginning Place*[31] respond to, respectively, the nineteenth-century novel, science fiction, and fantasy. They are self-conscious pieces, frequently ironic, and if not all outright revisions of their respective genres, metafictional in at least the second two cases. We can almost feel Le Guin chafing under the traditions that hold these literary types together. At least early on, her attempts at distancing herself from these traditions were not wholly successful.

That feminist discourse was pivotal in her reassessment of these genres is evident in *Malafrena*, a novel set in nineteenth-century Orsinia. Le Guin began *Malafrena* in the early fifties, while she was composing much of her Orsinian work. But it refused to come together, despite repeated efforts over the next two decades. Finally, thanks to her raised feminist awareness, Le Guin was able to complete the book. She says there were in it

> Things I needed to rethink entirely. Getting the women characters
> right. Itale was always OK, the men's story was easy, but I had a terrible
> time with the women. I didn't understand them. I especially didn't
> understand what was happening to Piera, the heroine. I know now
> why: I needed to become a conscious feminist to understand why my
> women were acting this way and what was happening in their relation-
> ships.[32]

Le Guin did get the book "unstuck" and published, though it has received little attention from critics. It is in some ways dissatisfying. It deflates the romance convention of the union of lovers that guarantees renewal, but it does not proffer a clear alternative.

Set on country estates, in small provincial towns, and in the drawing rooms, ghettoes and prisons of several large cities, *Malafrena* shows the influence of the major European nineteenth-century novelists. It reads like an Eliot or Tolstoy novel, tracking characters of both sexes and telling their interrelated stories in the period 1825–1830, during Malafrena's fight for independence from the Austrian empire. Le Guin had trouble completing the book, perhaps because the women characters, as they finally evolve, are out-of-place in a book set in the early nineteenth-century. The three main female characters, who come of age in the course of the story, seem to choke at the restraints of their gendered situation. They ruminate on it in ways that feel incongruous not just to their time but also to the traditional conventions of the historical novel. In her attempt to revise the book to fit her heightened feminist sensibility, Le Guin rewrites the scripts for the women characters, trying to find room for them to be something other than prospective wives. The effort falls somewhat short; despite the three-to-one ratio of female to male lead characters, it is the young man, Itale Sorde, who most stands out.[33] The female characters seem constrained by his narrative weight, and the scenes in which he is featured are the best developed and have the most convincing dialogue.

Itale is a young man of the landed gentry with a passionate commitment to freeing his country from Austrian domination. He leaves his family's estate to live in the capital city, Krasnoy, where he starts a radical journal and builds a group of friends from among the city's aristocrats and artists. Among them is Luisa Paludeskar, a wealthy young woman with whom Itale has an affair. When he is jailed for subversion, Luisa uses her money and political connections to rescue him. Though he is physically and emotionally scarred after two years in solitary confinement, he returns to the city and to his revolutionary activities. After a failed uprising, he is proscribed and returns to his country home in defeat. By the end of the story, however, his childhood friend Piera has convinced him that he must continue to create freedom for those who cannot go out and gain it for themselves.

Itale's fight to free his country from Austrian oppression is juxtaposed with the women's lack of freedom, of choice. The novel is filled with women's meditations on their lot in life. Piera is shown early on attempting to write a school essay on the "Duties of the Young Female." She cannot stop herself from doodling; there is little to write of other than obedience, marriage, and babies. In the course of the novel, though, she will break two engagements and commit herself to managing her family's estate, at which she excels. Piera differentiates between men's and women's freedom, thinking that "No one had ever spoken to her about what freedom is for a woman, what it might consist of and how it is to be won. Or not won, that seemed the wrong word for a woman's freedom; worked at, perhaps."[34] Later she understands, when Itale cannot, that the country's freedom depends on him resuming his revolutionary work, on refusing the easy, secure way. Piera, childish at first but eventually a mature woman, is contrasted with Luisa, Itale's aristocratic lover. Luisa seems sophisticated and self-assured, but she is consumed by both her love for Itale and her jealousy of the freedom that he enjoys as a man. Whereas she must depend on her looks and wealth to achieve what little power she will ever have, he is free to make his way in the world. She seems sexually liberated and initiates an affair with Itale, desiring no promises of love or marriage, but she is afraid of the loss of control in sexual abandon. As a woman she is allowed no part in Itale's cause, and she entertains dignitaries from the government he attempts to overthrow: "She saw no disloyalty in this. Why should she be loyal to a cause from which she was excluded? How could she be? She could not play the game, therefore she did not care who won it."[35] In fact, she uses these government contacts to free Itale from prison — something his family and political friends are unable to do.

Even given the high level of development in these and other female characters, *Malafrena* is Itale's story. His magnetism and fight for freedom make him seem like a romantic hero, though he more resembles Shelley than Byron. If Itale still holds center stage, it is perhaps because he fits our outdated sense of the protagonist as the one who acts, who is caught up in whatever drama impels the plot. This is less a result of Le Guin's unconscious bias and more a consequence of writing a historical romance. Yet Le Guin does comment ironically on the form in which she is writing. One of Itale's friends has written a popular romance in which Itale is the thinly disguised hero. As it will transpire, Itale's reality is far grimmer; after his imprisonment for treason and his two years in solitary confinement, even his lover does not know him and is loathe to touch him. Le Guin also deflates or rewrites the usual romance ending; though the reader expects that Itale and Piera will finally marry, they do not, and at Piera's insistence rather than Itale's.

Despite her love of the great nineteenth century novelists, *Malafrena* is Le Guin's only novel that borrows their forms. Along with her other Orsinian stories, it is of particular interest for her juxtaposition of how lives are shaped by city versus countryside, and for her examination of the forces that control history. But it is not among her best works. Her considerable skills, in particular her gift for compression, are not well suited to the conventions of the historical romance. Some sections of the novel and some interior monologues do not ring true (which is genuinely unusual in Le Guin's writing). More than that, she had not quite bridged the gap between the traditional characterization of women and the feminist. She would not publish another Orsinian story for over a decade. It would take the fall of Communism to restore her interest in her European country.

In the meantime, she was also losing interest in outer space, as indicated by her abrupt break with sf, the genre that made her famous. She would later tell an interviewer:

> Space was a metaphor for me. A beautiful, lovely, endlessly rich
> metaphor for me ... until it ended quite abruptly after *The Dispossessed*.

> I had a loss of faith.... I don't seem to be able to write about outer space anymore. The last outer-space story I did was ... "The Pathways of Desire," and it turns out to be a hoax in a sense. Apparently it's an expression of my loss of faith.[36]

"The Pathways of Desire" ironically plays on the limitations of science fiction conventions, as well as on the limitations of some science fiction writers and readers who uphold the crudest kinds of stereotypes. Le Guin's loss of faith is as much an expression of disgust.

"Pathways" tells the story of an anthropological team studying a tribal culture on a distant planet. One of the anthropologists, Bob, resembles the hero of action-adventure science fiction. He is blond, athletic, of superior mind; against his better judgment — if not against his will — he becomes sexually involved with the natives, known as the Ndif. The other two visitors are more like anti-heroes. Twenty-eight-year-old Tamara qualifies by this culture's standards as middle-aged; the linguist, Ramchandra, suffers from diarrhea and had two episodes of insanity following the death of his wife. The planet is a South Sea-style paradise of abundant food and good weather; the young people are all good looking and totally without sexual hang-ups. The team soon realizes that the youth culture is oddly oversimplified. The young men are almost totally occupied with hunting, the young women with erotic dancing and sexual practices. They have almost no storytelling tradition and in fact very little vocabulary. The fair-haired and deeply tanned Bob looks like a Ndif and thrives in this environment, but Tamara and Ramchandra quickly become restless studying the young Ndif. As Tamara says, "They're boring! No kinship systems, no social structure except stupid age-grading and detestable male dominance, no real skills, no arts — lousy carved spoons, all right, like a Hawaiian tourist trap..."[37] Even Bob remarks that they talk like Hemingway characters, since their only topics of conversation are their sexual exploits and their success at hunting. The anthropologists begin to realize that there is nothing truly alien about the culture. Ramchandra notices that Ndif is startlingly like English, too much so to be coincidental. In fact, the transliteration of English into Ndif is by his calculations laughably simple. It is finally revealed that the culture of the planet is the invention of a lonely and most likely sexually frustrated Earth teenager. This boy, like many imaginative people, has invented a science fictional world, a culture on another planet that is essentially a wish fulfillment, an expression of an immense desire he does not understand.

"Pathways" plays ironically on the limitations of the most facile science fiction.[38] The cultures described are often, as here, simple transplantations of our cultures to other planets; they are also ridiculously shallow, as a team of trained scientists would very soon discover. The invented languages are as unsophisticated. Ramchandra, discussing the simplicity of Ndif, remarks, "All female names ... end in 'a.' That is a cosmic constant established by H. Rider Haggard. Male names never end in 'a.' Never."[39] Bob is the standard science fiction hero except that he is drawn into a duel over a Ndif woman and is killed. The death of the blond hero skeptically comments on legions of science fiction heroes who have involved themselves in the affairs of other planets seemingly without ever coming to harm. The young Ndif women are given over wholly to expert sex and pleasing men; in them Le Guin lambastes one of the few stereotypes of women that conventional science fiction includes. The story does end happily, at least for Ramchandra and Tamara, who fall in love. Unlike the teenage boy who has created the place they are studying, they have the maturity to deal with a world of ambiguities, where true heroism is learning to create a mutually satisfying reality with another person. But science fiction, Le Guin seems to argue, indulges too often in adolescent wet dreams and fantasies of power. This simplistic version of life is not truly satisfying to anyone; it is an escape from reality, not a reflection of it. As such it may temporarily satisfy, but it can never help the reader understand the world better. Tamara and Ramchandra's mature, mutual relationship is the superior foundation on which to build.

Le Guin has much the same thing to say in *The Beginning Place*, which endorses the imaginative use of fantasy so long as the individual does not lose sight of reality. *Place* is, to use Brian Attebery's phrase, metafantasy — a fantasy about fantasy.[40] The novel tells of two young people, Hugh and Irene, who are drowning in their own lives. Though they don't know each other, they are unhappy in similar ways. Hugh is overweight, clumsy. His self-loathing and sense of confinement arise from his relationship with a neurotic mother who detests his physical being, yet insists on his constant presence. Irene feels equally trapped. She is consumed by her fear of physical attack, a fear founded on her friend's having been gang-raped and on her own stepfather's frequent attempts to molest her. Like Hugh, she puts her own best interests aside to remain near her mother, clinging to the belief that by doing so she can improve the quality of her mother's life. Both find escape in an enchanted forest, a mysterious place in which time runs very slowly, and where it is always twilight. Though there are humans living there, in the mountain town Tembreabrezi, there seem to be no birds or other animals in the woods. After discovering the place, both return again and again to escape their dreary lives. Irene finds the woods and the town long before Hugh does. The townspeople welcome her as an honorary daughter and she has learned something of their language and culture. She treats Hugh as a trespasser and is dismayed when the townspeople welcome him as a savior. Hugh, they believe, can save them from some unnamed horror that holds them in thrall.

The townspeople look and act like archetypes — the dark lord, the fair damsel, the wise man — and they draw Hugh and Irene into their fairy tale. Hugh is the brave knight who will rescue them (and win the fair maiden), while Irene is Hugh's interpreter and guide, or perhaps the sacrificial offering for the monster. If this is a fairy tale, it is a dark one. Hugh may be the appointed savior, but he is nonetheless still a clumsy supermarket checker. He imagines himself dying for the fair damsel (a young woman from Tembreabrezi), but his romantic fantasies are almost comic-heroic, such is the intensity of his adolescent fervor. And although the townspeople love Irene, they are not above using her as an offering for the monster they fear.

The monster itself is mysterious and deadly, "white, wrinkled, twice a man's height, dragging its bulk painfully and with terrible quickness, round mouth open in the hissing howl of hunger and insatiable pain, and blind."[41] Hugh and Irene first run from it, then confront it face-to-face, Irene baiting the monster and Hugh slaying it. But it remains unclear what this monster is.[42] It may be male. Hugh thinks it smells like semen, and there is the suggestion that the creature looks like him. Yet Irene sees it as female. Their varying interpretations suggest that they see in the monster projections of themselves: Hugh as huge bodied and grossly sexual, and Irene as overly defensive and shrill. It is, like the shadow in *Wizard*, an embodiment of the dark side of the self. That they have seen and in a sense come to terms with their own dark sides is further emphasized by the fact that slaying the monster changes them.

Once the monster is dead and the fairy tale over, Hugh and Irene realize that they love and feel responsible for each other. Though Hugh has been badly hurt in his fight with the monster, the two solidify their relationship by making love. When they emerge from the enchanted forest, they move to the city and set up housekeeping together. Hugh and

Irene know that they cannot ever go back to the enchanted place. It was a kind of escape for them, a retreat from real life problems and from the specter of mature sexuality. Hugh's confrontation with the dragon/monster has taught him to face his problems, including his neurotic mother, and so resolve them. Irene learns the value of partnership when she trusts Hugh to slay the monster and when she helps him find the way out of the forest. Though the real world that Hugh and Irene have to contend with is indeed grim, Le Guin clearly argues that it is necessary to live there. The fantasy world, while pleasant for a brief escape, and necessary for psychic renewal and wholeness, is not a place in which to linger. *Place* is, as Le Guin suggests fantasy should be, about "the journey to self-knowledge, to adulthood, to the light."[43] But it also contains a warning about the unconscious world that fantasy represents: it is a treacherous place in which to stay too long.

Other than "The White Donkey" with its sad suggestion that an arranged marriage will end a young girl's innocent meetings with a unicorn, Le Guin would write no more fantasy until *Fire and Stone* (1989) and *Tehanu* (1990). *Fire and Stone* is a children's story about how a village deals with the dragon that threatens it. It plays with the idea that "dragons" arise from the mythologizing of geography. A more serious treatment of dragons is found in *Tehanu*, Le Guin's next installment in the Earthsea series. *Tehanu*, discussed in the next chapter, sounds another cautionary note about the uses of fantasy. Le Guin is more overtly concerned here about the misuse of power, but she continues the critique of fantasy's feudal social systems and oversimplified archetypes that she began in *Place*. Clearly Le Guin is not disaffected from fantasy, as she professes to be from science fiction. But *Place* suggests a distance not at all evident in her earlier works.

South

By 1982, when she published the short story "Sur," Le Guin had left behind not only the traditional narratives and genres, but men too. "Sur" tells of a group of South American women who in 1909 go on an expedition to the South Pole several years before Amundsen and Scott. Their "goal was limited to observation and exploration. [They] hoped to go a little farther, and see a little more; if not, simply to go and see. A simple ambition ... and essentially a modest one."[44] They go for themselves, so as not to have lived a "life without danger, without uncertainty, without hope."[45] In other words, they do not go to conquer, to be the first or to claim the land in their country's name, but rather to have the experience itself. The story is told in retrospect by one of their number, in a diary she has no intention of publishing. She later leaves this record of their journey in an attic trunk in her suburban Lima home, hiding it from both fame and notoriety. The women, all of respected families, have of necessity cloaked their adventure in secrecy; their husbands do not know their destination. Even with this secrecy, their expedition proves difficult to assemble. Many potential candidates cannot release themselves from their responsibilities:

> An ailing parent; an anxious husband beset by business cares; a child at home with only ignorant or incompetent servants to look after it: These are not responsibilities lightly to be set aside. And those who wished to evade such claims were not the companions we wanted in hard work, risk, and privation.[46]

Yet their experience of living within a network of relationships and responsibilities serves them well in the tight quarters of their arctic camp and in the travails of the polar journey. They know the benefit of mutual cooperation. Though they appoint leaders whose voices would prevail in cases of urgent danger, they never make use of this hierarchy: "we nine were, and are, by birth and upbringing, unequivocally and irrevocably, all crew."[47]

When she sets foot on Antarctic ice, the narrator claims a sense of "familiarity. I felt that I was home at last."[48] She finds the camp built by Scott and recently used by Shackleton to be offensively unkempt; outside is a mass of rubbish and seal skins, inside a mean disarray of discarded tins, food, and dog turds. This experience alloys her pleasure, and she reflects on the fact that "the backside of heroism is often rather sad; women and servants know that. They know also that the heroism may be no less real for that. But achievement is smaller than men think. What is larger is the sky, the earth, the sea, the soul."[49] The women, rather than live in the place left uninhabitable by male explorers who went before them, live in a series of tunnels and warrens dug into the ice itself.

Though one group turns back without remorse before reaching the pole, the other women do reach it and leave no indication that they have been there: "there seemed no particular reason to do so. Anything we could do, anything we were, was insignificant, in that awful place."[50] Despite having achieved their goal, there is no elation among the women; they realize, even before they achieve the pole, that it is no place for human beings — they have no business there. The narrator relates how she "was glad even then that we had left no sign there, for some man longing to be first might come some day, and find it, and know then what a fool he had been, and break his heart."[51] Years later, the narrator goes back to her diary to add a last note. In a brief paragraph she sums up the lives of these nine women; some have died, one took the veil, all have grown old and drifted apart. A child born in the base camp, Rosa del Sur, died at five of scarlet fever. Of their trip to the pole the narrator says only that anyone who might read this record must not let Mr. Amundsen know. "He would be terribly embarrassed and disappointed. There is no need for him or anyone else outside the family to know. We left no footprints, even."[52]

Le Guin has said of this story that writing it "was one of the pleasantest experiences of my life" and that though she realizes she is "saying some rather hard things about heroism," she wrote the story as a way of joining the explorers of the Antarctic rather than as a means to chiding them. "Why couldn't a few of us, my kind of people, housewives, come along with them in my book ... or even come before them?"[53] The differences she implies between the way that these women view their Antarctic expedition and the way men do, however, are important and instructive. Le Guin may have enjoyed her imaginative expedition, but she definitely approached it far differently than did any of the men who really went there. She seems to have objected most to the idea that the pole is a place to be conquered, that anyone would go there in order to tell others that he had been, that he had overcome the forces of nature. For the women in her story, the pole itself is never the real goal. That they do reach the pole is not to them a matter of heroism. They have conquered nothing, for there was no battle put up against them by the Antarctic. The howling winds, impassable crevasses, bitter cold and blinding snow are not forces arrayed against them; nature is unaware of them. That awesome, awful place is not the domain of human beings, and it is, the narrator comes to decide, not a place where humans should be.

That they go at all is never treated ironically by Le Guin. While they ultimately question the wisdom of forging ahead to the pole, they do not regret the adventure they underwent; how else but in the knowledge that they had lived with danger could they continue in their otherwise quiet and predictable lives? That they succeeded where groups of men had failed is a tribute to skills they have developed as women, wives and mothers. As a reflection of Le Guin's mature feminism "Sur" again disappoints some readers. The narrator's diary — hidden away, to be discovered only after its writer's death or perhaps never to be read at all — seems to reenact the disappearance of so much women's writing, so many of the achievements that feminism has worked hard to uncover. The women's apparent passivity, their willingness to let the men take all the credit for discovering the pole, also seems a step backward. It is opposite the feminism of audacious action Rebecca West and Germaine Greer advocated, which called for women to disprove the male notion of their docility and femininity. Yet what seems a "kinder, gentler feminism," one that allows for feminism as long as we do not tell the men, has at its core something profound and subversive.

In "Sur" Le Guin simply rejects prevailing notions of success. Her views reflect Dale Spender's statement that "It is not a feminist principle that women should have half of what men have because it's not a feminist belief that men are the yardstick, or even that what they do is desirable."[54] What Le Guin writes about is a different way of being in the world, one that she believes will insure global survival by reversing Western notions of progress. It is not, she tells us, wise to stand in an adversarial relation to nature. For one thing, it is a delusion to believe that nature stands against us, waiting for opportunities to diminish and destroy us. Such an understanding of our relationship to nature denies our relative insignificance in the world. Rather than see ourselves as coexisting as strands of a web, the heroic stance insists on a hierarchy that isolates humankind from the rest of nature. Shackleton's careless treatment of his base camp also demonstrates that the adversarial relationship to nature leads to disrespect and wanton destruction. "Sur," defines a kind of "her-oism"; though the women's trip to the pole is "heroic," it is made so by their sense that the victory won is over the self. These women confront danger, uncertainty, and the unknown and they live to tell about it, but choose not to. Their heroism comes from taking on themselves the responsibility for the success or failure of the trip and judging for themselves the worthiness of their effort. In the meantime, they provide a model of a community that works not by hierarchy but by mutual aid and cooperation. They grumble, as those sharing tight quarters and hard work do, but they happily co-exist.

The Space Crone

In her non-fiction of this period, Le Guin began to write more frankly about women's lives. Her 1976 piece, "The Space Crone," is a lively essay exhorting women to enjoy or at least appreciate menopause as a woman's rite of passage, marking the end of her childbearing years but by no means the end of her life. Indeed, the real glory of menopause is the opportunity it gives women to become Crones. "There are things the Old Woman can do, say, and think that the Woman cannot do, say, or think."[55] She wields, moreover, a kind of power virgins and women of childbearing age do not: men are afraid of her. Le Guin wrote this essay, she says, at the same time that she was going through menopause. Though menopause had recently begun to receive attention from feminist thinkers, when Le Guin wrote her essay, it had been largely undiscussed in the women's movement. She has also dealt with the subject of abortion. Though certainly not a taboo topic in the women's movement, Le Guin allowed the public a rare glimpse into her private life by describing the circumstances around an abortion she had as an undergraduate. "The Princess" is an ironic fairy tale about a college co-ed who has an expensive and illegal abortion in the early fifties. The essay, she tells the reader, is based on her own experience. Though she says she is ashamed to have been ignorant enough to have gotten pregnant, she is not ashamed of the abortion itself. A lecture on abortion/family planning that Le Guin delivered during this period speaks more generally on her sense of women's relation to their reproductive capacity. For the survival of the species, she argues, we must allow women to make their own choices, assert their own morality about the reproductive process. Given the opportunity to do so, women will make a choice for life; that is, they will choose to limit family size and not to bear unwanted or deformed babies. Her implication is that because current laws on reproduction and abortion are made by men, the standards created have nothing to do with women's morality. She quotes Irene Claremont de Castillejo to contrast women's sense of morality with society's "man-made ethics." Claremont de Castillejo argues that although women have adopted male principles about the sacredness of life, "Women's basic instinct is not concerned with the *idea* of life, but with the *fact* of life. The ruthlessness of nature which discards unwanted life is deeply ingrained in her."[56]

Le Guin calls these comments "a suggestion of the kind of thing I and many, many others are groping towards."[57] But she seems a little uneasy with the essentialism implied. Ten years later, she notes that Claremont de Castillejo "runs the risk of implying that women are 'natural,' that their morality is 'natural' or 'instinctive.'"[58] She refers the reader to Gilligan's *In a Different Voice,* "one of the most useful guides into the difficult area of the cultural determination and enforcement of differences between male and female moral perception."[59] The idea that morality is not necessarily a matter of biological sex is in keeping with Le Guin's own experience; it was, after all, her father who told her that having an abortion "is a lesser sin than the crass irresponsibility of sacrificing your training, your talent, and the children you will want to have, in order to have one nobody wants to have."[60]

In 1980, Le Guin watched the eruption of Mt. St. Helens from a window of her Portland home. She describes the experience in a small collection, *In the Red Zone,* which combines poems and journal entries. The tone is both awed and humorous, and she is clearly delighted to have witnessed an event on the geologic scale. As she says, "everybody takes it personally."[61] For Le Guin, the "eruption was all mixed up with the women's movement. It may be silly but there it is."[62] The mountain is a "sister," displaying women's power to seem graceful and peaceful until the moment she decides not to be. Then, watch out. The mountain's eruption, its force and unpredictability, its participation in the geologic act of making and unmaking are "a threat: a terror: a fulfillment."[63] Le Guin is moving, as we shall see in the next chapter, to a more aggressive, openly political stance. She seems, in fact, to have become the crone who uses her experience and wisdom to critique society. She is, at the same time, Grandmother Spider, who spins in her web new versions of reality, visions of possible, better ways to live.

The spider/weaver/artist, ubiquitous in Le Guin's writing, is the subject of her children's book *Leese Webster.* Leese is an artistic spider that lives in a deserted palace and makes intricate webs following designs taken from the furnishings and carpets around her. The palace is to be converted into a museum, and the authorities in charge of its renovation mistake Leese's webs for tapestries. So fine is her work that the humans decide these delicate masterpieces must be kept under glass. Leese's cries that the glass will prevent her webs from catching her dinner go unheeded. Eventually she is discovered by a cleaning woman and is thrown out a window. Yet Leese finds the outdoors the ultimate place to build a web. Not only can she catch more flies, but she can copy the beautiful designs of nature. Even better, the morning dew that clings to her webs catches the early sunlight, adorning her work with jewels.

The loom and the spider as weaver recur regularly in Le Guin's writing. In *City of Illusions, Always Coming Home,* and "Buffalo Gals," Le Guin uses web-making or the loom to symbolize creation on a cosmic level. Whether Grandmother Spider or a lesser character, in Le Guin's fiction weavers have a deep connection to the life force. *Leese Webster,* despite its whimsy, has something serious to say about the nature of creation.[64] Leese embodies the commitment of the artist. She continues to work despite her loneliness and the disapproval of other spiders that believe webs need only be practical. Indeed Leese's first efforts at artistry are failures both as art and as webs for catching food. She learns to combine functionality with artistry, and becomes quite adept at copying designs. She cannot, however, make her work capture the quality of the jewels she has seen in the throne room; her webs never sparkle or give off color. She is delighted when her work is discovered, having toiled for so long without praise, but she is not so sure about having her webs glassed in, deprived of functionality. The freedom of the outdoors and the beauty of the natural world are exactly the remedy she needs.

Leese's story is not unlike Le Guin's. Having toiled in seclusion for many years, she was delighted when she finally became a published author. And like Leese, she was probably less delighted to have her work, in effect, isolated and scrutinized by a scholarly machinery that made of her an icon to be either worshipped or pulled down. She was at the same time being stereotyped both by critics and by the publishing industry. Like Leese, at least to an extent, she was copying from a sometimes arcane tradition, drawing artistic inspiration from other artists' perceptions of the world. For Le Guin, as for Leese, it must have been a relief to leave the palace and to breathe fresh air.

CHAPTER THREE

The Fisherwoman's Daughter

In a 1986 interview, Le Guin discussed the role the feminist movement played in changing her perceptions:

> I'm deeply grateful to feminism, because I feel it has liberated me in many ways. It's liberated me from ways of thinking and being that I didn't even know I was caught in. But I was caught. And now I'm free of certain rigidities—for instance, the fact that all my early books are about men, and women are very secondary.... That's very strange. I'm a woman. Why was I writing that way? [...] now I have my tradition as a woman, as a woman writer. I was afraid of it, apparently, I wasn't strong enough to use it.[1]

The depth of Le Guin's gratitude to feminist thinkers, those Le Guin calls her "unteachers," is evident in the non-fiction pieces collected in *Dancing at the Edge of the World*. These include commencement addresses, lectures, magazine articles, and theoretical essays. In these pieces, she thanks feminism openly and she herself preaches feminist ideas with joyful conviction. "The Fisherwoman's Daughter," which she originally delivered as a lecture, is an especially informative example of how far Le Guin has come as a feminist.[2] The last essay in *Dancing*, "Daughter" stands as a culmination of her feminist thinking, summing up where she has come from and to as a woman writer. We can thus use the essay as a point of entry for discussing Le Guin's emergence into full-blown feminism.

A resonant affirmation of women's creative and intellectual powers, "The Fisherwoman's Daughter" both overtly and subtly undermines our sense of the author as omniscient, the text as monolithic. Le Guin, for example, calls "Daughter" a collaboration. She says of it,

> This essay has been given as a lecture six or seven times. I rewrote it each time, guided by responses, questions, letters after the lecture. I look on it, gratefully, as a collaboration with my listeners, my editors

and all the writers whose works and words I pieced together in it—ancestors, strangers, and friends.[3]

"Daughter" thus undermines the conventional positioning of the author as authority and the reader/listener as acolyte. Instead of lecturing distantly from her podium, Le Guin initiates reciprocal relationships among herself, her audience, and the women writers who went before her. The collaborative acts that shaped the essay underline one of Le Guin's key points: women writers do not really work alone, are not given a "room of their own" where they write in uninterrupted solitude. According to Le Guin, male writers can sequester themselves from the business of life, adopt the stance of the artist as hero and so wrestle with their artistic demons in private. They are assured that they need not leave their cork-lined writing chambers, for their meals will be brought to them by kind, ministering angels (that is, their wives). Women writers, particularly those with children, have traditionally worked in a turbulent sea of conflicting demands. They write at the kitchen or parlor table, while running a household, tending to husbands and children, and trying to ignore the social criticism heaped upon them for diverting any attention from their "rightful duty." Unlike those of the hermetic male artist, women's acts of creation are entangled in the fabric of relationships that make up women's lives.

Rather than presenting this as a disadvantage, Le Guin sees benefits in this interconnection with the activity of the household. Against the old assumption that women who write cannot make books and babies, Le Guin argues that the writer/mother is in a unique and wonderful position. Who could be more qualified to write about life, to create from this raw material the stuff of art, than she who is in the middle of it? Not only is the woman writer, mother or not, capable of writing, she is certainly as capable as any male artist of writing which truthfully reflects life, perhaps more capable because she is more in tune with the subject. To prove her point, Le Guin gathers together in her essay a number of different sources, including excerpts from poems, books, letters and diaries. The essay is thus a loosely-knit collage, the working title for which was "Crazy Quilt."[4] This patching together of words and ideas from a number of writers again deflates the traditional sense of the author as working alone and of the text as sacred and inviolate, not to be cut and stitched together with vastly divergent works. Moreover, "Daughter" relies on the experience of women as a base of evidence, making women writers authorities on the value of their art and on the social appropriateness of combining writing, womanhood, and mothering. It belies the seeming historical evidence that there have been few women writers and no women's literary tradition, instead establishing a sense of a literary community of women writers, living and long-dead, forming a tradition that reaches back through literary time. Le Guin also discards the stance of objectivity and distance from her subject that has long been the favorite pose of intellectuals; in fact, she uses her own experience as a woman writer to prove her point.

"We think back through our mothers, if we are women," Virginia Woolf wrote[5]; "Daughter" is Le Guin's thinking back through her literary mothers and through her own literal literary mother, Theodora Kroeber. She is, in Alice Walker's phrase, in search of her mother's garden.[6] While Walker sought her mother's artistry in the non-literary, Le Guin looks to the wealth of women's writing to find her literary mothers, many of whom have only recently come back into print. These writers enable us all — and especially the writer/housewife who has long considered herself an oddity working against nature — to think back through generations of women writing. Le Guin's own greatest enabler, she says, has always been Woolf, whose work she read long before the feminist movement began to regain momentum.[7]

The title and central image of "Daughter" come from Woolf's "Professions for Women" in which the author likens the efforts of a woman engaged in writing to those of a woman fishing. In Woolf's scenario, the woman writing lowers her imagination into the depths of her consciousness. She cannot, however, let her imagination go free but must keep hold of it by the thin thread of reason. Should she let it loose, it would dart away "into the dark pool of extraordinary experience. The reason has to cry 'Stop!' The novelist has to pull on the line and haul the imagination to the surface."[8] Reason has checked imagination's efforts because it was going too far, taking the writer into realms male readers would be unwilling to go. Reason reminds the woman writer that "Men would be shocked!" Because of the strength of literary conventions and social stigma (Woolf delivered this essay in 1931), the woman writer is unable to write about her body, her passions, her experience of womanhood. Wait fifty years, reason says to the imagination, and we will be able to tell these truths. It was not only men who would be shocked. Earlier in the essay, Woolf describes the Victorian ideal of womanhood, the utterly charming, pure, and selfless wife and mother — the Angel in the House. This Angel threatens the woman writer as much as does the specter of male disapproval. Women must, the Angel says, flatter, cajole and deceive; their livelihoods as wives, mothers and homemakers depend on it. Woolf boldly disagrees: women must tell the truth as they know it. To be writers, they must exorcise this Angel and tell the truth about women's experiences and emotions.

In Le Guin's view, even in the 1980s, things had only just begun to change for women who write. They still combated both male disapproval and that of the womanly Angel. If they were given the seal of canonical approval — were the subject of critical exegesis, taught in college courses, included in anthologies — it was at the expense of their identity as women. If they insisted on their womanhood, and particularly if they incorporated issues of female sexuality, childrearing and housekeeping into their art, they were soon forgotten. As Le Guin points out, the so-called canon of English literature never included a woman who had children. "The received wisdom is ... that any attempt to combine art work with housework and family responsibility is impossible, unnatural. And the punishment for unnatural acts, among the critics and the Canoneers, is death."[9]

For the woman writer this can pose a crisis of identity. Should she negate her womanhood and write like a man (or at least sign herself with a man's name)?[10] Forgo children? Write of the experience she knows best but accept eventual obscurity? Le Guin herself struggled with these questions. A housewife and mother, she nonetheless pursued a career as a writer. But because she was told, even by feminists in some cases, that women could not and should not have both books and babies, she became used to the feeling that her "experience was faulty, not right — that it was wrong."[11] The attitude that her personal life was incompatible with her identity as a writer is apparent in her writing primarily by her omission of female main characters. As described in Chapter One, through the amazingly productive years of the late-sixties and early seventies when she wrote the novels that made her famous, her writing was at least in part like that of her male counterparts. She did subvert the conventions she used, even inventing an androgynous society by which to question the nature of gender. Yet her use of these conventions stymied her imagination. She continued writing like a man. Though her early writing has a smattering of important female characters, only one of these is a woman with children. Her women characters were peripheral, secondary.[12] "'Why don't you write about women?' my mother asked me. 'I don't know how, I said.'"[13]

That she has learned how to write about women Le Guin credits to the women writers who went before her, her literary mothers. In "The Fisherwoman's Daughter," to Woolf's image of the woman fishing, Le Guin adds a small child, a girl, who observes her mother at work. She sees the personified imagination pulled abruptly out of the water, brought up short by the restraints of convention. Yet the child is undaunted; she will write whatever she wants and have children too, if she chooses. Though Le Guin herself seems clearly enough to figure as a literary "mother" through whom future generations of women writers will think back, she stands in the essay for the daughter who benefits from the experience of the mothers who went before her. If she has more artistic freedom and self-awareness as a woman writer now than earlier in her career, it is because of the efforts of all those women who sat fishing on the banks, letting their imaginations have more line, bit by bit. Le Guin's metamorphosis from the "dutiful daughter of the patriarchate" to the "fisherwoman's daughter" came not by looking back through her father and his tradition, but by finding herself in her mother. This chapter focuses on how Le Guin turns increasingly to feminist thinkers and writers to redirect her art. In *Always Coming Home*, *Tehanu* and *Searoad*, she attempts to "write beyond the ending," to "write the body," in "white writing" or mother's milk, and to rewrite misogynistic literary history.[14]

Le Guin owes much to the feminists who went before her, American and French. She is more from the Anglo-American school of feminism, as is evident in critical writings in which she cites Anglo-American feminists and espouses their historical version of feminist theory. She frequently mentions the rediscovery of our literary mothers and applauds efforts like Gilbert and Gubar's *The Norton Anthology of Literature by Women* and the work of reprint houses like Virago Press. She angrily denounces the gender based exclusions of the academic canon and extends her anger to its exclusion of marginal genres as well. She argues for the social construction of gender, following the theories of Carol Gilligan and Jean Baker Miller, while she flatly derides Jacques Lacan for his male essentialist notion that women are excluded from discourse by virtue of their anatomy.[15] She also makes use of French feminism. She appreciates Hélène Cixous' playful and joyous engagement with language and her extreme confidence in womanhood.[16] In her writing of this period, particularly the story "Hernes," Le Guin opens up her narrative, using spaces, elisions, and mergings of identities that reflect Cixous' *l'écriture feminine*. Le Guin has also written about an "undifferentiated language," the language of conversation, of the household, what she calls the "Mother Tongue," the language our mothers teach us. The "Father Tongue" is the language of lectures; it is didactic, authoritative, and unidirectional. We learn this language in school, at church, wherever we are talked to and not with. Though Le Guin does not specifically follow Julia Kristeva in calling these the "semiotic" and the "symbolic," they carry some of the same connotations. Le Guin's proposal that we blend the mother and father tongues to form a third language, a "native tongue," is again a gesture of reconciliation. On the whole, though, Le Guin's feminism remains more in the American mode. While she increasingly aims to "break the sentence" and "break the sequence," as Woolf describes it, her grammar, syntax and semantics are never obscure or unreasonable to the reader brought up in the Western literary tradition.

Her feminism also informs her anger about the state of the world. She describes herself as "an angry, aging woman laying mightily about me with my handbag, fighting hoodlums off."[17] Increasingly her fiction and particularly her non-fiction make use of the persona of the "space crone," the post-menopausal woman who voices her considerable wisdom. Her writing has always had a tendency to the didactic, but while she worries still that this will affect her art, she now seems more willing to allow her personal views to be openly a part of it. Of course, Le Guin has always worked with contrary instincts. While she may subvert and rebel, at heart she wants still to be liked. That the dutiful daughter, or the Angel in the House, may still have some pull on her, is evidenced in her introduction to *Dancing at the Edge of the World*, in which she tells us that her goal is always "to subvert as much as possible without hurting anybody's feelings."[18] This dual impulse — toward subversion or more open rebellion on the one hand and toward conciliation on the other — is one that has tempered her feminism from the beginning. That women live a duality (even as feminists they must struggle between their self-perception as subject and the socially-imposed identity as object) has been noted by many feminists.[19] Le Guin is no exception.

Nonetheless, Le Guin had begun the process of becoming a woman-identified writer, learning to write the world through the eyes and experiences of women rather than of men. She began breaking out of the narrative modes to which she was so accustomed, to "write beyond the ending," Rachel Blau DuPlessis' term for "[t]he invention of strategies that sever the narrative from formerly conventional structures of fiction and consciousness about women."[20] Thus her stories take us beyond the conventional plots in which women either marry or die. Le Guin instead writes about the lives of women after they are widowed, or about women in untraditional relationships, or she defuses our romantic expectations by denying the happy or tragic ending. She was also learning to write what Woolf called the "woman's sentence," which DuPlessis defines as "writing unafraid of gender as an issue, undeferential to male judgment."[21] Woolf imagined the woman writer "tampering with the expected sequence. First she broke the sentence; now she has broken the sequence."[22] DuPlessis interprets this sketchy sense of what a woman's writing might be like:

> To break the sentence rejects ... rhythm, pace, flow, expression: the structuring of the female voice by the male voice, female tone and manner by male expectations, female writing by male emphasis, female writing by existing conventions of gender.[23]

On a larger scale, "Breaking the sequence is a rupture in habits of narrative order."[24]

In 1985, Le Guin published a short piece, "She Unnames Them," in which she playfully revises Genesis. In the story, Eve unnames all the animals that Adam and God gave names to, including herself. The animals are perfectly happy to discard what they had so long ignored; Eve says her own name has "been really useful, but it doesn't exactly seem to fit very well lately."[25] She fears Adam will think her ungrateful, but he has not paid much attention to her, and she slips out — for good — to join the nameless animals in the world outside the father/husband's house. She says, "My words must now be as slow, as new, as single, as tentative as the steps I took going down the path away from the house, between the dark-branched, tall dancers motionless against the winter shining."[26] Reminiscent of Luz in *The Eye of the Heron*, this now-nameless woman leaves behind a tradition that had objectified and defined her, making her both the innocent virgin and the evil temptress, the scapegoat for all the troubles of the world. But she will walk away from these definitions, simply slip away, and find new words. Likewise, Le Guin knows that she must carefully seek out a new way, choose her words well. She must relearn her native tongue, blend the undifferentiated discourse of the Mother Tongue with the authoritarian Father Tongue. "She Unnames Them" shows Le Guin's perfect sense that the Father Tongue, patriarchal language, no longer fits her, that in refusing this language its monolithic status, she comes into her true power as a woman writer.

Le Guin had begun in the 1970s to write her way out of the expected sequence, and to some extent out of the expected sentence. After about 1985, in *Always Coming Home, Tehanu* and *Searoad*, as well as in her poetry and short stories, she explores more fearlessly and more fully the territory of women — evidence of her reading in feminist theory and in fiction by women. Le Guin's feminism is unique for its eclecticism, particularly for her willingness to try out the stance of a feminist she admires, but with whom she does not necessarily agree. It can therefore be somewhat difficult to sort out Le Guin's own feminist position. The short piece "Woman/Wilderness," for example, includes a quote from Susan Griffin and seems clearly to relate Le Guin to so-called nature feminism. Yet Le Guin says the essay is "highly tendentious, it was meant to, and did, provoke lively discussion,"[27] and she has told me that it does not necessarily stand for what she herself really believes.[28] So I proceed, somewhat cautiously, by examining the variety of feminist ideas that her work reflects.

The Valley of the Na

In 1985, Le Guin published *Always Coming Home*, one of her most important works. Like *The Dispossessed, Home* is rooted in the utopian tradition, but it derives also from science fiction, magic realism, realism, and Native American poetics and oral tradition. A collage of elements, it is ostensibly an anthropologist's casebook and includes recipes, an extract from a novel, poems, the script of a play, maps, charts, field notes, autobiographies and much more. Descriptions of the book cannot do justice to the wealth of details and voices or to the variety of texts Le Guin explores in this work. Lest it seem a *tour de force, Home* humorously and self-consciously disallows its own authority, inviting the reader to share in constructing its meaning, while subtly deconstructing the reader's cultural biases.

Home describes a place (what we now call California's Napa Valley) and its inhabitants (the Kesh) who "might be going to have lived a long, long time from now."[29] We see the people and the place through the eyes of an ethnologist from our own time, Pandora, who has discovered the Kesh. We follow her progress as she interviews informants, gathers texts and records her impressions of the Kesh, piecing together the sexual, economic, cultural, ecological and sacred practices that constitute their way of life. There is no pretense of anthropological impartiality on the narrator's part. Pandora may influence the Kesh's presentation of themselves; yet, although she is ostensibly there to study the Kesh, we see that they are actually influencing her. And while she strives to efface herself, her attempts to understand the Kesh are constantly thwarted by her own cultural biases. It is her spiritual journey, her learning to question and perhaps put aside her twentieth-century cultural perceptions, that gives the books its real continuity. She has, by the end of her stay with the Kesh, learned to "join the dance." Pandora is both narrator/author and reader — she constructs the text at the same time that she records or "reads" Kesh culture. She is also text, since the record of her spiritual quest is a central aspect of the story and because her cultural predispositions necessarily slant her manner of interpreting the Kesh. We are also simultaneously reader and author as we piece together meaning, interpreting and reading at the same time. This dispersal of authority and the resultant lack of fixity allow us to find something new in the book every time we approach it.

In a clever blend of utopia and dystopia, *Home* acts as a warning as well as an example, for the Kesh world is not wholly utopian. The Kesh live with the aftermath of our current ecologically destructive practices. Some areas are still so contaminated that they cannot be visited. Large animals and humans, with their relatively slow evolutionary processes, suffer from devastating diseases, the effect of residual toxins. On the other hand, the Kesh have learned to exist in the world with ease and grace, and some readers will find their lifestyle idyllic. *Home* is covertly didactic, challenging and altering the reader's perceptions in subtle ways. What we have primarily to learn from the book is an inhabitory and interpersonal ethic that allows humans to live in the world without destroying it or each other. Le Guin's approach to this difficult topic is informed by her intimate knowledge of Native American inhabitory practice, her explorations of anarchy, her Taoism, and, underlying it all, her feminist sensibility. How that feminism interacts with her presentation of Kesh ecologic practice and social organization is the focus here.

Home is striking for its detailed evocation of physical place. While Le Guin can always make a place — real or imagined — vitally present to the reader, in *Home* place takes a more central position than in most of her previous writing. The Na Valley (as the Kesh call it) is itself (the Kesh would say "herself") a character and is depicted as a physical extension of every element of the story. That Le Guin is so well able to call forth this place into the reader's imagination is probably the result of her having spent many summers in the Napa Valley on her family's forty-acre ranch. This is the place where the Papago Indian, Juan Dolores, took Le Guin and her brothers on walks and taught them about native Californian inhabitory practice. Here, too, her father's native consultants would sometimes visit, and the Kroeber children would hear stories told in their original languages. Le Guin also undertook intensive study of the area's geography, climate, flora and fauna in preparation for this book. Her deep knowledge of the place, and indeed her personal identification with it, are integral aspects of the book's sense of place.

In a way, *Home* is wish fulfillment, if not for the author then for some readers. The Kesh seem almost a renaissance of the native populations who once inhabited the Valley. These new inhabitants, however, live with the physical and emotional after-effects of our present-day devastations. For anyone who has ever wondered what the Napa Valley looked like before current development, *Home* presents a chance to see the Valley returned, on the whole, to a natural environment. It is altered, of course, by weather patterns that have changed over time as well as by local seismic activity, but it is once more a place where bear, puma and coyote roam. The Kesh have some highly selected technology including computers, electricity and a train, but they are not progress-oriented. The human role in the ecosystem cannot be underestimated, for though the Valley has for the most part recovered from the ecological devastation of our time, it is still in a state of recovery and is ecologically vulnerable. The Kesh understand this well, and they therefore treat the Valley with reverent care. They also understand that their ancestors caused the ecological disaster. As humans, then, they must live carefully, mindfully, so as not to repeat the mistakes of the past. In order to prevent such a recurrence, they have learned to reverse the relationship of human to nature that is current in Western practice.

The Kesh consciously reject our separate and unequal relationship with nature, instead seeing themselves as part of the Valley's ecosystem. For the Kesh, all members of the system are equally valuable. This is reflected in their language. "People" in Kesh includes animals, plants, dream, and rocks. It is equally reflected in their beliefs. They see everything as having a spirit and so treat all accordingly. A rock, a sunrise, an animal or another human is greeted with *heya*, the word of praise. The

Kesh, of course, revere the Valley itself as their life-source and feel themselves literally rooted in it. This intense mindfulness leads them to limit their population, their technology and their lifestyle to what the delicate Valley ecosystem can easily sustain.

One way the Kesh maintain this careful attitude is by including the symbol or metaphor of the hinge in every aspect of their life, from the design of their towns to their sexual practices. This complex idea is akin to the Taoist symbol of yin and yang; both connote a balance of elements or extremes. Pandora describes the hinge as "the center of a spiral, the source of a gyring motion; hence a source of change, as well as a connection. [The hinge] is the eternal beginning, the process of energy arising and continuing."[30] The hinge is both a joining and the source for a reversal of that joining; it is visually represented as "two spirals centered upon the same (empty) space."[31] The idea of the hinge is central to the way the Kesh try to live, and can be seen, for example, in the generally moderate Kesh celebrating festivals focused on sexual and alcoholic binges. Living by the idea of the hinge means finding a balance for oneself, in part by accepting the existence and necessity for the opposite ends of the spectrum.

Not surprisingly, the Kesh attempt to treat each other with the mindful care they accord the Valley. There are exceptions —*Home* would be unrealistic without them — but social pressure is exerted against those who treat others in a wrong-minded way. Similarly, there is a tacit protection of the equality of the sexes. A few activities are sex-segregated (hunting is a male domain, butchering of domestic animals a female one) but child-care and house care are done indiscriminately by women and men. Rule is by consent and consensus, so there is no male or female in a seat of power over others. Despite this equality, the book overall emphasizes the female. Kesh kinship organization is matrilineal and living arrangements are matrilocal; a woman can end a relationship with her lover by putting his belongings outside the door, an action which leaves the ousted party no recourse.[32] Those traits we call "female" — being nurturing, communal, non-competitive — are praised by the Kesh regardless of biological sex. And the Valley is imbued with female attributes. The dormant volcano at the head of the Valley, for example, is called "Grandmother Mountain." The Kesh jokingly refer to the town Kastoha as "Granny's Twat" because it lies between the spread legs of the mountain. Hearing this, a small child imagines the town "to be set among fir and redwood trees and to be a cave, dark and mysterious, with the River running out of it."[33] Coyote, who figures in Kesh literature as creator and trickster, is female, while the only word in Kesh for nature is *she*. The Kesh word for house, which denotes both a living space and a social/cosmic principle, is *ma*. Her pairing of sound ecological practice and gender issues demonstrates Le Guin's engagement with ecological feminism.[34] Ecofeminism begins with the premise that the domination of women and of nature arise from the same source — a patriarchal society that exploits both women and the natural world. As Sherry Ortner points out, in such societies, women are viewed as closer to nature than man, and both nature and women are considered to be beneath men.[35] Both, moreover, are seen as needing subduing. Men are linked with the mind, women with the body, and the body with nature. This mind/body separation elevates the mind over the body and over nature. For ecofeminists, understanding the connection between the exploitation of women and of nature is essential to ending both forms of patriarchal dominance. Ynestra King argues that this means women have a higher stake than men in healing the rift between humans and nature; end the domination of nature and it will end for women as well.[36] Ecofeminists in general stress a holistic approach to living, a recognition of the planet as a single, interacting ecosystem in which all forms of life are interdependent. Again as a general principle, ecofeminists emphasize the importance of non-hierarchical systems and of careful attention to process rather than to progress.[37]

Eco-feminist theories about how to end the interlocking oppression of women and nature vary. One common approach is the "re-affirmation of female consciousness, which [ecofeminists] associate with wholeness and interdependence."[38] What is valued is less likely to be exploited. Some ecofeminists advocate the creation of a culture that honors women and nature. This culture's myths, rituals and philosophies would recognize and value women while emphasizing human interdependence with the natural world, essentially recreating the matriarchal cultures that flourished before the advent of Judeo-Christian values. Another approach is to eliminate the difference in male and female psychologies by relegating childrearing responsibilities to men and women equally. This argument is based on the theories of Nancy Chodorow and Dorothy Dinnerstein, who believe that boys develop psychologically by differentiating from their female caregivers, thus leading to a psychology of separation or alienation from the "other."[39] With men sharing equally in the parenting, boys will identify with their biologically similar caregiver, avoiding the fear of and alienation from women. Male attitudes will thus change, while "women's work" will be integrated into the male domain. Yet ecofeminism, like feminism itself, is marked by a radical split in beliefs. Some ecofeminists, like Susan Griffin and Mary Daly — known as "nature feminists" — believe that the perceived closeness between woman and nature is both true and good.[40] For these nature feminists, the connection should be cultivated, especially through a spirituality that celebrates women's closeness to nature. Their opponents, social feminists, feel that arguing for a special link between women and nature can only perpetuate the sex-role stereotyping that has contributed to the subjugation of both women and nature.

This fundamental disagreement between nature and social feminists should sound familiar: it is the "nature versus nurture" or "androgyny versus essentialism" argument with an ecological spin. There is, of course, some danger for arguing either extreme. Karen J. Warren notes that both schools of thought persist in the notion of a nature/culture dichotomy: "by locating women on either the nature or the culture side ... [this polarization] mistakenly perpetuates the sort of oppositional, dualistic thinking for which patriarchal conceptual frameworks are criticized."[41] Joan Griscom agrees that the question of whether women are closer to nature is itself flawed since men and women are equally part of nature. This nature/culture dichotomy can be resolved by seeing some male or female qualities as innate, others as the result of socialization.[42]

In *Home*, Le Guin makes the connection between woman and wilderness quite explicit, particularly by giving the Valley female attributes, as noted above. She also clearly links patriarchal culture and the domination of women and nature. To make this latter connection clear, Le Guin includes the People of the Condor, an aggressive tribe that threatens the Kesh. The Condor are an extreme patriarchal-supremacist society, serving a theocratic dictator. Sex roles are rigidly stratified. The men are mostly soldiers; the women of the ruling class are kept in purdah and have no choice but to marry and bear children. Slaves do all menial work. At the time they appear in *Home*, the Condor are attempting to widen their sphere of power and come into the Valley with the ultimate aim of taking it over.

The link between their patriarchal culture, exploitation of women, and devastation of nature is made primarily in two ways. One is through the autobiography of Stone Telling, a Kesh woman whose father is Condor and who chooses to spend part of her life as a Condor woman. Her deep connection with the Valley and her love for the natural world — as well as the freedom she enjoys as a Kesh female — are contrasted sharply with the life she lives as a Condor, particularly in that she is kept indoors almost entirely. From her vantage point, we see that the Condors live an unnatural life in the service of their social ideals; rather than prepare for shortages of food, they pillage from those they conquer. When their warfaring goes wrong, they starve.

More disturbing is the influence that the Condor have on the Kesh. During the time that they are stationed in the Valley, the Condor have a profound if not enduring effect. Their presence prompts the formation of a cult lodge among the Kesh men. This cult, called the Warrior lodge, reinvents the mind/body or spirit/matter split that Sherry Ortner describes. This split is shown in a discussion between Spear, a young warrior, and Stone Telling:

> Spear said that there had never been sacredness in rocks or springs, but in the mindsoul, the spirit only. The rock and the spring and the body, he said, were screens, that kept the spirit from pure sacredness, true power. I said *heyiya* [sacredness] was not like that; it was the rock, it was the water running, it was the person living. If you gave Blue Rock nothing, what could it give you? Easy enough to turn from it and say, "The sacredness has gone out of it." But it was you that had changed, not the rock; you had broken the relation.[43]

The warrior emphasis on mind rejects the relation between the body and the mind, the self and the material world that the Kesh so revere. The Warriors also claim that women corrupt the mind's purity. They say that women, moreover, are incapable of understanding Warrior rites. The women's version of the Warrior cult, the Lamb Lodge, teaches that women are only to love, serve, obey and sacrifice for the men; they cannot themselves understand the higher mysteries. Le Guin is clearly suggesting that the mind/body split — as practiced by both men and women — leads to alienation between the sexes and from the natural world, opening the way to exploitation at the hands of men.

The ideal Kesh way, that of mindful relationship, integrates matter and spirit, leading to total identification between humans and the physical world. In fact, the Kesh feel that their own bodies are physically part of the valley. Their identification with it is so total that one of their worst fears is to die outside the Valley and so be buried elsewhere. Stone Telling relates that on embarking for a long journey

I began to feel the Valley behind me like a body, my own body. My feet
were the sea-channels of the River, the organs and passages of my body
were the places and streams and my bones were the rocks and my head
was the Mountain.[44]

This full identification with the land is perhaps the best guard against
exploitation of it; any harm done to the land is done to the self. Importantly, Le Guin does not make this identification specific to women; Kesh
men are equally capable of this deep identification with the Valley, despite
the Kesh conception of the Valley as female. And whereas in the Western
tradition we have tended to make nature female in order to express a relation of dominance and control, the Kesh make the Valley female in order
to remember their debt to it as life source.[45]

All Kesh are taught, furthermore, not simply to be mindful of nature
and to revere it, but to look to the natural world for spiritual guidance.
At various times in their lives, when the Kesh need to reaffirm the bond
between self and Valley, they embark on spiritual guests. Over four or
more days, solitary and carrying only offerings, a Kesh will ask guidance
of all the members of the Valley ecosystem he or she encounters. Cautionary tales tell of spiritual questers who fail to ask for help and advice of
deer, oak, hawk or Mountain. Being willing to request and to heed such
advice means seeing the value of each element of the whole, asking of ant
as well as of Coyote. "A Poem Said with the Drum" illustrates this leveling:

The hawk turns crying, gyring.
There is a tick stuck in my scalp.
If I soar with the hawk
I have to suck with the tick.[46]

These quests remind the Kesh that they are simply an equal part of an
interdependent, non-hierarchical ecosystem. This humbling subverts a
tendency to value human intellect as higher or better than other forms of
sentience; it reminds the Kesh of the danger in believing they can fully
understand and thus control nature, an error in thinking that historically
has had devastating consequences. Stone Telling writes,

We have to learn what we can, but remain mindful that our knowledge
not close the circle, close out the void, so that we forget that what we
do not know remains boundless, without limit or bottom, and that
what we do know may have to share the quality of being known with
what denies it.[47]

113

In nature is found the manifestation of the hinge, that Kesh symbol of process without closure. The Kesh look not to explain the world fully but to live in it as best they can.

Home easily falls within the parameters of ecofeminism: Le Guin links women and nature while connecting their exploitation to a progress-oriented society that values mind over body and man over woman and nature. We have seen Le Guin in earlier works positioning herself on the side of androcentric, though sometimes unintentionally showing herself to have androcentric essentialist leanings. This is due to her unconscious mirroring of male-oriented biases. But has her awareness of these biases and her education in feminist thought changed her take on androgyny as opposed to essentialism? She has indicated to me that *Always Coming Home* is, like *The Left Hand of Darkness* and *Very Far Away from Anywhere Else*, an experiment in androgyny.[48] That this is so is very much visible in the text: the Kesh work hard to maintain a way of life where gender does not limit choices. But the balance does shift to the female; that is, not simply to female values, which men as well as women can equally share (true androgyny), but to women themselves. *Home* sometimes posits an innate difference in men and women, giving women an edge in terms of social power and prestige. In fact, some Kesh women belittle men because they are not female. There is some implication in the text that women have a closer alliance with animals than do men, and there is a cultural disposition to believe that men are less spiritual than women. This latter is evidently a hazard of a culture that sees "female" characteristics as more valuable than "male" characteristics.

We reach tenuous ground here, for in a psychologically androgynous society there would be no traits that could be identified as innately "female" or "male"; neither would either sex be seen as the good or the bad one. Moreover, if psychologists Chodorow and Dinnerstein are correct, then the Kesh distribution of childcare and domestic duties would have gone further to bringing male and female psychologies together. This is not to say that the Kesh male is mistreated or even much maligned, but the door is open for discrimination among the Kesh on the basis of sex. Sex-typing the Valley does suggest, too, the possibility that Kesh men would consider themselves to be "other" and so see true union with nature impossible. While this may have been another thought experiment in androgyny, the truth that Le Guin arrives at through the text is that androgyny is not really possible given the innate differences between men and women. The Kesh view of nature as female, as life giver, must stem from their observation of female humans and animals as the bearers of off-spring. But the values that accrue around this identification are problematic in the sense that the opposite values will always be identified with the male; no matter how hard a Kesh man might try, his biology is his destiny. Thus mindfulness would be at core a more difficult task for a male to achieve than a female. In the book itself, of course, Le Guin avoids such easy characterization; a Kesh woman is as likely as her male counterpart to be ill-willed or unmindful. Yet in Kesh society, women have an advantage over men.

Home represents, in part, Le Guin's revision of the utopian tradition — including of her own previous, though qualified, utopian novel. In "A Non-Euclidean View of California as a Cold Place to Be," composed during the time that she was writing *Home*, she says that the utopian tradition has been Euclidean, European and masculine: "Utopia has been yang. In one way or another, from Plato on, utopia has been the big yang motorcycle trip. Bright, dry, clear, strong, firm, active, aggressive, lineal, progressive, creative, expanding, advancing, and hot."[49] These are the traits that have brought our civilization into its current disastrous state. In order to speculate on an inhabitable future, Le Guin argues, we must imagine a utopia that is the opposite, a yin utopia. "It would be dark, wet, obscure, weak, yielding, passive, participatory, circular, cyclical, peaceful, nurturant, retreating, contracting, and cold."[50] *The Dispossessed*, she argues, was a good attempt at a yin utopia, but it suffered from excess yang: "though the utopia was (in fact and in fiction) founded by a woman, the protagonist is a man; and he dominates it in, I must say, a very masculine fashion."[51] *Home*, with its many female stories and characters, on the other hand, may have excess yin.

Earthsea Revisited

Home was a return to an actual place, a literal homeland, but the following years would see Le Guin return to some of the places she had imagined. She would write a new Orsinian story, updating the political history of that much-besieged place, and a new story gathering together many of the widely scattered elements of her Hainish universe. In 1990 she published what probably seemed to many readers an unexpected gift, a fourth

Earthsea novel: *Tehanu: The Last Book of Earthsea*. Earthsea fans have been surprised — some happily, some not — with the change in perspective in this fourth book. Eighteen years had passed since Le Guin published the previous Earthsea book, *The Farthest Shore*. She had tried to write a fourth book almost immediately, but as with her attempts to finish *Malafrena*, she found that she did not understand the central female character well enough. As with that Orsinian novel, the feminist movement was what made her completion of the book possible.[52] The result is a return to a familiar place, but almost, it seems, with a different author for our guide. To compare *Tehanu* with the earlier books is to see how much Le Guin has altered from a woman writing male-style adventure books to a woman writing about women.

Le Guin says of the early books that they were "written totally within the classic Western tradition ... this kind of vaguely medieval, vaguely European context of an unquestioned patriarchal system where only men are wizards, only men have power."[53] The hero of the Earthsea Trilogy is the Archmage Ged, whose life we follow from his childhood to his loss of power in advanced middle age. Although *The Tombs of Atuan* and *The Farthest Shore* each features a young person coming into her or his maturity, Ged's is the unifying presence in all three books. In the second two books, his is also the voice of authority as he instructs and enlightens his younger companions, guiding them along the difficult paths they must follow. As archmage in a land where magic is power and only men practice real magic (as noted earlier, women's magic is either "weak" or "wicked"), Ged embodies male rule. He is also the ultimate hero: he is a loner yet he inspires great loyalty; he is a very great wizard, legendary even among dragons; he has conquered personal and universal demons, giving up his own power in order to heal the world and bring a king once again to the throne of Earthsea.

In *Tehanu*, however, much is changed. This book centers on Tenar, whom we met as a young girl first serving and then breaking free of the dark powers in *The Tombs of Atuan*. That this fourth book is Tenar's story reorients our reading of the first three books, making Ged and Tenar more co-equally the protagonists of this series. Ged, who appears in all the books up to this point, is still the more considerable presence, probably because he fits the heroic mode so well; yet the balance of the storytelling dramatically shifts in *Tehanu*. Ged has lost his magic and hence his power; he feels he has no identity. Tenar shows him how to live without power — a skill at which, as a woman, she is adept. But this is not the story of how Tenar saves Ged, and so a fourth part in the story of Ged. This is fully Tenar's story, a meditation on what it means to live in a society that does not much value women. As such, it is a very different book from the first three: there is little magic performed, there are no great sea voyages or decisive acts, and no visionary revelations. There is not even physical security. The first few chapters deal with death, misogyny and the rape and mutilation of a young girl. The mood throughout is equally dark.

There is no hope, as in the earlier books, for a hero's resolution of the difficulties the characters face. No wizardry can repair the girl's grossly disfiguring wounds or save Tenar from the wrath of an errant wizard who hates her because she is a woman. There are no easy answers of any kind in this story. The first three books of the series feature relatively long passages in which a mage explains the workings of the world's equilibrium or the nature of magic to an attentive student. In *Tehanu* there are dialogues rather than lectures; characters share their understandings without arriving at definitive answers. So, for example, Tenar and the village witch Moss discuss the differences between men and women, exchanging opinions without really settling the matter. The earlier books deal with the things and the world of men; even *Tombs*, set though it is in a women-and-eunuchs only religious enclave, is about women who serve a patriarchal deity. *Tehanu* deals with things that have traditionally been the realm of women. Childrearing, housekeeping, cooking and gardening are natural and integrated elements of the story. We are fully aware of Tenar as the tender of the hearth; whether this is her own kind of magic or power is a question central to the narrative.

Tehanu does have more in common with *Tombs* than with the other two early Earthsea books. Tenar is the protagonist of both, and it is her story that the books follow. Like *Tehanu* with its emphasis on women, *Tombs* features a world populated almost entirely by women and it teems with images of the female. For example, the labyrinth where much of the action takes place is decidedly symbolic; it is a place where light never enters, described as a large central vault with winding passageways and a single door to the outside world. Whereas the female world in *Tehanu* is presented as hearth and haven, in *Tombs* it is overwhelmingly negative. The women in power in *Tombs* are unsexed and uncaring; they collude with the male-dominated religious state to deny Tenar her youth and innocence. They live in a desert world, a place where human life does not flourish, leading cloistered, celibate lives and perpetuating dark rituals. In *Tehanu* a reversal takes place; instead of denying life, the women in this novel create and sustain life while men seem bent on destroying it, particularly those aspects of life associated with women. Frequent images of Tenar trying hard to make a good life for those she loves — feeding them, keeping the house and farm in order, tending to the ill and injured — are juxtaposed with the ever-present threat of physical violence against women and children. For the first time in the series, the nature and indeed the wisdom of male rule undergo probing scrutiny, particularly in light of male abuses of power that lead to violence against women and children and against the delicate balance of the world itself. The nature of what power women might have and the essential differences between men and women are also questioned.

Tehanu begins before *The Farthest Shore* ends, establishing Tenar as a middle-aged widow and relating how she came to adopt Therru, the child whose father raped her and threw her into a fire. Sometime later, Ged appears on the back of the dragon Kalessin, having just returned from the journey related in *Shore*. While battling the wizard Cob, who had discovered the secret of immortality, Ged used every bit of his own power. No longer a mage, completely without power, Ged is an elderly virgin, a man without a home or livelihood. Tenar, in the meantime, is undergoing an identity crisis of her own. Few on Gont realize that she is Tenar of the Ring. They know her as Flint's wife and later Flint's widow, and always as the mother of Flint's children. When the dragon Kalessin speaks to Tenar, a vague sense of remembering or reawakening stirs within her. If a dragon lord is a man with whom dragons talk, and she is a woman who speaks with dragons, what does that make her?

The nature of female power is further illuminated through the damaged child Therru. Early in the novel Ogion and the witch Ivy had noted that Therru possessed enormous power. Ogion exhorts Tenar to teach Therru, saying "Teach her all! Not Roke. They are afraid."[54] Even Ivy fears Therru's power. She says, "What power she is, I don't know, I don't say ... Beware. Beware her, the day she finds her strength."[55] This strength is never entirely explained, but Therru is clearly linked with the dragons, is a daughter of the dragons. Therru speaks to Kalessin in the Language of the Making, the language of dragons and of magic, which she knows instinctively; Ged calls it her mother tongue. She addresses the dragon as Segoy, who according to Earthsea creation myth is the maker of all things.

And Segoy/Kalessin calls Therru by her true name, Tehanu, and asks whether she will go to the land of the dragons or stay with Ged and Tenar. She will stay with them for the time being, she says. Kalessin approves, saying that Therru has work to do there. Her story mirrors the tale of the Woman of Kemay. Ogion had met this woman and immediately recognized that she was simultaneously a dragon and a woman. She told Ogion of a time when dragons and humans were one winged race. It eventually separated into two — a wild, dragon race and a flightless human one. Those among the humans who saved the language of the dragons — the True Language of the Making — became wizards; among the dragons were some who remembered their kinship with humans. What the story does not reveal, but the dragon/woman of Kemay herself indicated, is that there are among humans some who have not lost their dragon nature. Therru must be such a person. Throughout the story there are hints of this. Due to her disfigurement, she even looks half-human, half-dragon: her right hand is claw-like; the right side of her face, eyeless and cheekless, is slabbed like a dragon's mail; her voice, affected by her having lain in fire when she was beaten and left to burn to death, is scratchy like Kalessin's. What is never clear is whether Therru was born a dragon or made into one by her ordeal. Some questions like this, but not all, will be answered in *The Other Wind*, which is discussed in Chapter Four.

In Tenar's ruminations and Therru's apparently great magical powers the book explores the nature of magery, of power. It considers in particular the seemingly gendered nature of magic. Ged differentiates between the power that a king has, which is given to him, and that of a mage, which is his own, himself. Furthermore, he says, the mage's is a male power; women cannot become mages because they do not have this power. Yet the mages of Roke have received a clue in their search for an archmage to replace Ged: "A woman on Gont." The clue prompts them to look for some woman who could be the mother, sister, or even teacher of a male who is to be the new mage. That the woman might herself be the future archmage is not a possibility they will entertain. Ged says:

> No woman can be archmage. She'd unmake what she became in becoming it. The Mages of Roke are men — their power is the power of men, their knowledge is the knowledge of men. Both manhood and magery are built on one rock: power belongs to men. If women had power, what would men be but women who can't bear children? And what would women be but men who can?[56]

The village witch Moss seems to agree with this one-dimensional view of men. She argues that men are like shells packed with their manhood or power; when the shell is emptied out — as in Ged's case — there is nothing left. The events of the novel seem to discredit them both. Ged himself, after he is emptied of his power as a mage, finds a new identity; Tenar, despite Ged's statement, once did have power but willingly gave it up. Kalessin's arrival prompts further questions. If knowing the Language of the Making is part of what makes a man a mage, then what of Tenar and Therru to whom this language comes easily? There is also the frequent suggestion in *Tehanu* that women are closer to dragons than men. Men, Tenar remembers when she meets Kalessin, must not look into a dragon's eyes. Yet, she thinks, that is nothing to her; she looks directly at Kalessin without consequence.

The connection between women and dragons is reminiscent of the relationship that Susan Griffin posits between women and nature. Like nature, the dragons are wild; they are entities unwilling to be civilized, who with rare exceptions are inaccessible to humans. The fact that men cannot look dragons in the eye but women can parallels Griffin's sense of women's accessibility to the wild. The subtitle of Griffin's book, *The Roaring Inside Her*, suggests the linked anger of women and nature at the acts of rape and suppression they have endured. In this context, Therru's power seems like a product of the heinous crime against her; what the witch Ivy seems to warn against is the power she will display when she comes to full realization of her own anger. She seems then like an emblem or warning: those on Roke would do well to fear her. Yet whether Therru's dragon nature is innate or whether she learned dragon nature as the result of her anger over being raped and disfigured is not entirely clear. Therru's ability to speak the Language of the Making, however, seems to indicate an innate link with the dragons and therefore an essentialist view of women's nature. Le Guin would return to Earthsea once more, in 2001, when she published the novel *The Other Wind* and the story collection *Tales from Earthsea*, both of which continue to engage these issues.

On the Searoad

For *Always Coming Home*, Le Guin says she needed to learn "dirt words" to write that place, and indeed the book touches earth again and again, grounding the whole and the reader in the dirt, rocks, and wild oats of the Valley. Le Guin's other recent works are also made up of the elements of the earth. *Buffalo Gals* (1987), with its intensity of light and long, rimrock vistas is a story made of air or sky words; *Tehanu* is a story of fire. For her collection of linked stories, *Searoad* (1991), Le Guin learned the language of water.

In *Searoad* Le Guin exchanges our myth of Neptune and his horses for images of women in the rain and surf. The book opens with a short piece "Foam Women, Rain Women." The foam women "lie at the longest reach of the waves, rounded and curded, shaking and trembling, shivering hips and quivering buttocks, torn by the stiff, piercing wind, dispersed to nothing, gone ... till the long wave breaks again," while the

> Rain women are very tall; their heads are in the clouds. Their gait is the pace of the storm-wind, swift and stately.... They move northward, inland, upward to the hills. They enter the clefts of the hills unresisting, unresisted, light into darkness, mist into forest, rain into earth.[57]

"Foam Women, Rain Women" sets the tone for the collection of stories. More so than in *Home* or *Tehanu*, Le Guin looks here at the continuities in the lives of women. This focus on women, and in particular on generations of mothers and daughters, is underscored throughout by the continuous, dully heard roar of surf as the tidal forces carry the waves forward, draw them back, and plunge them forward again. As "Foam Women, Rain Women" makes clear, these women are the very cycle of life, of tidal rhythm, of death and rebirth.

Klatsand, the imaginary but not-fantastic town these stories are set in, is located somewhere along the Northern Oregon coast. It is home for a few, a vacation spot for many, and Le Guin tells stories of both its temporary and permanent residents. These stories are among Le Guin's most bleak: manic depression, rape, approaching old age, cancer, death and guilt are the subjects. It is mainly a book about coping, about how we all get through the difficulties of life. Some, as in "Sleepwalkers," simply shut out the suffering of others; in "The Ship Ahoy," the owner of the story's eponymous motel escapes her unhappy life through fantasy. There are, in a number of these stories, workable solutions, if no happy endings. The protagonist of "True Love" eventually finds happiness not with the vain and self-satisfied man she has been dating, but with her beloved books. In "Crosswords," "In and Out," and "Quoits" women help each other through difficult times. In "Hernes," the main story in the collection, a woman seeks escape through her art. In all these stories, the sea is a kind of magnet, a source of solace, or at least of continuity.

In *Searoad* Le Guin explores women's lives and women's issues in new ways. *Always Coming Home* includes homosexual couples but does not examine their lives in any detail. In "Quoits," Le Guin goes for the first time inside a lesbian household, taking the point of view of a woman coping with the recent death of her partner and her uneasy relationship with her partner's grief-stricken daughter. The woman's anger over the inadequacy of our language to account for or encompass her relationship with her dead lover reflects Le Guin's heightened awareness of the marginal status of lesbian women:

> There aren't any words that mean anything. For us. For any of us. We can't say who we are. Even men can't any more.... We don't have words for what we do! Wife, husband, lover, ex, post, step, it's all leftovers from some other civilization, nothing to do with us.[58]

For the first time Le Guin really looks at the different experiences of non-white, non-middle-class, and homosexual women. But while she does write about working class and poor white women in the first person, when she includes a black woman character — a waitress whose son is dying of AIDS — she does not look through that woman's eyes. Le Guin had previously made many of her main characters non-white (Genly Ai, for example, is black) without taking much note of it, subtly undermining the primacy of the white main character. But this rather glib technique does not account for race as an influence on experience. In *Searoad*, she reflects the then current sense in feminism that, as a white woman, she could not know how to write about women of color. At the same time, Le Guin seems to have lost much of her earlier interest in writing from the male point of view, or even about men. When she does, the characters tend to be deflated. In "Geezers," a successful, smug, middle-aged man is demoralized when he is routinely mistaken for a member of a seniors' club. "Bill Weisler" is the sad and sympathetic story of a potter who is of diminished mental capacity and is also depressive; he is being taken advantage of by his distributor but has no skills with which to confront him. Moreover, the generations of women in "Hernes" seem unable to choose good men — one marries a philanderer, her daughter bears a child by a rapist, a third marries a controlling, chauvinistic academic.

Le Guin's attention is turned to and tuned into the female, as the aptly titled "Hernes" and the similarly multi-generational, multi-voiced

"Hand Cup Shell" indicate. Le Guin says, "Hernes is fairly unconventional in style and I feel it as a breakthrough piece for me — getting a little closure to the essence of what I want to get at."[59] The stylistic breakthrough in "Hernes" is Le Guin's renunciation of linear narrative, of continuous plot. While in *Home* we had the voice of Pandora to guide us, in "Hernes" we catch only a moment of thought, a bit of dialogue. We must piece the narrative together ourselves, bridge the ellipses in the text, make the connections. Le Guin gives us only a name and a date at the top of each entry as specific clues, forcing us to read and reread in order to understand the chronology. To facilitate matters, Le Guin has appended biographies for each main character to the end of the story. Even so, there are long gaps in time, and many unanswered questions. In "Hernes," Le Guin brings much of her experimentation in feminism to the forefront. The style is reminiscent of Toni Morrison's "participatory reading," where the author leaves holes and spaces so that the reader can come into the story, or of Woolf's *The Waves*. With its multiple points of entry, its tidal rhythm, its non-linearity, *Searoad* recalls *l'écriture féminine*. Yet it also reflects Le Guin's concept of a socially constructed women's psychology, as described by Jean Baker Miller and Carol Gilligan, of women's attention as diffuse, widely encompassing and connective. *Searoad* is Le Guin at her most experimental, though as narratives the stories are less satisfying than Le Guin's best.

The Overcorrections

Just as her anger and frustration over the Vietnam War led her to write a novel, *The Word for World Is Forest*, that was sometimes more didactic than well written, her anger in this period led to some reverse sexism, to depicting men as unrelenting drags on female empowerment. This isn't always true of her work. During this time, for example, she wrote the screenplay *King Dog*, centering on male characters who try desperately to do the right thing. But on the whole, there are fewer well-rounded male characters in this decade's writing. That this is a result of her immersion in feminism seems likely given that many of us, once politicized by reading feminist theory, went through periods of reactive and sometimes retributive anger. Most of us, of course, do not have the skill or reputation to leave a body of work that documents this, but that makes it no less true.

It would be dishonest and destructive in the long term not to acknowledge, and while painful, it is not disloyal to look at the rhetorical excesses of the period, to ask why feminism has the reputation it does, why it is in need of some new methods. Of course, the rhetoric flies in both directions as Thomas Disch's frequently quoted invective against Le Guin in *The Dreams Our Stuff Is Made Of* (1998) demonstrates. Interestingly, Disch starts by dissecting some of Robert Heinlein's more objectionable chauvinism, in a manner of which any feminist would approve. But this is merely the lead-in to his discussion of women's entry into science fiction, in particular Le Guin's, and what he considers her singular focus on feminism.

> Le Guin's feminism is less overtly phobic of the male sex than that of Andrea Dworkin, but it is no less absolute. She requires nothing less, if one credits her utopian romance of 1985, *Always Coming Home*, than the abolition of Western civilization as we've known it and the (re)institution of a benevolent, holistic, shamanistic matriarchy. Science fiction, with its opportunity to posit other worlds designed to showcase one's own ideological convictions, is a godsend to any polemicist.[60]

Disch actually has some reasonable things to say about feminism and political correctness, and his discussion of *The Word for World Is Forest* fairly represents some of that work's shortcomings. But his rhetorical manner is extreme, personal and sometimes petty, particularly when he dissects Marleen S. Barr's essay on *Searoad*.[61] Nonetheless, Disch's tirade is instructive for reasons he probably did not intend. His criticism of *Word*, while vehement, does not raise the reader's hackles, perhaps because that war is so far behind us, and it is no longer politically incorrect to question anything written about it. It is only when he attacks the texts and theorists of high feminism that he awakes the reader's ire. Modern feminism is still a loaded topic and despite it having co-originated with Vietnam War protests, it is still politically dangerous to criticize.

To dig deeper into this, Le Guin, who is generally a weigher of words, makes some reproachable comments about men. For example, in a performance piece from the early nineties, she rebukes Ernest Hemingway both for his writing style and for his having committed suicide. "Hemingway would have died rather than get old. And he did. He shot himself. A short sentence. Anything rather than a long sentence, a life sentence. Death sentences are short and very, very manly."[62] This comment, besides making light of suicide, misses the irony that Virginia Woolf, one of Le

Guin's "literary mothers," herself committed suicide, doubtless while struggling as Hemingway did with clinical depression. True to form, however,
Le Guin's comments are mixed with self-examination, and even in the text
quoted above, she is talking mainly about her own experience of coming
into old age.

The short story "Limberlost" (1989) provides an example of how Le
Guin moves sidewise into critique of masculinity, in this case specifically
of the "Wild Man" movement of the eighties and nineties led by the poet
Robert Bly. Yet instead of a full-on assault of the preoccupation of men's
groups with segregation and quasi-tribal ritual, she brings us into the
action through the point of view of a novelist who is in residence at a writing retreat.[63] The retreat is led by a male poet, presumably meant to be
Bly, who is first depicted swimming nearly naked — he has kept on his
boxers — in a scene suggesting the man's vanishing vitality. He tells the
narrator that "The Men have raised a Great Phallus farther up the river ...
I'd show you, but it's off limits to the Women."[64] And, as the story continues, the narrator contrasts her own hesitation and half-hearted self-
affirmations with the strangeness of men howling throughout the night in
male-only rituals. The narrator, who seems to have entered some kind of
twilight world under these massive trees, suddenly remembers that she
had been to camp there as a girl, an abiding memory of which was the
bridge separating the male and female campers, with the boys' side marked
as forbidden territory. While clearly making fun of the "wildmen," the story
is nonetheless a poignant portrayal of how it felt to the girl camper to want
to play with the boys only to find many signs telling her to keep out.

In her explorations of yin utopias, androgynous human relations, and
inhabitable futures, Le Guin imagined better ways of living in the world,
and living with each other. She also paid attention to the ways in which
we tell stories and the reasons for our doing so. In "Why Are We Huddling About the Campfire?" she suggests that we tell stories as a way of
constructing reality, of making ourselves understand both that we do exist
and offering explanations for why we exist. If we tell stories about men
only, feminist theory has taught her, women will not exist. Her writing of
this period has been in the service of women, telling their stories. What
she has learned from feminism, are ways in which to narrate the lives that
do not fit in men's stories. As her fiction shows us, not only are there
diverting and riveting ways to tell the women's story, but there is much of
moral value to be learned from them.

CHAPTER FOUR

Repairing the Sequence

In 1990, Le Guin published "The Shobies' Story," which tells of the first group to test churten technology, a method for instantaneously traveling through space and the culmination of theories developed by Shevek, the physicist in *The Dispossessed*. As the walls of the spacecraft dissolve around them, the terrified crewmembers huddle together and report their quite different ideas about what is happening. Because their stories are so different, one no more plausible than another, they build a consensus reality by agreeing that each of them is right. As they do so, the walls again become solid, and the space ship returns to port with none of its members permanently harmed. The key to the churten drive, a universe-shrinking technology that ends exile by time dilation, is storytelling. How this works is not completely clear. It seems, though, that an existential crisis arises within the traveler when he or she disappears from one point in space and reappears at another with no loss of time. To resolve that crisis, participants remake reality by storytelling, combining experiences to create a kind of transitional object to ease their journey across space.[1] As a metaphor for Le Guin's writing of the period covered in this chapter, from about 1990 to 2001, this represents a repairing of the sequence, a return to the broken science fiction narrative, but one refreshed by a new approach to the genre. For one thing, Le Guin returns willing to invent her own rules. More importantly, though, if her initial writing had been all about men, then her writing of the high feminist period might be said to be all about women. Here, while gender is still an issue, the writing balances stories of both awomen and men.

For Le Guin's readers, "The Shobies' Story" was another unexpected too-much-to-be-hoped-for return, this time to the Ekumen of Worlds that Le Gun had appeared to abandon after "The Pathways of Desire." It was later included in *A Fisherman of the Inland Sea* (1994), a collection of

Hainish stories. Three other book-length works featuring the Ekumen appeared in the next decade: the story suite *Four Ways to Forgiveness* (1995); a novel, *The Telling* (2000); and the collection *The Birthday of the World* (2002), which includes several Hainish stories. Unlike *Tehanu*, the novel in which Le Guin similarly surprised readers by returning to Earthsea, these stories are more continuous with earlier works like *The Dispossessed*, *The Left Hand of Darkness* and "Vaster than Empires." The new work covers in familiar terrain, both geographically and in terms of style and mode. Unlike *Tehanu*, which dramatically shifted the tone and focus of the early trilogy, these stories fit fairly seamlessly into the Hainish tradition. The author retains the general sensibilities developed through feminism, especially in her engagement with issues of gender, but her tone is more level, her narrative styling more traditional, and her characterization of males more complex. In this decade she also made another return to Earthsea, this time focusing on bringing her old world into line with her new world view. Unlike *Tehanu*, however, with its unblinking look at the evil men can do, the novel *The Other Wind* (2001) and the story collection *Tales from Earthsea* (2001) are more determined than angry. Le Guin has a task to perform with these stories: utterly shifting the underpinnings of Earthsea, effecting a total change in the series' philosophy of gender roles and the afterlife. Despite this radical agenda, the narratives are more satisfying than in *Tehanu*, in particular because the characters are better developed and the action, while dramatic, is better realized. As with her solving Shevek's theoretical dilemma by inventing the churten drive, in these stories she is also repairing the sequence. In this case, though, she is finishing the distaff narrative she began to develop in *Tehanu*, balancing the old male-focused trilogy with more female focus. In the meantime, she reshapes Earthsea into the kind of place that reflects her altered sensibilities.

I asked Le Guin in 1991 why she had returned to both Earthsea and the Hainish Universe. "I'm getting older," she joked.[2] But given her earlier disengagement with both science fiction and fantasy, clearly something had changed. She had a renewed belief in science fiction and fantasy as viable forms for her stories. I believe a key change was her belief, reinforced by feminism, that there was little to be gained by adhering too closely to traditions, including those governing genres. In terms of science fiction, she simply disregarded the old dictum that things in an invented universe had to make sense, that they must conform to the laws of physics.

This old rule, established by Hugo Gernsback and enforced for decades by editors like John Campbell, is well encapsulated in Gernsback's belief that sf had to be built on, and the stories themselves had to contain, "scientific facts."[3] Rather than balance the contrary instincts discussed in Chapter One, in her return to science fiction, Le Guin largely ignores propriety and plays by her own rules. Early in her return to sf, she published "Newton's Sleep" (1991), about the danger of relying too heavily on logic. Taking its title from Blake's poem in which he hopes to be spared "single vision and Newton's sleep," the story considers the dangers of blind adherence to logic and of denying the messiness of reality.[4] Le Guin does not disparage logic or tidy solutions; she suggests instead that they be balanced with imagination and openness. This philosophy is attributable to the way that feminist poetics, and perhaps age and the very considerable weight of her reputation, gave her the freedom to mix science and magical thinking. By doing so, she solved the abiding problem of her early narratives: the exile from place, time, and people that is created by space travel. Her solution, transilience, is "an absolutely, inexcusably implausible notion, not extrapolated from any existing technology, not justifiable by any current theory of physics."[5] Le Guin's willingness to disobey the laws of physics and the science fiction tradition clearly opened up pathways into the genres, suggesting stories to tell and new solutions to old problems. There is an unmistakable note of joy here, and a sense of return to the impulses of the maverick child writer who uses time travel to end a story as she wishes. Returning to science fiction and fantasy, and indeed to her very own, long ago established places, runs the risk of once again being constrained by forms. But Le Guin works within those structures and rewires them, creates from them a hybrid between what existed and what is now true for her. The results are surprising in that the more conservative form, fantasy, seems in fact to yield more opportunity for real rebuilding.

While during this period Le Guin engaged less with theory, her writing reflects the thinking current in the nineties, especially post-feminism and to an extent both post-structuralism and post-colonialism. In fact, the hallmark of post-feminism is embracing multiple points of view and choosing eclectically from other schools of thought. Though Le Guin has not written about post-feminism *per se*, her work exhibits many of post-feminism's signature moves. The writing is more inclusive of people from the spectrums of preferences, sexual, political and religious; while lesbian characters, for example, deal with the difficulties associated with their sexual preference, they are main characters, not peripheral ones. There is more focus on sexuality, including unorthodox practices. The variety of roles humans can take on is embraced. Devotion to childrearing, for example, is not treated as a capitulation to patriarchy. There is less essentialism and less feminist experimentation with form, sentence, and diction. Women's and men's individual stories share space with those of couples working out the rules of engagement. While several stories focus on women as the last slaves in a post-colonial world, in two of them, men are pivotal players in helping women win their freedom. In other words, these stories balance perspective more than the work of the 1980s did. Another emphasis is on finding truth through personal story and using multiple narrators to achieve this. Following post-feminist inclusiveness, the individual perspective is privileged, so that stories taken together construct reality. As demonstrated through analysis of the new Hainish work and of the completion of the Earthsea cycle, Le Guin has moved on from second wave feminism. She has not disowned it nor disparaged it by any means, but she has moved into the next, post-feminist phase.

Telling Stories

Story, the act of storytelling and how it creates multiple, equally true realities, is a major focus of Le Guin's science fiction of this period. As she points out, the transilience stories "The Shobies' Story" (1990), "The Dancing to Ganam" (1993) and "Another Story" (1994) are all "metafictions, stories about story."[6] Like science fictional versions of *Rashomon*, the stories explore the co-existence of multiple narratives, emphasizing the relativity of perception. While not by any means a new idea, this is nonetheless a central tenet of postmodernism: the impossibility of a master narrative, except in the sense that the stories, taken together, form reality — consensus arriving only in the acceptance of multiplicity.[7] This differs from the relaying of personal experience that was central to the early women's movement. In that form of consciousness-raising, women told their stories in a group setting to bring the hidden and therefore deniable out into the open; it created truth or reality by repetition and reinforcement of experience (as in, "I know date rape exists because she, and she, and I have all experienced it"). These efforts universalized the experience of womanhood, building an individual's sense of empowerment through the assurance of others that what she was relaying was true and that others had had the same experience. In the post-feminist scenario, the stories are individual and are told together to establish the textures of existence, to establish existence itself—the stories, told together as story, are reality.

The first of these three metafictions, "The Shobies' Story," is also metaphorical for Le Guin's Ekumen. In a way that she had rarely done before, she brings her created worlds into relation: the Shobies' crew includes an Annaresti, a Hain, Terrans, and a family of Gethenians. Of course, as the products of the Hain's universe seeding, they are all distantly related despite their outward differences. The story involves the first group test of churten technology, which moves mass across space with no loss of time. The crew of ten should jump across light years of space with no time duration; it is instantaneous "transilience." Though they spend a month bonding as a crew and trying to understand the technology, it is far too technical for all but the Cetian physicists who themselves are incapable of explaining it in lay terms. They are making a real leap of faith in this unproven, poorly understood technology. The Shobies spend their last evening before the experiment gathered around a (fake) fire, telling bedtime stories. When they attempt the jump, all cohesion and coherence is lost. They all experience different and increasingly diffuse realities, from not having jumped at all to being utterly lost in a disintegrating ship. They only begin to cohere again when they regroup around the proverbial fire, the ship's hearth, and begin telling their individual versions of what happened. "Tai gestured at the cave of firelight around them and the dark beyond it. 'Where are we? Are we here? Where is here? What's the story?'"[8] They share stories, not attempting to make them meld. One of them sees chuten drive as ushering in a new manner of being, a new unity among peoples. "They got lost. But they found the way."[9]

Despite the profound hope this statement implies, the next churten story, "Dancing to Ganam" is a cautionary tale. Because churten drive is somehow powered by story, when the group is too small, or one among them has the kind of charismatic personality that can reframe the perception of others, churtening can allow one person to "entrain" the reality of others. In the story, Dalzul has this power. An egomaniac, he sees himself as a savior who can use chruten theory as a means to bring humankind together, to allow them all to "rejoin unity."[10] The danger, of course, is that his understanding of reality is wildly out of keeping with how others perceive it; his misreading of events leads the crew of this Churten test group into danger and reinforces the sense that no one view of reality can be privileged.

"Another Story or A Fisherman of the Inland Sea," discussed briefly in the Introduction, takes its central image from the Terran story of the fisherman who is seduced by a sea goddess, spends a night or two with her in her underwater palace, and awakens to find everything he knows gone, centuries having passed. The story is here a cautionary tale, told by a mother who has left her homeworld to settle on O. She relates the story to her son, Hideo, to warn him of the loss inherent in space travel, churten travel not having yet been invented. Despite his mother's warnings, that will be the pursuit of the boy Hideo as he becomes a physicist and leaves behind his homeworld, his family, and the woman he loves in pursuit of science. Eventually, Hideo becomes ill with homesickness. While in an earlier story Le Guin would have Hideo learn to adapt to the new place, learn to love the land and become part of a family, she finds an unexpected solution here. One day while experimenting with the churten drive he has helped to invent, Hideo ends up back on his homeworld O, but he has traveled back in time as well. Though he has not lost the years he spent away, he has returned to O only a short time after he left it many years before. Everyone is just as they were; for them no time has passed. They cannot explain why Hideo looks older; they simply accept him back. He is reunited with his love and settles down into the life he once discarded, living as a farmer instead of a physicist. It is a cosmic do-over, only complicated by the fact that he will have to experience the stretch of time he has already lived through twice. In a bittersweet twist, Hideo knows how the coming years will play out for his family. But having learned to appreciate his people and his place, he uses this knowledge to keep himself centered, to appreciate what he has. Hideo is whole and healthy when he lives in context, sick and empty when he is not. This casts another shadow on churten theory, a typical Le Guinian complication. "Event without interval," or moving huge distances without experiencing it, invites rootlessness and an inability to process reality.[11] Nonetheless, the story is remarkable for its atypical happy ending. Le Guin's exiles have been many: virtually every person who travels in space becomes exiled from their time, their people, their place. They rarely go home again and if they do, it is to a place that has changed in their very long absence. As such, the conclusion to "Another Story" is a dramatic departure from form, though as noted in the Introduction, if Le Guin's account of the story she wrote when she was ten is accurate, she did write such an ending before she became invested in the "rules" of sf. Her scientists in that story solve a problem they have created by going back in time, something that only inadvertently happens to Hideo and yet opens the door to the possibility of time travel.

Another take on the power of story is offered in the novel *The Telling*, which mirrors the history of Tibet under communist Chinese occupation or of Afghanistan under the Taliban. *The Telling* is about a Terran envoy, Sutty, sent to the planet Aka to discover the linguistic, literary and philosophical history suppressed by Aka's scientific-capitalist totalitarian regime. Hidden within this Orwellian dystopia of cultural suppression, she discovers remnants of the planet's quasi Buddhist/Taoist religion, including a trove of banned texts. "The Telling" refers to this religion's use of story to attend to its spiritual health; the stories "tell" the world, creating reality whether related orally or in writing. Having escaped a religious totalitarian society on Earth, Sutty has lessons to learn here, among them how to trust in the miraculous and how to tolerate and understand others. Her nenemsis on Aka is a fanatic monitor from the totalitarian culture, sent to keep her under control and in particular to keep her away from the remnant religion. The story bears some resemblances to *The Left Hand of Darkness*, though as an essentially widowed homosexual, an Anglo-Indian, and an ex-Terran, Sutty is far more an exile than Genly. While blinded by her own prejudices, she is more politically aware, especially of the dangers that surround the Ekumenical envoy. Yara, the monitor, is no Estraven; he is as in need of enlightenment as Sutty, but as in *The Left Hand of Darkness*, it is in a tent in a remote region that the two of them learn to understand one another. Through hearing Yara's story, Sutty finds the key that makes Aka's entry into the Ekumen possible; it is the private story that leads to widespread change.

In recent criticism on these works, both Deirdre Byrne and Warren Rochelle pay particular attention to story. Byrne uses Lyotard in her discussion of storytelling, history and narrative. In her view, "The Shobies' Story" illustrates the synergizing power of micro-narrative: telling stories coalesces reality. Moreover, historical truth requires the intersection of history with biography or autobiography, these "little narratives" making up the "grand narrative."[12] She compares "truth through storytelling" to the work of the South African Truth and Reconciliation Commission. The

Commission solicited the testimony of Apartheid victims in the belief that storytelling would both uncover the hidden history, making it real, and allow victims to heal. Byrne's theories apply even more strongly to the stories in *Four Ways to Forgiveness*, about a world recovering from slavery. Warren Rochelle similarly writes about storytelling, relating it to Le Guin's trope of community. While he focuses primarily on myth, his ideas are equally applicable to the use of story, which he argues emphasizes "the small, the private, the local."[13] Story, being a metaphor for knowledge and values, leads us into what he calls "communities of the heart."[14]

Finding Forgiveness

The story suite *Four Ways to Forgiveness* focuses on the aftermath of a slave rebellion that utterly remakes two worlds, Werel and its former colony Yeowe.[15] As the people struggle to remake reality, they are also in the midst of a bid to join the Ekumen. Overtly post-colonial in nature, the narratives are told from the vantage points of slave and owner, as well as those of the Ekumen mobiles. Rather than large social questions, the stories consider recovery on a personal level. How do people move past events and mindsets to forge new ground, to forgive each other? How do the enslaved learn to be free? What is the effect of ownership on the ruling class? How are sexual conventions redefined in a society where assets, as the slaves were known, were often sexually abused? The stories take on difficult issues, including those that have long informed the feminist debate, such as the connections between gender, sexual conduct and social status. But the collection's title is quite telling. These stories are not intended to obscure or excuse the past. What is post-feminist here is the attempt to move forward, the conscious decision to find points of connection and to proceed together. The stories in *Four Ways*, as well as "Old Music and the Slave Women" from the later collection *The Birthday of the World*, are about connecting the sexes and the classes to cultivate the ground on which equal relationships can exist.

We have seen the themes of the first two stories in *Four Ways to Forgiveness* ("Betrayals" and "Forgiveness Day") before. Each tells of two people from greatly different backgrounds forced together by circumstances. Despite an initial hesitation or even animosity, they come to understand and love each other, and in the process heal wounds within themselves.

133

In both cases, the characters must learn to hold fast "the one noble thing," the essential connection between people, hold each other dear above all else. The first story, "Betrayals," is about Yoss, an older woman who has moved to an isolated home in the marshes, ostensibly to renounce worldly pleasures and find peace. She eventually admits to herself that she has to come to mourn the loss of her daughter and grandchildren who have departed in an Ekumen ship. Due to time dilation, they will never see each other again. She has come to the marshes to be figuratively what she is to them literally: "dead."[16] Out on the marshes she meets another exile, the Learesque Abberkam, former chief of the rebel World Party, a man who has betrayed his ideals and his people. He is a shell of his former self, ill and literally howling in the wilderness from shame, anger and loss. Yoss knows who he is and what he has done, to herself among millions of others. Yet recognizing in him the signs of a life-threatening respiratory disease, she nurses him to health and in the process grows out of her own period of grieving. Never good at renouncing the pleasures of life, including good wine and conversation, she gives up the pretext of deprivation. But as a woman from a former slave society where women, even when freed, are still essentially enslaved, Yoss must hold her ground in the presence of the larger-than-life Abberkam. She is emotionally stronger than he, strong enough to see that his pain and grief make them equals; she will "not let him have power" over her.[17] This is essential because of their people's history of misogyny. But Abberkam is a huge man, and after recovering from his illness is still charismatic and wearing the swagger of the public figure. But his ego and physical powers are checked when, in a Rochesterian moment, he is injured by a falling beam as he attempts to rescue Yoss' pet from her burning house, an event that leaves him at least temporarily maimed. This accident brings them to a more equal footing, for the loss of her hideaway forces Yoss to do what she had come to the marshes for, be truly divested of material things and forced to "hold fast the noble thing," a basic tenet of her religion. Abberkam's act of creating a bedroom for her, which he hopes but does not assume they will share, shows his sense of their equality. Howard Sklar sees this as a story of reconciliation; "'Betrayals' is a deep and enduring expression of the dynamics that enable individuals who are divided to feel and care for each other."[18] I agree but would add that it is equally a story about healing the self.

The same can be said of "Forgiveness Day," told from the alternating viewpoints of Solly, a half-Terran Ekumenical envoy, and Teyeo, the former solider who is her bodyguard. Teyeo is a member of the veot, a soldier class brought up with a strong code of chivalry. Though attracted to the sexually liberated Solly, Teyeo is repulsed by what he perceives as her immorality and disregard for decorum. He is steeped in the Werelian owner/asset mindset, according to which even an owner woman is an asset to her husband. But his faith in this way of thinking has been tested by the treatment he received when he returned from Yeowe, where he fought to repress the slave rebellion. In an analog to the treatment of soldiers returning from Vietnam, Teyeo finds his service has become politically incorrect, himself and his fellow soldiers scapegoated by the government. Solly, brought up in a classless system, is in many ways Teyeo's opposite. She is introduced as a "space brat," and is painted from the outset as naïve and probably not yet well equipped to be an envoy, despite having been raised on a series of Ekumen ships. Her generally easy life has not taught her to value her own freedom or to recognize the lack of it in others. On Werel she has a lover, an actor/asset named Batikam, who seems at first to be freely her lover and later to be more of a prostitute. He tells her, "You're the only person I've ever known who was neither owned nor owner. That is freedom. *That* is freedom. I wonder if you know it."[19] In this story, reminiscent of *The Left Hand of Darkness*, Solly will learn how to be a good envoy through her relationship with Teyeo. Unlike Genly and Estraven, though, these two become lovers and their story ends happily. This comes about when they are kidnapped and held hostage by a rebel faction. Their enforced togetherness leads to understanding and eventually love. Moreover, they learn the essential thing that will make them complete: Solly learns to value her freedom only through being imprisoned, while Teyeo learns from her how to think like a free person.

"A Man of the People" concerns Havzhiva, an envoy who helps bring about a massive women's resistance movement on Yeowe, the former slave colony struggling to recover from its history. For ex-slaves, it takes time to learn how to be free. As one woman says, "You kill the boss and you become the boss."[20] While the revolution ended the owning of "assets," Yeowe's women are still all but enslaved. When Havzhiva gently suggests to Yeowe's president that women are not yet treated as equals, he is met with the comment that "A freeman's women are free."[21] Through subtle diplomacy, Havzhiva helps to bring about the end of female enslavement. In the story's pivotal moment, he is a guest of Yeowe's new leaders, made up of former slaves. They invite him to watch an initiation rite, essentially a ritual rape, with the young boys as much victims as the girls. His hosts clearly have no sense of the wrongness of this ceremony; they have lived it themselves, experienced it as a cultural norm. Havzhiva's horrified reaction opens up an alternate view on the scene, showing that other cultures find such a ritual unthinkable. Galvanized by this, the women of Yeowe organize and agitate, adopting a form of passive resistance to secure their rights. In huge groups, they disrupt government and commerce by lying down on train tracks and in houses of state, fomenting a non-violent rebellion.

"A Woman's Liberation" is about Rakam, an ex-slave who becomes a leader in the women's movement. Rakam must unlearn slavery and learn freedom. She leaves Yeowe for Werel, where she becomes a historian and starts a press, bringing the written word to the ex-slaves. Her freedom is complete when she meets Havzhiva and opens her heart to him, the symbolic gate that frees her from the plantation. Having been sexually enslaved from childhood, for Rakam learning freedom is as much a matter of reclaiming her sexual self as it is of becoming educated, gaining self-confidence and learning to set boundaries for those who try to take advantage of her. Consent is an essential aspect of her freedom, as she tells a woman who kisses her without asking first. Havzhiva, here referred to by his proper name of Yehedarhed, asks if he can make love to her. Rakam considers this consensual sexual act to be the first time she makes love.

Though not published until 2002, when it was included in the collection *The Birthday of the World*, "Old Music and the Slave Women" is the fifth member of this story cycle. It tells of the Hainish ambassador, Old Music, last seen ushering slaves through an underground railroad in "A Woman's Liberation." In this story, set in the waning days of the rebellion, Old Music is kidnapped first by a government faction and later by rebels. Though a somewhat elderly statesman, and as an ambassador seemingly immune to political uses, Old Music is taken to a former slave estate where he is held captive and tortured.[22] When the rebel faction storms the plantation, rather than free Old Music, they also use him as a political pawn. Once slaves themselves, they are nonetheless ruthless, even killing any "house slaves" they see as having collaborated with the owners in pre-rebellion times. Old Music holds onto his humanity by befriending the few women slaves still living there, left behind after the rebellion because they could not travel with a sick child. As in "A Man of the People," here the male lead softens what might be read as an anti-male story. Though it is full of men who do terrible things, its strength resides in the main character, a man of integrity who lives through a terrible ordeal with dignity. The story suggests that malevolence recognizes no boundaries; anyone can fall victim, even an envoy from the powerful Ekumen. As the historian Henennemores puts it, "In war everyone is a prisoner."[23]

While *Four Ways* does not have the conscious narrative experimentation of a story suite like *Searoad*, Le Guin is certainly using narrative invention to make a point. The quartet of *Four Ways* uses a different storytelling frame in each; the first is told from Yoss' perspective while "Forgiveness Day" is told from both Solly's and Teyeo's. The next two stories, "A Man of the People" and "A Woman's Liberation" separately tell the stories of the same two people who will by the end of the quartet become a couple. The stories also provide a variety of viewpoints, including those of owners, assets, and free people, as well as Hains and Terrans. And while the stories are not arranged chronologically, they do intersect: Abberkam is the leader of the World Party that tries to assassinate Havzhiva; Solly, who is a young envoy when we meet her, will later send Havzhiva to Yeowe, where he will meet Rakam, leader of the women's liberation movement. Jane Donawerth argues that *Four Ways* is "mobile not collage,"[24] stretching the "polyvocal form of the novel."[25] This kind of storytelling, however, is still vintage Le Guin, reminiscent of the alternating times and places in chapters of *The Dispossessed* or the various materials and points of view included in *The Left Hand of Darkness*.

The Joy of Sex

Feminism has gained a reputation for sexual prudery, probably because the anti-pornography efforts of activists like Andrea Dworkin have been taken to be anti-sex or anti-erotic. Feminists who critique pornography are concerned with the images of violence against women present in much pornography and with the social effects of selling products using images of the eroticized female body. Nonetheless, the perception lingers that feminists are censorious and against sex. In reaction to this, and in conjunction with gender analysis that argues for a wide range of sexual practices regardless of gender, post-feminists have sought to reclaim the sexualized or erotic. In this formulation, the Pussycat Dolls, for example, can be read as empowered — as women gaining from the display of their sexuality. In another instance where Le Guin seems to be keeping pace with emerging post-feminist sensibility, her writing of this period lingers over sexual detail more than in her earlier work. In making love, Solly and Teyeo, for example,

> reached out to each other. They clasped each other, cleaved together, in blind haste, greed, need, crying out together the name of God in their different languages and then like animals in the wordless voice. They huddled together, spent, sticky, sweaty, exhausted, reviving, rejoined, reborn in the body's tenderness, in the endless exploration, the ancient discovery, the long flight to the new world.[26]

Reflecting on their union, Teyeo thinks, "Sex, comfort, tenderness, love, trust, no word was the right word, the whole word."[27] Le Guin is certainly not pornographic and her characters have never been squeamish, but there is a new element here. In "Coming of Age in Karhide," she meets head-on the critics of Gethenian sexuality as she depicted it in *The Left Hand of Darkness*. These androgynes, when they come into their monthly period of sexual activity, seem far more alien than they did earlier, their choice of mates infringing on the reader's sense of taboo. Unlike the Terran experience, where the onset of menstruation is not ritually associated with loss of virginity, on Gethen the first kemmer is accompanied by the first experience of the kemmer house, where those who are in their active sexual period congregate. While the very thought of the experience terrifies the young protagonist of the story, it is a rite remembered with great fondness and treated with complex care by the older Gethenians. Gethenians seem to share the French feminist view of the polymorphously perverse, to bask in *jouissance*. Since Gethenians can be male or female, have no incest taboos, and spend only a few days a month in kemmer, they make the most of it. One can have any variety of consensual sexual experience desired with the exception of the scrupulous care taken with birth control. The lack of boundaries is in line with post-feminist rethinkings of sexuality, in particular in its refusal to link or rather to judge the relationship of the sex act and power, quite unlike early branches of feminist theory in which every sex act was considered to be rape. In "A Woman's Liberation," Rakam writes of how she was repeatedly sexually abused by first her female master and then by a fellow slave. While not condoning these acts, she nevertheless recognizes a complexity in her response to them: "Perhaps you will say that I could not or should not have had pleasure in being used without my consent by my mistress, and if I did, I should not speak of it, showing even so little good in so great an evil. But I knew nothing of consent or refusal. Those are freedom words."[28] Le Guin more fully builds the homosexual experience into her characterization. Sutty in *The Telling* is lesbian, her sexual preference outlawed on both religious totalitarian Terra and science-driven Aka, which needs its citizens to continue producing new consumers. In "Mountain Ways," a gay woman pretends to be a man in order to marry into a group that requires two men and two women. This is her only means to be married to the woman she loves. Her transgression is not that she is homosexual, since bisexuality is a given in this society. Rather, she has broken the most essential unit of society: the matched quartet.

The Lot of Men

For some time in Le Guin's writing, sympathetic male characters were easily outmatched by sometimes one-dimensional men, whether they were depicted as evil or as objects of fun, as with the husband in "First Contact with the Gorgonids." *Searoad*, for example, has almost no men who are not weak-willed, domineering, mentally diminished, vain or otherwise unpleasant. *Always Coming Home* is more balanced, but the Condors and the Kesh boys who join them seem to be more present on the page than their gentler male counterparts. In this return to the Ekumen, Le Guin displays a renewed sense of the male character. Clearly, Teyeo, Havzhiva and Old Music demonstrate that men can be other than warmongers, rapists or self-centered ex-lovers. Teyeo's story, in particular, reflects on how boys are shaped to become soldiers. He gave his youth to a useless war, lost his beloved wife, and returned to find his kind disgraced and treated as pariahs. Whereas in the last chapter we saw Le Guin depicting men somewhat unsympathetically or leaving them out altogether, in these stories we see the return of the kind of men that made Le Guin's earlier fiction palatable to both sexes. Because post-feminism makes room for men as well as women, it has incorporated critiques of masculinity gleaned from gender studies.

That Le Guin has turned her keen eye toward the lot of men — the social construction of male identity more than the essential traits — is most evident in "The Matter of Seggri," which began as a thought experiment about the cultural effects of child rationing in China.[29] What happens in a culture where most parents select for a male child? In this story she reverses the scenario, making males the minority gender. This might seem on its face to be another of Le Guin's reversals to create distance, a story meant to bring the plight of current-day women to light. Instead it evokes pity for men over the gendered restrictions placed on them. The story is composed of short pieces, told from the viewpoint of Ekumen explorers as they observe and later live incognito among the planet's inhabitants. The touch-and-go first glance, written in the style of Captain Cook, depicts the men as god-like, living for sport and pleasure while the women do all the work. Initially "The Matter of Seggri" seems almost comic. As the pieces progress, however, the tone becomes urgent and a sense of danger grows. As the story layers unpeel, it becomes clear that far from being treated as gods, the men are virtually enslaved. Torn from their loving families as adolescents and forced to live in the men's compound, the targets of bullies and tyrants, they are in constant danger of being ambushed and beaten or raped by their captors. Their only path to "glory" is sport and studding. Because it is believed that schooling might ruin their capacity for reproducing, they are uneducated; they have no survival skills and no place to live outside the men's compound. They are completely entrapped by gender. In this society which prizes extreme sport and favors rule by bullies and tyrants, most men die young. All in all, the narrative is too extreme, too tragic, and the masculine details too gender-specific to work as illumination by reversal.[30] Instead, the cumulative effect is to reverse our reading of some rites of masculinity — sports, for example, and to see them as pseudo-glory, a disguise for men's lack of options.

Interestingly, in this period Le Guin introduces more complexity into her vision of the Ekumen. For one thing, it is clearly dangerous to be an envoy. Solly and Teyeo are held hostage, Havzhiva is nearly killed, and Old Music is tortured. And not all planets are eager to join the Ekumen, despite its stated benevolence. Entry into the Ekumen seems to have chaos as an accompaniment, as the envoys discover. The consequences of joining are unknowable and uncontrollable, as we saw with Hideo who cannot anticipate what his decision to board a NAFAL spaceship will cost him, or in *The Telling*, where cultural contamination leads to totalitarianism. In some respects the Ekumen is the ultimate colonizer; it aims to bring everyone in under the family umbrella, to universalize knowledge and to establish racial unity. Moreover, the goals of the universe-seeders, the Hain, are called into question by several characters that remark on the perversity of the Hain, their willingness to experiment with life. Finally, if the Hainish seeded the universe, put humans here on Earth to blend in with whatever fauna already existed, presumably including monkeys, then what does that say about the Terran fossil record? It certainly makes a clear statement about the existence of a creator god.

Again, Earthsea

As discussed in Chapter Three, eighteen years after *The Farthest Shore*, Le Guin surprised readers with the Earthsea book, *Tehanu*. Le Guin provided a bridge between the older story and the new by overlapping the timeframe of *Tehanu* with that of *The Farthest Shore* and by completing storylines left open. Ged and Tenar become a couple, and Lebannen becomes king. That story introduced us to the damaged child, Tehanu, who is adopted by Tenar and who, it seems, is the daughter of dragons. While subtitled *The Last Book of Earthsea*, the novel ends, almost literally, with a cliffhanger. There is no attempt to explain fully how the burnt human child could be part dragon. This loose end hints at some narrative unease boiling in the depths of Le Guin's consciousness. Clearly her feminist evolution had uprooted some of her deeply held concepts of the place, but it had not supplied the means for finishing out the story. She had returned to Earthsea with her compass points shifted and with an altered perspective on her earlier work. She questioned the assumptions underlying her construction of the trilogy, in particular why men were mages and women were not and "where were the women in Earthsea?"[31] She was evolving a new paradigm for Earthsea, but in *Tehanu* it has not fully taken shape. When Le Guin returned to Earthsea, in 2001 with *The Other Wind* and *Tales from Earthsea*, she resolved this problem and comes to the storytelling with a specific purpose — to align the place with her 21st century sensibility. Yet, rather than rewrite or revise the trilogy, as she did in response to criticism of *The Left Hand of Darkness*, she shifted the narrative focus, created a parallax view of Earthsea, a distaff point of view.

To tell the other side of the Earthsea story, Le Guin had to deal with vestiges of her own pre-feminist thinking. In the early books, the men held the power and women were secondary. Women did not do magic, except wrongly, especially as evidenced in the aphorisms "Weak as woman's magic

... Wicked as woman's magic"[32] Mages could only be men and, as it turns out, had to be celibate. To set things right, she recasts the vilification of women as a projection of male fear of female power, in particular procreative power. Mages deny this fear by abstaining from women, shielding themselves from sexual contact and hiding behind their ironically phallic staffs. Their celibacy cuts mages off from more than sex. In Le Guin's new conception, women are linked to the "Old Powers," a primeval force far stronger than the power of mages. The Old Powers, deeply rooted in the earth, are consistently portrayed using female sexual imagery. A mage's abstinence from women thus becomes a metaphor for his denial of the life force. Abstaining from a full experience of life, he denies its necessary end, death.

In retrospect, it seems ironic that in *The Farthest Shore*, which is about the necessity of accepting death, that the dead of Earthsea do not die but journey to the Dry Lands to exist forever as shadows of their earthly selves. By the time she wrote *The Other Wind*, Le Guin had recognized and resolved this contradiction. In order to bring Earthsea in line with her new sensibility, this concept of death would need complete revising. In fact, she links the imbalance of male and female power with this denial of death. In a brilliant reversal, she corrects both problems through a narrative that appropriates the romance quest. This is the main plot that drives the novel, the quest to discover why Earthsea, although ruled by the rightful king, has not found peace. Nominally led by Lebannen, the effort to repair Earthsea depends on the shared knowledge of women, dragons, laymen and mages. Together they find a link between the lack of peace and the mages' fear of death, the hero-centric quest mitigated by the novel's collective point of view.

As they discover, the imbalance in Earthsea results from a breach by mages of the *Vedurnan* (*verw nadan*), an ancient agreement between humans and dragons. Long ago one people, they split into two races: humans chose material goods and mortality and dragons chose the freedom of "the other wind" and seeming immortality. Afraid of death, mages broke this agreement, stealing dragon territory and walling it off to create the Dry Lands. The disquiet of the newer books results from dragon anger about this theft and from the voices of the dead clamoring to be allowed truly to die. The Earthsea series ends with the harrowing of the Dry Lands and the release of its souls into oblivion. The dragons, their lands restored, leave Earthsea for good. The mages, their core beliefs in tatters, must reexamine their exclusionary practices. Far from her noble depiction of wizards in the original trilogy, Le Guin here places full blame for Earthsea's problems on the masters of Roke. More radically, Le Guin's dismantling of the Dry Lands is akin to refuting the Christian heaven. The history of Roke becomes a cognitive parallel to Western history, with mages standing in for the leaders of the early Christian church who, in some accounts, closed ranks around a male prerogative, writing women out of church history, vowing celibacy and vilifying women.

There is a further matter to resolve. What kind of peace will reign in a kingdom ruled by a bachelor (if hardly celibate) king, a man as unschooled in the fullness of life as any mage? The chastising element of the new books, where wizardly celibacy misleads and endangers, is counterbalanced by the serio-comic romance of Lebannen and the Kargish princess Seserakh. Forced upon each other, they slowly arrive at a détente and eventually a passion. Their sexual congress is the final step in a return to fertility and hence the full healing of the land. While we never see what it will become, their marriage is also meant to symbolize not just the unity of Archipelago and Kargad but also the co-equal rule of male and female. That they charge the air with sexual longing is so much the better. A marriage plot seems conservative in comparison with the radical inversion of the afterlife paradigm; however, Le Guin paints Seserakh as more than a match for the king. Assuming they are equals, their marriage will unite Havnor and Kargad, promising peace for all Earthsea.

Real Mages Do It with Their Staffs

Celibacy appears elsewhere in Le Guin's work. In *The Left Hand of Darkness*, indwellers of the Handdara vow celibacy as a discipline, a form of self-concentration and a step toward full awareness.[33] We see the same concept in *Always Coming Home*, where young people "live on the coast," willingly forgoing physical contact as they learn to control their sexual energies.[34] In both cases, celibacy is treated gently, with respect for the discipline and self-sacrifice of those on a spiritual path. In the early Earthsea books, celibacy is unquestioned and even unmentioned. The closest we get to sexual content in the trilogy is Ged, staff in hand, wandering the obviously symbolic maze of Atuan (a place where women have power but, like mages, don't have sex). Le Guin first calls this celibacy to our attention in *Tehanu*. When we left Ged at the end of book three, he had sacrificed his magic powers to close the doorway from death back to life. Having lost his power, he leaves his useless staff behind. When we see him again early in book four, he has lost everything: his powers, his home on Roke, and his profession. Of him, the witch Moss says, "It's a queer thing for an old man to be a boy of fifteen, no doubt!"[35] Tenar realizes for the first time that Ged is a virgin. Wondering why, despite an almost life-long friendship, she never felt attracted to him sexually, Tenar asks, "is it a spell?" Moss tells her a theory which she has heard, but which she, too practical for abstinence, does not believe: "They witch 'emselves. Some'll tell you they make a trade-off, like a marriage turned backward, with vows and all, and so get their power then."[36] Le Guin's specific attention to celibacy is thus a major shift away from the first three books. She forces the question of where the belief that mages must be celibate to have power originates. Celibacy protects the non-magical from a mage's abuse of power for sexual ends, but must a mage exchange sex for power?

That wizards do hoard their power by insulating themselves from sex is shown in *Tales from Earthsea*. A young mage in training is told that "to make love is to unmake power."[37] In "Darkrose and Diamond," Hemlock puts a protective spell on his apprentice Diamond. Like a dose of saltpeter, the spell dampens sexual longing. It also protects the boy from sexual advances. When Diamond objects, Hemlock says, "The bargain, boy. The power we give for our power. The lesser state of being we forgo. Surely you know that every true man of power is celibate."[38] In the collection's back matter, Le Guin connects the origins of celibacy among wizards to the Dark Time, a period in Earthsea history when the throne of Havnor sat empty and the school on Roke had yet to be formed. "Women, witchery, and the Old Powers had all come to be considered unclean, the belief was already widespread that men must prepare themselves to work 'high magic' by scrupulously avoiding 'base spells,' 'Earthlore,' and women."[39] "The Finder," about the mage Medra, tells the history of the founding of Roke. It locates the origins of wizardly celibacy in a fear of female power. In the Dark Time women and men were equally capable of magic, but magic itself was feared. Roke Island was a haven for witches and some mages who hid from persecution and coexisted with no restrictions on sexual activity. They founded a school on Roke to teach those gifted in magic. From within their own ranks came a separatist movement of mages who vilified women, casting them as carnal and as users of dark magic. Even though

Roke Knoll is a center of the Old Powers, these separatists feared the powers of the Earth. As Medra's partner, the witch Elehal, describes these mages,

> they are men, and they make that important beyond anything else. To them, the Old Powers are abominable. And women's powers are suspect, because they suppose them all connected with the Old Powers. As if these Powers were to be controlled or used by any mortal soul! But they put men where we put the world. And so they hold that a true wizard must be a man. And celibate.[40]

Equating women with these powers enabled the separatists to control them; meanwhile, historical revisionism and a smear campaign worked to subjugate women all over Earthsea. Yet Medra shows that a mage can be powerful, sexually active, and even partnered. As a finder, his gift is sensing water and minerals in the earth under his feet; his power arises from his connection to the earth, which he calls "mother." At one point he escapes capture by asking the earth to open up and take him in. After some coaxing of "open to me," the ground parts and Medra enters a huge cavern that leads onto a long passage to safety.[41] As in *The Tombs of Atuan*, the earth is rendered as womb-like and immensely powerful. Medra's willingness to take refuge in the earth mirrors his comfort in sharing his life with Elehal. They are both people of great power, yet their sexual relationship strengthens them. Medra is a model of possibility, an alternative to the story of mage as celibate. But despite the founders' intention that Roke school males and females equally, the separatist movement won the day, and wizardry became the domain only of celibate males.

At least these mages had their staffs to keep them warm at night. Although we don't need much prompting to see the staff as a symbolic penis, its phallic nature is evident in a monologue directed by the mage Dulse to his staff in "The Bones of the Earth":

> "Stand!" He said to it in its language, and let go of it. It stood as if he had driven it into a socket.
> "To the root," he said impatiently, in the Language of the Making. "To the root!"
> He watched the staff that stood on the shining floor. In a little while he saw it quiver very slightly, a shiver, a tremble.... The staff swayed, was still, shivered again.
> "Enough of that my dear," Dulse said, laying his hand on it.[42]

As another of Le Guin's good wizards, a man whose power does not depend on female subjugation, Dulse is perhaps the wrong example to use here.

Like Medra, he operates by merger and empathy, quelling an earthquake by "getting in with it ... Inside."[43] Again like Medra, Dulse's teacher was a woman, the witch Ard, who taught him "old" magic, scorned by Roke and aligned with the dirt and rocks of the place itself. Yet Dulse hides the gender of his teacher, even from his own apprentice Ogion, because it is not the way of Roke. And, like any wizard, Dulse lives a celibate, nearly monastic life. His relationship to his staff hints at sexual narcissism, or at least sexual immaturity. That a boy becomes a mage only when given his staff by his teacher suggests a homogametic quality, a kind of asexual reproduction. Further, since the staff amplifies and directs the magic words of the wizard, it might remind us of Gilbert and Gubar's famous question about the penis and the pen. Illustrating the concept of phallogocentrism, they argue that men have equated pen and penis, thereby implying that only a man can write.[44] Here, we might extend the equation: is a staff a metaphorical penis? Is that why only men do magic?

This leads us on to the question of women, whose knowledge and bravery will ultimately save these mages from themselves. Le Guin's feminist awakening caused her to wonder why she never wrote about women: "all my early books are about men, and women are very secondary. In the first and third Earthsea books there really aren't any women to speak of. That's very strange. I'm a woman. Why was I writing that way?"[45] As noted in Chapter Three, starting with *Tehanu*, women are more central, more powerful, and much wiser than in the early books. If anything, women and the powers associated with them — the Old Powers of the Earth and, as we shall see, those of the dragons — are privileged above the male powers associated with Roke. What emerges is a feminist essentialist perspective, one that argues for nature over nurture and which here elevates female nature over male. As Ged, Dulse and Medra illustrate, however, this is not a separatist paradigm. Some men are more "female" than others, are able to submerge their egos in the stream of life rather than try to control its flow. There are good men and bad here, though it must be admitted that there are no bad women.

Even in the first trilogy, we saw the Old Powers equated repeatedly with the female body. Le Guin herself has described *The Tombs of Atuan* as being "about sex."[46] Indeed, the underground mazes, the hidden treasury, the virgin priestess, and the violation of the tombs by a man, staff in hand, are almost too symbolic. As Tenar and Ged escape the labyrinth, Ged holds back the tunnel's spasms. The book even ends in an orgasmic collapse of the tombs, underscoring the might of the Dark Powers residing there:

> The earth of the valley rippled and bucked; a kind of wave ran up the hillside, and a huge crack opened among the Tombstones, gaping on the blackness underneath ... then with a crash that seemed to echo off the sky itself, the raw black lips of the crack closed together and the hills shook once, and grew still.[47]

The femaleness of the earth is even more overt in the recent books, where its powers are far stronger and much older than those of the Roke mages. At the same time, these powers are accorded little reverence. In *The Other Wind*, a cave called the "Lips of Paor" is described as "a sacred place, full of power."[48] Its powers as an oracle long-forgotten, it is now used as a dump: "all around was a litter of rancid scraps of half-cured leather and a stink of rot and urine."[49]

Then there are the dragons. In the early trilogy, they are essentially run-of-the-mill: impressive but not vital to the story. They know the Old Speech, the Speech of the Making, and being so old, they remember things lost to human knowledge. But as characters they are flat. In the new books, the difference is immediate and immense. In *Tehanu*, we hear early on the story of the Woman of Kemay — a woman who is also a dragon. She tells of an ancient time when dragons and humans were all one race. Eventually, some chose the dragon's path — a wild life, free of material possessions, spent flying on "the other wind."[50] The others chose the human path, of material possessions, flightless and protected. Some people, it emerges, are both. Le Guin has said the dragon "rejects gender."[51] Of course, both people we meet who cross the boundary from human to dragon are female, the burned child Tehanu and Dragonfly, a young woman turned away by the masters of Roke. Both have suffered sexually at the hands of men, including their own fathers. Clearly, the catalyst that arouses dragon-nature is human rage, in particular female rage. In *Earthsea Revisioned*, Le Guin writes,

> The dragon ... is wildness seen not only as dangerous beauty but as dangerous anger ... It meets the fire of human rage, the cruel anger of the weak, which wreaks itself on the weaker in the endless circle of human violence. It meets that fire and consumes it, for "a wrong that cannot be repaired must be transcended."[52]

This wildness and righteous anger are akin to what Susan Griffin describes in *Woman and Nature*, which warns of the anger of the oppressed female.

In *Tehanu*, when Tenar and Ged are being tortured, the dragon Kalessin saves them by burning their captors to death. Kalessin, also called Segoy (creator of Earthsea), is depicted as awesome, immense, and ancient. Kalessin calls Tehanu "child" and indicates that Tehanu will join the dragons one day, when her "work among the humans is done."[53] Particularly as embodied in Tehanu herself, woman/dragon is reminiscent of Medusa, whose punishment for being raped is to be turned into a monster, one that men cannot look directly upon. Hélène Cixous' "Laugh of the Medusa" reclaims the myth, seeing it as an imposition of male fear of castration arising, as Freud would put it, from the snakes adorning Medusa's monstrous head like so many severed penises. Though she doesn't fully explain her meaning, Cixous says that the Medusa, if actually looked upon, is beautiful, even laughing. These images accord with Le Guin's description of Kalessin, on whom Tenar is not afraid to look: "She had been told that men must not look into a dragon's eyes, but that was nothing to her."[54] Like the women who are also dragons, Medusa has a double identity; she is both the young woman raped and "punished" and the feared/fearful Gorgon. In her landmark essay, Cixous also claims for women the power of flight: "Flying is woman's gesture—flying in language and making it fly ... women take after birds."[55] Further, Cixous argues,

> Unlike man, who holds so dearly to his title and his titles, his pouches of value ... woman couldn't care less about the fear of decapitation (or castration), adventuring, without the masculine temerity, into anonymity, which she can merge with without annihilating herself.[56]

This sounds much like the territorial differences between human and dragon—the division of the material and the immaterial. Importantly Cixous, like Le Guin, leaves room here for men; she says, "there are some men (all too few) who aren't afraid of femininity."[57]

"All changed"

Lebannen follows the mode of Le Guin's men who distinguish themselves by considering women (and dragons) his equals. In Arthurian style, he takes council with a Palnish sorcerer, the poor mender Alder, middle-aged Tenar, the maimed Tehanu, and the dragon Orm Irian, who is also the woman Dragonfly. Reluctantly he includes Seserakh, the Kargish princess forced upon him by her father. Along with those few Roke mages

148

capable of self-evaluation, these are his quest companions. Le Guin revises the chauvinism of the earlier books that present the Archipelago (Roke and the associated islands) as the geological and ethical center of Earthsea. Instead, we find that the warrior Kargs and the dark sorcerers of Paln have retained essential knowledge long forgotten in Roke. In fact, the story of the Vedurnan comes from Seserakh, who herself is Kargish.

In sharp contrast to the Archipelagans, the Kargs neither practice magic nor believe in an afterlife. When Seserakh learns she is to marry Lebannen, she is terrified that, "I won't be able to die. I'll have to live forever without my body, a bird that can't fly, and never be reborn."[58] Kargs do not fear death. They believe in rebirth in the strictly biological sense: return to the earth and thus to the cycles of nature. In contrast, Orm Irian says of the Archipelagans, "Men fear death as dragons do not. Men want to own life, possess it, as if it were a jewel in a box. Those ancient mages craved everlasting life. They learned to use true names to keep men from dying. But those who cannot die can never be reborn."[59] The wizards who broke the ancient bargain dreamed of something akin to the Christian heaven: "a great land of rivers and mountains and beautiful cities, where there is no suffering or pain, and where the self endures, unchanged, unchanging, forever."[60] Their mistake was in thinking that they had created a paradise. Instead, walling off the land also walled off water, wind and sunlight. The dead there clamor to be let free. "It is not life they yearn for. It is death. To be one with the earth again. To rejoin it."[61] In the pivotal scene of *The Other Wind*, men, mages and dragons together tear down the wall that keeps the dead from death. The Dry Lands are returned to the dragons and the dead go free. The price paid is immortality. As Peter Hollindale has argued, the Earthsea series' great theme is "the use and abuse of death."[62]

The final elements needed to restore Earthsea's balance are the shared rule of male and female, the reunification of nations and the promise of fertility. Male/female balance was suggested but never fully realized in *The Tombs of Atuan*. The symbolically female labyrinth is penetrated by the staff-carrying Ged. And while this seems a Taoist balance, the dark Ged and the white Tenar, the ring of Erreth-Akbe and the sword of Havnor, Ged's celibacy denies fertility and thus rejuvenation. The true resolution of this element comes only in *The Other Wind*. In a plot pulled straight out of *Henry the V*, the long-promised peace comes through the marriage of Lebannen and Seserakh. They overcome cultural and linguistic misunderstandings to unify the lands. Again, the imagery is almost too obviously symbolic: their coupling, he dark skinned, she light, forms a perfect Taoist circle. This heterosexual marriage plot may seem reactionary. Seserakh, raised in purdah then forced to marry a stranger, initially strikes the reader as a victim; yet her red veils not only suggest fertility, they warn of the hidden dragon. Of Lebannen, Tenar says, "'he's met his match.'"[63] This pairing of equals who will clearly share a passionate sex life counterbalances *Tombs'* unconsummated and unequal relationship between the mage Ged and the girl Tenar.

Here the newer books come closest to illustrating Darko Suvin's argument that *Tehanu, Tales from Earthsea* and *The Other Wind* constitute a second Earthsea trilogy. They also seem to illustrate Comoletti and Drout's suggestion that the newer books are a "feminist intervention." Without disagreeing, I would suggest that Le Guin did not intend to negate or deny the original trilogy. She is not rewriting it. Instead, the new books speak in the "other voice" present but to a degree hidden in the trilogy. They form a companion set, albeit one whose values are presented as superior to those of the first. In fact, the newer books are as female essentialist as the first three are male essentialist. Any essentialist perspective, however, is problematic. What good (or perhaps what harm) does it do to equate women to wild nature given the contempt with which nature itself is regarded? To suggest that women are at heart dragons and ought to be feared? Or that the damaged girl can achieve wholeness only as a dragon, flying wild on an immaterial "other wind?"

Imagine There's No Heaven

Colin Manlove describes the first three Earthsea novels as "profoundly conservative," in as much as they strive to preserve "balance, moderation, and the celebration of the way things are."[64] This balance is achieved in part by acceptance of death. On their way to the Dry Lands, Ged tells Lebannen that "nothing is immortal. But only to us is it given to know that we must die. And that is a great gift."[65] Yet, as Le Guin parses out in the later books, these "mortals" are not truly relinquishing life. They go to the Dry Lands, where they are shades of themselves, not to the Earth, where they would become part of nature's great recycling program. This lies at the heart of Le Guin's disquiet with her own trilogy: it insists on mortality but provides for a kind of immortality. Ironically, celibacy insures that mages will never enjoy the "immortality" inherent in passing on their genes. The recent books, knocking out this immortality clause, could then be read as more consistently conservative, truer to the author's intention, than they were before. Certainly, they now fall more clearly in line with Le Gun's Taoist sensibility. That would be denying their radical agenda, however.

As Darko Suvin argues, this "second" trilogy has the property of cognition, what he calls "a transitive understanding, which the readers can transfer from the pages of fiction to their own personal and collective lives."[66] The new books reach past their fantasy packaging to suggest ways that we might enact change in our own lives. The recent additions to the Earthsea series do not just argue for living in the present. Like Phillip Pullman's *His Dark Materials*, they force a reexamination of the Christian tradition, a questioning of the origins of its core beliefs. The many parallels to the history of the Christian church, from its early inclusion of women, to the internal takeover by a male-oriented faction, its avowal of celibacy, and its campaign of disinformation about women, are too analogous to dismiss.[67] To draw the analogy out, if Earthsea's mages are responsible for many of its social ills, to whom do we affix blame in our cognitive reality? Here, Le Guin seems clearly to be assigning blame to a Western Judeo-Christian culture that denied death and excluded women from power. As a work of fantasy, a genre that critics have long considered to reinforce existing values rather than introduce new ones, this demonstrates another version of Le Guin feeling free to invent her own rules.

The Post-Feminist Le Guin

In Le Guin's world, true journey is return and her evolution into post-feminism marks a spiral trajectory, nearly coming back to origins. She does not reject her feminism but builds it into her mental architecture in a way that makes it second nature, so that the writing that springs from it seems more organic. But she moves on from some of the fervor of high feminism, including its experimentalism, essentialism and exclusions. Le Guin has not engaged in discussions of post-feminism. Nonetheless, the work of this period shows a clear backing away from the experimental, non-linear narratives of her high feminist period. She is certainly assessing the lot of men differently as well, as comparisons of her Condor society in *Always Coming Home* and "The Matter of Seggri" demonstrate. There is less universalizing of the male experience, more dimensionality and more recognition that men can be as constrained by social roles as women. Le Guin has always been exceptionally conscious of the power of story. Her Mobiles of the Ekumen have made their reports in the form of a story from the beginning. Nonetheless, the focus on story as reality creation, on simultaneous, multiple building of reality through story is considerably greater here. There is also a new disregard for the master narratives of sf and fantasy and a desire to rewrite the rules or disregard them altogether.

CHAPTER FIVE

Landing on Middle Ground

In the years since the last Earthsea books, Le Guin has continued to be impressively productive.[1] She "discovered" another place and hence another series, the young adult Western Shore books, *Gifts* (2004), *Voices* (2006), and *Powers* (2007). She continued to blur the edges of genre in *Changing Planes* (2003), a collection of quasi-science fiction stories with magic realist leanings. And she wrote the subtle masterpiece, *Lavinia* (2008), a work of historical fiction that similarly tilts toward magic realism. Like all of us, during these years she went about the business of daily living while watching consensus reality devolve, as the World Trade Towers collapsed, the United States went to war, and global economic disaster descended. She also approached old age, turning 80 in October 2009. Not surprisingly, her writing during this time reflects these public and private events, as is most directly evidenced by a collection of poems, *Incredible Good Fortune* (2006). Here she considers mortality, words, nature, war, and the aftermath of colonialism. These themes, as discussed below, are central concerns during this period.

Certainly war and power are her primary and commingled themes. For someone as committed to peace as Le Guin, the events of 9/11 and the subsequent wars in the Middle East must have been deeply disturbing. Her poem "Peace Vigil, March, 2003" reflects the nation's dazed disorientation. A ragged and bewildered man wanders into a circle of protestors who stand holding candles. He sits in the circle's center and is given a candle, which he shields from the spring rain. When the protesters disband, he remains, still holding his candle. His staying there while the others have left could symbolize hope, but instead it seems to capture our collective powerlessness. Indeed in the same year, Le Guin published an essay, "A War Without End," which contains as depressing a statement about human nature as she has made. She wonders whether a "hierarchy of power [is] a biological imperative,"[2] and concludes that freedom may more "remain a quality of the mind or spirit" than an actuality.[3] Nonetheless, the humanist in her still believes in a "middle ground between defense and attack, a ground of flexible resistance, a space opened for change."[4] As she did during the Vietnam War, she used fiction as a form of protest against the wars in Iraq and Afghanistan, though less baldly than in *The Word for World Is Forest*.[5] Le Guin does not invoke these crises directly, but the fiction represents an attempt to conceptualize the middle ground she mentions above. *Changing Planes* argues for cultural relativity. The Western Shore books are populated with characters that tread softly, carefully wielding their power. *Lavinia*, while painting war as inevitable, deflates any glamour attached to conflict.

Mortality also seems to be on Le Guin's mind, particularly in *Lavinia*. It is tempting to read *Lavinia* as a kind of swan song, but no one who has worked on Le Guin's oeuvre would be foolish enough to suggest that she would in any way slow down. Yet the story's insistence that Lavinia is "contingent," relying for her existence upon Vergil who created her and the reader who continually revitalizes her, forces consideration of the idea that literature confers immortality. There is also a sense of conserving words, hoarding them: like that of many great writers, Le Guin's work has become more compressed, her words and details ever more artfully chosen as she has aged. Indeed, the final paragraph of *Lavinia*, as the title character fades from life into poetic immortality, hearing both the sounds of nature and the machines of war, is as beautiful a passage as any she has written.

As she did in the nineties, Le Guin explores the idea of freedom, and in particular how the formerly oppressed learn to be free. Continuing in her post-feminist vein, she looks at how this is true for both women and men. *Powers*, for example, is the story of a former slave, Gavir, and his quest to become truly free. At the same time, she does differentiate between the kinds of oppression that men and women suffer, recognizing women's greater vulnerability to sexual abuse. She also continues what has become a feminist tradition, writing or rewriting the story of a female character from a classic work, here Lavinia, the third wife of Aeneas who is only briefly mentioned in Vergil's *Aeneid*. But as much as the novel makes an argument against war, it is the story of a woman who knowingly causes a war by the choice she makes. Here and in sections of *Changing Planes*, Le Guin does not lay responsibility for conflict at the feet of men alone. She also continues to write in the more linear, character-driven style she returned to in the nineties, and sustains, or even heightens, her attention to the individual story. This is still a writer working in a post-feminist mode. I believe, however, that her attention shifts from engagement in gender theory to consideration of the broader social problems that plagued the first decade of the twenty-first century. She is at the same time facing her own mortality head-on. These works mark the progress of a new kind of thinking through, another paradigm shift: in the wake of such events, how does one make sense of human nature or understand the impact she has had on the world?

Now Voyager

In 2003, Le Guin published *Changing Planes*, a collection of stories about imaginatively experiencing other people's realities. The underlying premise is that travelers can use waits in airport terminals as launching points for mind voyages. Its humorous descriptions of what the voyager encounters — living teddy bears with mice-like habits, for example — initially suggest that the book is more whimsical than serious. But there is more to it than first meets the eye. The narrator is reminiscent of Pandora from *Always Coming Home*, a cultural observer from another place, a kind of dream-time traveler; she is there to take it all in. The other "planes" to which she travels exist in separate but parallel realities, none more real or true than another. Like an anthropologist, the narrator listens without passing judgment, getting inside the culture as much as possible. This can be trying, as the places and people she encounters are both bizarre and quirky. On one plane, the narrator meets a woman who is part corn, in a story that seems to warn of the dangers of genetic manipulation. On another plane, she hears from a hybrid bird/man about his people's migrations and mating habits, which are strikingly similar to those of penguins. War is also a recurrent element, with an emphasis on its futility and wastefulness. A section called "Woeful Tales from Mahigul" includes a number of stories about that plane's bloody history. In one story, "The Black Dog," warriors from opposing villages orchestrate their battles. They agree that, rather than attack without warning, it is much more agreeable to hold raids outside village limits so as not to harm the elderly or the women and children. Their ritualistic skirmishes are disrupted by a huge black mongrel, a literal Dog of War, that both kills them and goads them into battle. Women from the warring communities conspire to kill this dog and restore the villages' natural order. But Le Guin does not make war a male activity only; in another story, women create and perpetuate a long-term war.

Marleen S. Barr reads this collection as a response to 9/11, an acknowledgement that in the unreality of the early twenty-first century, science fiction is the only way to describe reality.[6] Everything changed after the attacks, she argues, except male hegemony, which the narrator escapes through her imagination. "Traveling far far away from patriarchy constitutes the ultimate freedom for women."[7] Barr also links *Changing Planes* to more radically feminist science fiction of the preceding century, like Joanna Russ' "When It Changed." Barr sees Le Guin as more feminist in this story suite than she has ever been, now fully aligning herself with seventies sf, breaking gender and heterosexuality barriers in ways she had previously eschewed. As much as I agree that Le Guin is writing from a post–9/11 paradigm, I think Le Guin looks backwards but is moving forward, writing in a post-feminist mode in stories that plead for cultural relativity, for consideration of how power should be welded, and for admitting the costs of war and avoiding it when possible. While the attacks of 9/11 and the subsequent wars seem to have been designed and carried out by members of surprisingly similar patriarchies, there is in *Changing Planes* little lumping of men into a warmongering heap, and even less sense that only women desire to escape from the Kafka-esque nightmare of the new millennium.

Mightier than the Sword

In the *Western Shore Series*, Le Guin creates a land reminiscent of Earthsea — pre-industrial, provincial, sparsely populated. It is permeated by magic in the form of "gifts," specific skills that run like genetic anomalies through families, inherited by some members but not all, and seemingly heritable by either sex. It is Le Guin's most mythically rendered place, combining as it does elements of the Celtic and Roman. Its honored cattle, traveling shanachie, feudal compounds, raids, kilts and scabbed highlands, combine with magical powers, temple virgins, oracles, and multiple household gods. In the parlance of the Hollywood pitch, it is the *Tain bo Cuailnge* meets *The Aeneid*. To date, the series consists of three

156

novels, which are linked by two characters, Orrec Caspro and Gry Barre. But each novel has its own focal character — Orrec in *Gifts*, Memer in *Voices*, and Gavir in *Powers*— each of whom come of age in the course of their novels. They similarly struggle to understand their gifts: of storytelling, channeling an oracle, and foretelling respectively. But they are also linked by their gift for words; by the end of the three novels, they will be living together in a university town, scholars committed to a life of letters.

We first meet Orrec and Gry in *Gifts*, which also introduces us to the concept that drives the series, that some people are born with special skills or "gifts" that might be considered magical powers. Gifts are family-specific. Orrec's family has the gift of the "unmaking," the ability to destroy life with a glance, while Gry's family can communicate with animals. Orrec's father, Canoc, lord of a once-thriving farmhold, is widely feared for his gift. While Canoc doesn't use his power often, like the classic deterrence methods of the Cold War, it discourages war with the neighboring landowners, all of whom have their own dangerous talents. They live in a perpetual standoff. Orrec's father is eager that his son have, or be reputed to have, the most extreme form of the family gift, the "wild eye" that indiscriminately destroys whatever it looks upon. When he discovers that Orrec has not inherited the family trait at all, Canoc tricks his son and everyone in the vicinity into believing that he does. So dangerous does Orrec believe himself to be that he dons a blindfold and for the next two years is effectively sightless. In so doing, he loses the chance to look at his mother once more before her death, but he also uses the time to discover that, like his mother, he has the gift of making or storytelling. It is the reverse form of his father's gift, and it will not keep his family safe from their hostile neighbors. In the meantime, Gry learns she shares her mother's gift for communicating with animals. She can call them to her at will. Her mother uses the gift to lead hunting parties, but Gry refuses to do this. Like Orrec, she must leave her parents' household so she can explore her gift and use it in the manner she chooses.

These characters, like Ged and Tenar, or as Mike Cadden points out, Owen and Natalie of *Very Far Away from Anywhere Else*, help each other to learn the true nature of their gifts and to use them as ethically as possible. As Cadden argues, when Orrec and Gry leave home, it is not running away but going where they can use their gifts appropriately.[8] They are at the same time claiming ownership and control over their gifts, taking on the power inherent in their talents. Indeed all the books in the *West-*

ern Shore Series turn on the question of power. The gift confers considerable responsibility on the one who wields it. As in Earthsea, attention must be paid to the price of using that power. In the Western Shore, this is "the gift's gift," which might be the price paid for using the gift, as in a "pound for a pound," or it may be the hidden prize using the gift confers, an unsought but pleasant byproduct, like the better lives Orrec and Gry create for themselves when they are forced to leave home.

The second book, *Voices* (2006), features a female coming-of-age story even as it depicts the rebellion of an enslaved people against the colonial power that has overtaken them. Unlike the first book, this is more Roman than Celt, with its oracle and its pagan ritual worship of the household gods. It is also more centered in place, particularly since we see it through the eyes of the main character whose job it is to clean, shop for food, and tend to the house's deities. But like the world of *Gifts*, this is a place in decline, threatened by dangerous people. The reality of violence is embodied in the half-caste Memer, born of the rape of her mother by invading soldiers. She lives in Oracle House, once the seat of learning in the city Ansul, a place renowned for its scholarly community. At the time of the story, the city is occupied by the Ald, monotheists fanatically intent on destroying the Obatth, the enemy of their god. They seek what they call the "Night Mouth," the seat of Obatth. It is described as a place where

> all the foulness of earth gathers together, darkness drawing inward into earth, the reverse of light shining out from the sun. It is an anti-sun that eats light. It is black, wet, cold, vile. As the sun is being, it is unbeing. A void, a great hole in the earth, deep beyond depth.[9]

This description, like that of the Lips of Paor the entry to the oracle in Earthsea, suggests great power, but a dark and female power. The Alds rightly fear it, in the same way they seem to fear and thus closely control women. Having heard rumors that the "Night Mouth" is associated with Oracle House, they imprison the master of the house, the Waylord, and torture him to discover its location. He has sworn an oath of secrecy and is able to resist them, but he is left crippled. Since the Alds believe that reading and writing are evil, they also attempt to destroy the library at Oracle House. Though they set fire to much of the large estate, the main building with its hidden library is made of stone and doesn't burn. The library itself is built on top of the oracle, which in actuality seems to be the Night Mouth the Alds seek, but magical powers of some kind, more than the stone walls, protect it.

Despite being stigmatized for her half-caste appearance, Memer is a member of the household, and only she and the Waylord have access to the library and retain the family gift for speaking with the oracle. But she alone has the ability to ask the right question, as essential here as it is when questioning the Oracle of Delphi or the Foreteller in *The Left Hand of Darkness*. The oracle's power is evident to Memer from the first time she enters the hidden library, which houses the remnants of Ansul's once great collection. She is terrified of the oracle's power, and of what it means that only she can read the oracle's prophecies, which are written in blood. Because of the oracle's association with the female, and the fact that Memer comes fully into this power only when she approaches adulthood, the blood seems linked to her sexual maturity. This maturation is accelerated when Orrec and Gry come to Ansul, seeking the library. Orrec is by this time a renowned storyteller and poet, while Gry's gift with animals is evidenced by her companion, a half-lion. Gry becomes a surrogate mother to the orphaned Memer. Her fearless handling of horses and her delight in wearing men's clothing so she can walk freely in the Alds' world demonstrate for Memer an alternative version of womanhood. Gry teaches her how to be brave, which Memer will need to be so she can confront the oracle. At the same time, Orrec, the first living author Memer has met, opens for her the understanding that literature is vital, created by real people. A pivotal moment in Memer's evolution comes when she stays up all night reading Orrec's *Chaos and Spirit: The Cosmogonies*.

The "voices" in the book are not only the oracle's. Orrec is a legendary storyteller who is also famous for his "Caspro's Hymn," a rallying cry for liberty. His stories stir the people to rebellion against the Alds, resulting in a bloody insurrection but also in the freeing of the city. It is Memer's power with words, though, that ultimately saves them all. She alone can read the prophecy of the oracle, and in the confrontation with Ansul's oppressors, she seems to speak in the voice of the oracle. That she has an extraordinary gift for words is clear from the first line of the story: "The first thing I can remember clearly is writing the way into the secret room."[10] When the Alds ransacked Oracle House, burning all that was not made of stone, Memer and her mother had hidden there, so her association with the place and its books runs deep. The library is her sanctuary, her "kingdom of solitude."[11] She tells us, "Books are at the heart of this book I'm writing. Books caused the danger we were in, the risks we ran, and books gave us our power. The Alds are right to fear them."[12] Memer is like Orrec in seeing her life's work as collecting and protecting the literary heritage of the Western Shore. *Voices* is reminiscent of *The Telling* in its story of protecting the cultural heritage represented by books from those who consider books demonic or non-scientific and who set out to destroy them.

Voices also makes a plea for cultural relativity. Clearly the people of Ansul have developed a way of life and forms of worship that honor the place where they live, that arise from and are adapted to the symbiotic relationship between place and its inhabitants. Memer knows that her way of life is right for her, "Our gods, our books, our ways."[13] It takes no stretch of the imagination to see a parallel in the gutting of Ansul's library and the Taliban's systematic destruction of any art or literature that denies a strict interpretation of the *Koran*, or to American religious groups attempting to ban such writings as the Harry Potter series, or to the manifest destiny approach of the United States government in the first decade of the twenty-first century, bringing American style democracy to the cradle of civilization. In her poem, "Here, There, at the Marsh," Le Guin says, "my head is full of the anguish of battles / and the ruin of ancient cities."[14] Like *The Telling*, *Gifts* nonetheless assures us that cultures can abide, by subversion if necessary, despite totalitarian attempts to end them. At the same time, both books focus on the healing that must happen from within. Sutty and Memer are both crippled to some degree by hatred, and the oracle's declaration that "broken mend broken" applies to Memer as much as to anything else.[15] She must also learn to accept her gift, despite her fear of the oracle and its dark powers. Accepting the Ald half of herself and embracing her gift brings Memer fully into maturity.

Powers is about a slave, Gavir, who can see future events. As the title suggests, the book is about more than the power of Gavir's gift. The story moves along in a series of picaresque events, though young Gavir is a runaway slave and not a rogue. But the people he encounters, primarily men, prove the old adage that absolute power corrupts absolutely. The story begins with Gavir as a boy; he and his sister were abducted and brought up alongside their master's children, and they live as well educated house slaves, so deeply inculcated with the slavery mindset that they willingly live by the household's rules. Despite the relatively humane way in which they are raised, they are at the mercy of the master and his sadistic son. When his sister is raped and killed, Gavir loses faith in the paradigm he has long accepted and runs away. He eventually joins a Robinhood-esque band, The Heart of the Forest, led by the charismatic Barna, a former slave who is far more a dictator than his jovial persona initially would suggest. Barna and his inner circle seem to be living the high life, but their lifestyle depends on the exploitation of others, including the sexual enslavement of women they kidnap. From his experience with the Heart of the Forest, Gavir learns that even ex-slaves are prone to abusing power and betraying trust. His journey continues as he searches for the home in the Marshes from which he was abducted. When he does find it, he learns that his gift of foresight is a family trait, but also that even there he is not at home. Not having been raised in the culture of his birth family, he has no sense of attachment or understanding of it.

He does, however, have the gift of words. He has a talent for memorization and is prized as a storyteller. Though well-educated, Gavir was forbidden from reading "modern" literature, meaning that even in his reading he was not free. Part of his journey is discovering the place where he can be free not just physically, but intellectually as well. Throughout his travels, he carries a copy of Orrec's *Cosmogonies*, the same volume that is Memer's introduction to the writing of a living author, and he sets off for the university town in the free state where Orrec lives. One more adventure awaits him, and here the narrative takes on imagery from *Uncle Tom's Cabin*, of Eliza crossing the frozen river her child in her arms and the slave catchers at her heels. Gavir, who is escorting a young girl he has saved from extreme sexual abuse, is similarly being hunted, by his childhood nemesis, a slave from the family he has escaped. Gavir and his young charge cross the river into freedom, with this pursuer close behind. They are saved by Gavir's gift of foretelling, relying on a vision Gavir has had about how to ford the dangerous waters while the slave who pursues them drowns. They join the household of Gry, Orrec and Memer in the university town of Mesun, where presumably they will all live out their days using their gifts to write and to preserve their literary heritage.

Powers repeatedly plays upon the question of how power is used and abused, suggesting that even those who have experienced slavery firsthand are capable of immoral and brutal mistreatment of others. Like Memer, brought up to feel like a slave, Gavir must learn how to be free, though he continually finds himself at the mercy of individuals who want to control him. His story is quite different than Memer's or Orrec's, however, in that his gift, while frightening and something he keeps to himself, does not have the burden of power attached to it. Like them, his real gift seems to be for words, and he often wins entry into temporary shelters though his talent for storytelling. Ultimately, though, his story is still about choice: how will he negotiate the opportunities he does have to influence others? While living in Barna's household, for instance, unlike the other men, he does not tolerate the sexual enslavement of the young women who are brought there. Choice is also a key element in the story in *Gifts* of how Orrec's parents met. His mother, Melle, had been living a dull, chaste life in a strict family. When his father, Canoc, raids her village, using his gift in a quick display of power meant to intimidate the villagers into surrendering their goods and daughters, she sees not only a handsome man but a choice, a way out, and she volunteers to go with him, thus "saving" the other virgins in her town. She has quickly intuited that this man is not as dangerous as he pretends to be, and she has the presence of mind to claim her right to the choice he represents. Above all, the stories of the Western Shore are about how our choices shape our lives.

A Life Contingent

Moments of choice lie at the heart of *Lavinia*, a novel in which the title character must continually consider *fas* and *nefas*: what needs be done and what ought not be done.[16] Le Guin starts with Vergil's brief description of Aeneas' marriage to Lavinia, than fleshes out the story of the young woman who married Aeneas despite knowing that choosing him over her other suitors would cause a short but costly war. But the story is very little about their brief marriage and mostly about the many years before and after their meeting. It is the distaff tale, the untold woman's side of the story. While it takes a few coy liberties — chiding Vergil for getting the color of Lavinia's hair wrong, for example — it stays true to the events of the poem and even while embroidering all around those. Le Guin clearly prepared for writing the novel not just by translating Vergil and so getting inside the poet's ethos, but by learning what she could about the culture of Lavinia's time. When the spirit of Vergil visits Lavinia, he asks her to tell him of the world of women, of the daily chores that make up their lives: "Tell me how you unlock and clean out the storeroom early in summer, and leave it open for a few days, praying to the Penates that it be refilled with the harvest."[17] In the novel we get much of the daily life of a household in Lavinia's time, as seen through the woman who runs it. In counterbalance to the wars and power struggles that propel much of the action of the novel, this is at heart a quiet story of a woman's lifetime, from girlhood to her fading into immortality.

Of course, Lavinia is kept alive as long as we read Vergil's poem; as she frequently remarks, she is "contingent." There is throughout the novel a curious tension between her awareness of herself as a product of Vergil's imagination, bound to the fate he has written for her, and of her insistence on following her own inner compass. Despite the suggestion that the poet himself is the *deus ex machina* driving the events of Lavinia's life forward, for example by pretending to be an oracle that instructs her father, this is Lavinia's life. And since Vergil did not write her death, she is immortal. She does not fault the poet for her spare presencee in the poem; he'd already told two love stories and was running out of space and time. But she will not to be held back by the lack of her voice speaking in the poem. Her epic stature comes from her refusal to be bullied into an unwanted marriage, her unflinching look at her own involvement in the war, her ability to live in the moment despite knowing her years with her husband will be short, and especially her efforts to shield her son from danger. She is also pious, and like Memer from *Voices*, she oversees the household worship of the gods. As in that novel, Lavinia's piety arises from her attention to and embeddedness in place; when she marries, her allegiance switches to the gods of her husband's household, a logical shift given that her piety adjusts to her new place.

In his "Note" on *Lavinia*, Richard Erlich praises the novel but marks its silence on the dubious history behind the founding of Rome, including the rape of the Sabine women, or on Vergil himself as a "poet of Empire and imperialism."[18] Yet Le Guin portrays Vergil as despondent and near death; he is uncertain about what he has written, hoping that his poem will be read as something other than a glorification of war. When Lavinia reflects that Aeneas slays "like a butcher," Vergil responds that he has to "because that is how empires are founded. Or so I hope Augustus will understand it. But I do not think he will."[19] Le Guin's own responses to questions on the politics of the novel show that she intended the brutality of the battle scenes, even from the distanced vantage point of the sidelines or nursing stations, to indicate her sense of war as profoundly wrong. She told an interviewer that the book conveys her "moral outrage ... *Lavinia* is an antiwar book, as is the *Aeneid*."[20] That she has no easy explantations for how wars come about or why they are so common in our history is evidenced by Lavinia's role in bringing about war. Critics will certainly continue to grapple with the novel's complexities. If Lavinia, and for that matter the equally honorable Aeneas, are following their deeply engrained sense of piety and duty, what does that say about war and our ability to bring about peace? If the best among us can rationalize carnage, are we predestined to war? *Lavinia* presents no easy answers.

Legislating the World

In a 2008 acceptance speech for the Maxine Cushing Gray Award, Le Guin argued vehemently for the importance of literature, especially as a guard against tyranny and government censure. She quoted an early favorite poet, Percy Bysshe Shelley, who wrote, "The imagination is the great instrument of moral good."[21] Indeed Shelley's statement applies easily to Le Guin's writings. Her work has always orbited tightly around her own moral core, reflecting not commercial concerns but her working out of ethical ideas and making meaning of the changing world. While themes like freedom, justice and equality have been constant, others have appeared over time to reflect Le Guin's engagement with the world. Like rings in a redwood tree, these themes bear evidence of her responses to the changing environment over the fifty years of her career. For Le Guin, art "is a social act, and its social function is to affirm community, the human community, and the wider household of being."[22] Shelley also defends the importance of the artist as an agent of social good. Here again, Le Guin easily fits Shelley's sense that the artist plays an activist role. She is, however, very aware that activism can affect artistic quality:

> Art that preaches or teaches overtly is lessened by the sermon and the lecture; art in the service of an ideology is a servant and not a free creature; the artist must assert unconditional freedom of choice and follow thought and passion, not obeying any outer control or conforming to other people's standards.[23]

Le Guin has at times struggled with balancing art and activism, and at times the activism has won out, as in *The Word for World Is Forest* and in some of the writings of her high feminist period. But the balance is widely in favor of Le Guin writing both authentically and artistically, which accounts for her popularity and enduring legacy. It is too early to know how history will remember her, of course, but the fact that there are two new essay collections on *The Dispossessed,* a book published in 1974, is telling.

Early in this study, I suggested that Le Guin could stand as a perfect model for how feminism affected a major artist. In the form of her creative and theoretical writing, she has left considerable evidence of her thinking about feminism before she embraced it, through the period of high feminist practice, and later as she came to embody the ideals of post-feminism. Clearly, her thinking and writing have been much influenced by her engagement with feminist thought. Since September 11, 2001, her focus has narrowed somewhat as she concentrates on the pressing matters of the day, among them bringing about peace and safeguarding intellectual freedom. How much more writing we can expect from her is impossible to judge, though given her parents' long lives and her own productivity, we can hope for more. Whether she returns to the Ekumenical worlds, to Earthsea or Orsinia, or continues to explore the Western Shore, we can expect to find Le Guin's impeccable sense of detail, her deft characterization, and her ear for the perfectly tuned endnote. And we are sure to find her engaged with the things that matter most. If this study does nothing else, I hope it illustrates that Ursula Le Guin writes with her eyes open, taking in and making sense of the world, helping us all find that middle ground of flexible resistance.

Chapter Notes

Introduction

1. From *The Official Website of Ursula K. Le Guin,* http://www.ursulakleguin.com.

2. I will address many of these throughout the book. Donna White's history of Le Guin criticism, *Dancing with Dragons,* is the best general overview; Ransom's review of more recent Le Guin criticism carries on from White.

3. Joe De Bolt, "A Le Guin Biography," in *Ursula K. Le Guin.*

4. I discuss this in detail in Chapter One, but a prominent example is Joanna Russ, in "The Image of Women."

5. Le Guin, "Is Gender Necessary?" 168.

6. Le Guin, letter to the author, March 1991.

7. De Bolt, 25.

8. Interview, O'Connell, 36–37.

9. Le Guin, "The Fisherwoman's Daughter," 234.

10. This concept, explored in depth in Chapter Four, is best explained in the two essays cited just above. Le Guin borrows ideas from Virginia Woolf, Hélène Cixous, and Rachel Blau du Plessis, among others.

11. Interview, Broughton, 32.

12. Woolf, *A Room of One's Own,* 82.

13. Le Guin, *The Eye of the Heron,* 110.

14. Le Guin, "Is Gender Necessary? Redux," 15.

15. In her "Foreword" to *The Birthday of the World,* Le Guin describes the Ekumen as "a non-directive, information-gathering consortium of worlds" (vii) named after the Greek *oikumene.* It is also known as the League of Planets and the Hainish Universe.

16. Le Guin, *Language,* 27.

17. "Sf" is the academic abbreviation for science fiction, and I use it throughout this book.

18. Le Guin, *Language,* 27.

19. *Ibid.,* 27.

20. Interview, *Mother Jones,* 52–53.

21. Interview, "Author Spotlight."

22. See Sinclair on this theme.

23. Le Guin, *Rocannon's World,* 2.

24. Le Guin, *Fisherman,* 191.

25. Article and chapter-length studies on Le Guin's feminism include: Adams; Anderson; Arbur, "Beyond Feminism" and "Le Guin's 'Song'"; Attebery, "Gender"; Barr, "Changing Planes," *Lost in Space,* "Searoad"; Barrow and Barrow, "*The Left Hand*"; Brown, "Feminist Myth," and "*The Left Hand*"; Cassell; Clarke (all); Comoletti and Drout; Cummins, "The Land-lady's Homebirth"; Donawerth; Hemmings; Jacobs; Junko; Khanna; Klarer; LaBar; Lefanu; Lindow, "Becoming Dragon"; Littlefield; Lothian; McLean, "The Power of Women"; Malikki; Murphy, "The High and Low"; Nodelman; Pennington; Petersen; Rhodes; Sobat; and Suvin, "On U. K. Le Guin's second Earthsea."

26. Spender makes a convincing argument for how women's writing "disappears" in *Women of Ideas*.

27. For example, Friedan writes that women can do everything they are already doing plus hold a job. She neglects the possibility that a spouse might take on some of the childrearing and household duties. This attitude has led to the "second shift," that is, women coming home from work to another full-time job. Nonetheless, as Spender points out, one area of great significance for later feminist study was Friedan's validation of women's experience as evidence. Friedan also drew on her own experience, thus breaking the academic stance of objectivity from the subject under study. See Spender, *For the Record*, 8.

28. This attitude was encapsulated in Stokley Carmichael's infamous statement that: "The only position for women in SNCC is prone." Quoted in Sara Evans, 87.

29. Juliet Mitchell's influential article "Women: The Longest Revolution" appeared at this time.

30. Eisenstein, *Contemporary Feminist Thought*, xix–xx.

31. *Ibid.*, xx.

32. See, for example, the work of hooks in *Ain't I a Woman* and *Feminist Theory*, and of Moraga and Anzaldua in *This Bridge Called My Back*.

33. See Daly, *Gyn/Ecology*.

34. Here "sex" is the purely physiological differences between men and women; gender is socially constructed, the learned characteristics that accrue around the fact of physiological sex.

35. The myth of androgyny and its problems as a literary trope are discussed in Chapter Two.

36. Feminist criticism was written before the movement, though it was not identified as such. Woolf's work is an obvious — and outstanding — example. Millett, however, ignited a virtual explosion of literary activity.

37. Showalter, *The New Feminist Criticism*, 5.

38. See, for example, Baym; Gilbert and Gubar, *The Madwoman in the Attic* and *The Norton Anthology of Literature by Women*; Moers; Showalter, *A Literature of Their Own*; Spacks; and Tompkins.

39. This is Nathaniel Hawthorne's description of the popular women writers of the time who were making a good living by writing while he and other "real" writers struggled to be published. Quoted in Person, 24.

40. The "Great Books" is a list compiled by Mortimer Adler of work that meets his criteria of being endlessly rereadable, concerning the "great ideas," and retaining relevance. Adler's list, updated in 1972, includes one female author out of a list of 140. Information derived from the Great Books Foundation website.

41. Todd, in *Feminist Literary History*, rightly reminds us that there is no thematically continuous tradition; instead, what feminist criticism uncovered was far more women's writing than was previously thought to exist.

42. See Woolf's *A Room of One's Own* for her discussion of how women's writing might be different from men's. See also Rachel Blau du Plessis, *Writing Beyond the Ending*.

43. Like any generic labeling, these categories obscure finer shadings. "American feminists" were not only Americans, while French feminism included feminists who were not French. The categories also overlook the Marxist element of Anglo criticism, for example. Yet the American and the French have often been cast as polar adversaries.

44. See, for example, Cixous, "Laugh"; Cixous and Clément, *The Newly Born Woman*; Moi, *The Kristeva Reader*; and Marks and Courtivron.

45. I discuss this below in my analysis of the advent of post-feminism.

46. Gilbert and Gubar, *No Man's Land.* For example, Gilbert and Gubar counter Lacan's theory that women's "castration" has written them out of the symbolic contract. They suggest instead that Lacan, following Freud, has invented women's castration to allay male fears about women's primal relationship to language. Lacanian analysis of Le Guin is undertaken in Selinger and Robinson.

47. Whelehan, 127.

48. Spivak, 524.

49. See Reger, Whelehan, and Brooks as starting points.

50. Rebecca Walker's theoretical disagreements with her mother Alice are only one, very visible, example.

51. Henry, "Solitary Sisterhood," 81.

52. Vavrus writes entertainingly on this subject.

53. Reger's and Tasker and Negra's collections contain interesting essays on this topic.

54. Henry, "Solitary Sisterhood," 82.

55. Interview with Rebecca Walker.

56. Elam, 8.

57. The term is new enough that there still is no firm sense of whether it is hyphenated or not; I use the hyphen to emphasize the differences between feminism and post-feminism.

58. Useful sources on media postfeminism include Tasker and Negra, Faludi, Coppock et al., and Whelehan.

59. Faludi, xviii.

60. This is frequently cited as the first use of the term, for example, in Coppock et al. The concept of an "after feminism," Faludi would argue, first appeared in the 1920s, in reaction to the gains of the first wave.

61. Coppock et al., 3.

62. Tasker and Negra, 8.

63. Hubel, 19.

64. Brooks, 97.

65. Kavka, 29.

66. Brooks, 4.

67. I use the terms marginal and liminal as in van Gennep and in Turner's *Forest of Symbols* and "Variations." The liminoid is both part of society and at the fringes of it; such a person is in a position to comment on the society by virtue of knowing it well yet having some objectivity on it.

68. Le Guin, *Dancing*, 234.

69. Le Guin, "A Woman Writing or The Fisherwoman's Daughter" (New Orleans: Graduate School of Tulane University, 1987), 19. This is not greatly different than the final version, though it does more directly state some of the ideas that are pertinent to my approach in this introduction. I hope that as Le Guin uses an early version of the Woolf essay, she would not object to my use of an earlier (published) version of hers.

Chapter One

1. *Dancing*, vii.

2. Woolf, *Room*, 51.

3. *Dancing*, 234.

4. Le Guin, "The Wave in the Mind," 218.

5. Scholes, in his essay by that name.

6. Some examples are: Jameson, "World Reduction"; Manlove, "Conservatism"; and McGuirk, "Optimism." I discuss critiques of her "male-orientation" at length later in the chapter.

7. Two useful sources of biography are De Bolt and Hersh.

8. Theodora Kroeber, *Alfred Kroeber*, 235.

9. Interview, McCaffery, 235.

10. This household, filled with German refugees, intellectuals, and Native Americans, must have been stimulating to the young Le Guin. In *The Language of the Night* (111), Le Guin says she modeled the physicist Shevek on Robert Oppenheimer.

11. Biographical details on Theodora Kroeber are from Le Guin's essay "The Fisherwoman's Daughter," from *Alfred Kroeber*, and from Brower, "Preface."

12. See her interviews with McCaffery and Rountree as well as "Daughter."

13. In her interview with Rountree, she describes her mother as hating the "women libbers," 61.

14. Brower, 104.

15. Interview, *Mother Jones*, 26; See her article "Indian Uncles."

16. Interview, McCaffery, 154.

17. *Ibid.*, 157.

18. See interview with Rountree, 66–67.

19. *Dancing*, 165–170.

20. *Dancing*, 179–187.

21. On this topic see Le Guin "Prospects," in *Dancing*, 176–178; Russ, *How to Suppress*; and Spender, *Man Made Language*.

22. By, for example, Wyndham Lewis in *Men Without Art*.

23. Le Guin, "A Response to the Le Guin Issue," 4. She goes on, "Among contemporaries, Solzhenitsyn, Boll, Wilson, Drabble, Calvino, Dick." Le Guin no longer lists influences, fearing to leave out too many.

24. Interview, McCaffery, 173–174.

25. Very little has been written about Le Guin's poetry. See Arbour, "Le Guin's Song," and Murphy, "The High and Low" and "The Left Hand."

26. Interview, Broughton, 322. She credits feminism with helping her to discover her poetic voice.

27. *Language*, 107 and 116.

28. "On Sappho's Theme" was published in *The Husk* and does not appear in Le Guin's chapbooks. I am indebted to the Kidd Agency for allowing me to include several of Le Guin's poems.

29. She derived the name Orsinia from her own first name; Ursula comes from the Latin *ursa*, as in the Italian *orsino* or "bearish."

30. Interview, McCaffery, 158.

31. *Ibid.*, 159.

32. Interview, Broughton, 337.

33. *Ibid.*, 337.

34. Le Guin told Elizabeth Cummins that she felt her apprenticeship ended with "A Week in the Country." See *Understanding Ursula K. Le Guin*, 127. In *Approaches*, James Bittner presents a solid case for considering Orsinia the bedrock of Le Guin's opus, her first invented place and her first real body of work.

35. "*An die Musik*" originally appeared in the *Western Humanities Review*, typical of the kind of literary journal that first published her work but that did not meet her need for a wider audience or a sense of being "published."

36. *Language*, 28.

37. *Ibid.*, 28.

38. Some of the most influential of these are: Tolkien, "On Fairy Stories"; Todorov, *The Fantastic*; Rabkin, *The Fantastic in Literature*; Manlove, *Modern Fantasy*; Jackson, *Fantasy*; Kroeber, *Romantic Fantasy*; and Russ, "Subjunctivity."

39. See Chapter 2 of *The Fantastic*.

40. Jackson, 8.

41. Scholes, *Structural Fabulation*.

42. Delany, *The Jewel-Hinged Jaw*.

43. *Language*, 172.

44. Le Guin, "Introduction," *The Book of Fantasy*, 10.

45. *Language*, 58.

46. McCaffery likewise says science fiction has "the capacity to *defamiliarize* our science-fictional lives and thereby force us to temporarily inhabit worlds whose cognitive distortions and poetic figurations of our social relations…make us suddenly see our world in sharper relief," 3–4.

47. In *The Jewel-Hinged Jaw*.

48. *Language*, 62.

49. *Ibid.*, 124.

50. A number of essays in *Language* attest to her working out the differences between these genres.

51. Bittner, *Approaches*, xii.

52. Quoted in Bittner, *Approaches*, 7.

53. *Language*, 135.

54. Tolkien, 113.

55. *Ibid.*, 113.

56. *Ibid.,* 135.

57. *Ibid.,* 144.

58. Manlove, *Modern Fantasy,* 1.

59. Kroeber, *Romantic Fantasy,* 1.

60. Manlove, "Conservatism," 287.

61. *Language,* 26.

62. *Ibid.,* 26.

63. In the Introduction to *Rune,* Le Guin says she was nineteen when she wrote the story; in a phone conversation of 28 March 1991, she identified herself as twenty when she wrote both *Rune* and *Solomon.* Both works were published in limited private editions in the early 1980s; *Solomon* was published in 1983 as an illustrated children's book.

64. *Language,* 50.

65. The two that were published are "The Word of Unbinding" and "The Rules of Names." Both are reprinted in *The Wind's Twelve Quarters.*

66. *Language,* 55.

67. Le Guin discusses Jung at length in "The Child and the Shadow," in *Language.*

68. With its mazes and trapped hero, *Tombs* seems a variation on the story of Ariadne and the Minotaur, with some interesting reversals.

69. *Language,* 55.

70. Interview, *Locus,* 5.

71. *Coyote,* 101.

72. Some useful sources in science fiction theory are: Aldiss, *Trillion Year Spree;* Clareson, *Understanding Contemporary Science Fiction;* Hartwell, *Age of Wonder;* Parrinder, *Science Fiction;* Russ, "'What if'"; Suvin, *Metamorphosis;* Westfahl, *Mechanics of Wonder.*

73. Aldiss, 27.

74. Suvin, in Chapter One, he lays out his theory of cognitive estrangement.

75. Le Guin, "On Norman Spinrad's *The Iron Dream*" 44.

76. Russ, "'What if,'" 197.

77. Zaki, *Phoenix Revisited,* 31.

78. Interview, Broughton, 315–316.

79. See Russ, "The Image of Women in Science Fiction"; Friend, "Virgin Territory"; and Moskowitz, "When Women Rule."

80. Sargent, "Introduction," xv-xvi.

81. Maddern, in "True Stories," argues for Le Guin's very significant contributions to science fiction.

82. The quote is from *Language,* 26. In her Introduction to "April in Paris," in *The Wind's Twelve Quarters,* she wrote that she sent the story to *Astounding* when she was twelve. This may be more accurate. Here she specifies the year (1942) and the editor who rejected it (John Campbell).

83. *Language,* 27.

84. These stories are "April in Paris," "The Darkness Box," "The Dowry of Angyar," "The Masters," "The Rule of Names," "The Word of Unbinding" and "Selection." All but "Selection" are reprinted in *The Wind's Twelve Quarters.*

85. *Language,* 28 and 29.

86. Lewis, *The American Adam;* Rochelle makes a similar connection in *Communities of the Heart.*

87. *Rocannon's World,* 1.

88. See, for example, Parrinder, "The Alien Encounter."

89. "Science Fiction and Mrs. Brown," *Language,* 101–119.

90. On this issue see Jameson.

91. *Language,* 141.

92. In her essay by that title.

93. Interview, McCaffery, 160.

94. Though the Gethenians are usually referred to as androgynes, they are physically hermaphrodites since they possess both male and female sexual organs and can exhibit the behavioral pattern of either sex during the periodic reproductive phase called kemmer.

95. That this novel clearly links sexual difference to major social problems including war, sex crimes, and ecological exploitation is interesting in light of Le Guin's statement, quoted elsewhere, that she does not see sexual injustice as the root cause of all injustice.

96. *Hand,* 248.

97. Before *Hand*, there were few explorations of androgyny. Theodore Sturgeon was the first to write about it at length, in *Venus Plus X*. In Sturgeon's novel, a young man is kidnapped by androgynes. As in *Hand*, the man's culturally conditioned sense of gender becomes clear through his interactions with these genderless people. Sturgeon faced much criticism for this novel, none aimed at the sex of his protagonist. We might question whether Le Guin would have been criticized for using a male protagonist if she had not been female.

98. A number of critics have looked specifically at the gender issue. For unfavorable criticism see Annas; Grimstad and Rennie; Lefanu; Rhodes; Rosinsky; Russ, "Images of Women." For defenses of Le Guin see Hayles; Brown, *"The Left Hand"*; LaBar; and Barrows and Barrows, *"The Left Hand of Darkness."*

99. As feminists like Elaine Morgan argued, though these are the generic pronouns in practice they call to mind a man, not a man and/or a woman. See *The Descent of Women*.

100. "Winter's King" was originally published with male pronouns in *Orbit 5*. Le Guin revised it, using female pronouns throughout, when she included it in *The Wind's Twelve Quarters*.

101. Lem, "Lost Opportunities."

102. Grimstad and Rennie further argue that when femaleness is depicted, it is in a negative way. However, these references to the female tend to be made from the viewpoint of the male protagonist — a human male — who is meant to be depicted as somewhat sexist. Negative comments on women are intended to reflect Genly Ai's views, not the author's.

103. In Rhodes, "Ursula Le Guin's."

104. For discussion of Le Guin's use of the androgyny myth, see Rosinsky, Rhodes, Hayles, and Brown. See also Sargent's introduction to *Women of Wonder* for an account of Stanisław Lem's and

Le Guin's exchange on her use of the idea of androgyny.

105. Heilbrun, x.

106. See the *Women's Studies* special issue for a generalized discussion of the androcentric essentialism inherent in the myth, and Rhodes, Rosinsky, Lamb, and Vieth.

107. In Rhodes, "Ursula Le Guin's."

108. Quoted in *Women's Studies*, 119.

109. I summarize the debate that ensued after the book's publication; more recently, Veronica Hollinger applied a queer studies approach. See her "(Re)reading."

110. *Hand*, 90.

111. See, for example, Delany, Moylan, and LeFanu.

112. Moylan, *Demand*, 102.

113. *Dispossessed*, 42.

114. *Ibid.*, 43.

115. *Ibid.*, 43.

116. Though this may be due to a severe famine.

117. *Dispossessed*, 261.

118. *Ibid.*, 266.

119. Rochelle argues against this reading, seeing instead the small, private personal story being told here, the "small journeys of the mundane," in *Communities*, 60.

120. *Dispossessed*, 150.

121. See *The Jewel-Hinged Jaw*. I find Delany's criticism of Takver, Bedap, and Rulag to be generally very good. But I do not agree that Le Guin insinuates — intentionally or not — that Bedap's homosexuality is causing his unhappiness. Bedap could have been more cleverly fleshed out as a character, but I see no support for the assertion that Le Guin thinks homosexuality is unnatural.

122. Moylan, in *Demand the Impossible*.

123. *Dancing*, 11.

124. Bittner, *Approaches*, 25.

125. Russ, "Images," 91.

126. LeFanu, 146.

127. Barrows and Barrows, 84.

128. *Ibid.*, 85.
129. Quoted in Bittner, *Approaches*, 25.
130. Interview, *Mother Jones*, 26.
131. Marge Piercy, for example, in *Woman on the Edge of Time*, uses "per," while Dorothy Brant, in *The Kin of Ata Are Waiting for You* uses "kin."
132. *Language*, 168. As I discuss elsewhere, Le Guin revised this essay in 1987, quite firmly reversing her stand on the generic pronoun, and on other matters in the original essay. I respect her request that references to the older version of the essay not appear without some inclusion of her reconsiderations. As I am charting her increasing feminist awareness, I only make footnoted reference to her changes of mind here, but treat the matter at greater length later on.
133. Interview, O'Connell, 37.
134. *Dancing*, 15. This quote is given in italics in the original to denote that it is a revision by the author of the earlier text.
135. *Ibid.*, 15.
136. *Ibid.*, 16.

Chapter Two

1. Interview, *Mother Jones*, 52.
2. *Hard Words*, 5. This reading is supported by Danae's age, 46, which is how old Le Guin was in 1975–76 — eighteen months or so after *The Dispossessed* was published (though other sources indicate she was writing the book as early as 1971). George Hersh makes much the same point in his dissertation.
3. Suvin, "Parables."
4. *Ibid.*, 299.
5. *Ibid.*, 300. See Wymer, "Text and Pre-texts," for an alternative reading.
6. *Compass Rose*, 18.
7. *Ibid.*, 21.
8. *Ibid.*, 21.
9. *Compass Rose*, 122. Sorde's last name is the same as Itale's from *Malafrena*, which Le Guin was revising during this time. This of course could be coincidence, but it suggests the possibility of a totalitarian future, Orsinia, not unlikely given that place's history.
10. We see also a number of men with limps in Le Guin's later fiction, for example Stone Listening. This may be a way to mitigate masculinity, as Charlotte Brontë does with Rochester.
11. She has described these before. *Tombs*, for example, is about Tenar's coming of age. What I am tracing is a more concerted attention to the stages of women's lives and the variety of women's characters.
12. *Tombs* is mostly Tenar's book, but her destiny is usually controlled by others. At the end, she is being led away by Ged who seems to know what would be best for her. *Eye* is different in that Luz is in control of her own destiny at the end of the book and shows others a possible way out as well.
13. Le Guin has described it this way on several occasions including in the Broughton interview and in a colloquium at Davis, California, 9 May 1991.
14. Interview, Broughton, 325.
15. In a colloquium at Davis, California, 9 May 1991.
16. Rolery and Luz are, in fact, very much alike. Both are culturally marginal, Rolery because she is born out of season, and Luz because of her independence. Both leave their homes to join forces with their perceived enemies; both are attracted to leaders of those enemies; both are escaping the inevitability of a loveless marriage. The departures of both are precipitated by heroic acts: Rolery saves Agat after he is attacked, and Luz warns the Shanty Towners of an impending attack. As liminoids, both see some truth about the new culture — Rolery that Agat's people have adapted physiologically to the planet, and Luz that the People of the Peace's commitment to

their ideals is imprisoning them rather than freeing them. Bucknall makes the same point.

17. *Eye,* 76–77.

18. These ideas will be repeated closely by the witch Moss in *Tehanu,* published twelve years later. This does not indicate that they are Le Guin's ideas — though what Vera says fits Ged quite well.

19. Quoted in *Dancing,* 162.

20. Erlich writes on this symbol in *Coyote,* though he associates it more with Lev, 197; writing in a co-authored article, "Herons, Ringtrees, and Mud," he associates Luz with mud, 198.

21. *Eye,* 113–114.

22. *Ibid.,* 114.

23. *Language,* 142. In "American SF and the Other," she claims that the larger problem is the fear of the sexual, social, cultural or racial other; see *Language,* 97.

24. Despite her praise of radical feminists, she says that she herself cannot "take her answers from the current ideology of her movement," *Language,* 143.

25. *Language,* 143.

26. *Ibid.,* 143.

27. Bordo and Graham, 71–75.

28. *Eye,* 110.

29. *Language,* 141.

30. In *Hard Words,* 7.

31. *The Beginning Place* was serialized in *Redbook* in 1979.

32. Interview, McCaffery, 159.

33. Support for this view is found in Spivack's reliable *Ursula K. Le Guin,* where she summarizes the hero's (Itale's) storyline and barely mentions the female characters, 114–116.

34. *Malafrena,* 225.

35. *Ibid.,* 149.

36. Interview, *Mother Jones,* 52–53.

37. *Compass Rose,* 184.

38. See Erlich, *Coyote,* on this topic, 204–205.

39. *Ibid.,* 183.

40. This novel has proved difficult for readers and critics alike. Attebery's "*The*

Beginning Place: Le Guin's Metafantasy," is useful, as is Franko's "Acts of Attention," and Jacqueline Wytenbroek's dissertation. See also my article in the *Magill Guide.*

41. *Place,* 145.

42. Bucknall suggests the monster is the embodiment of Hugh's mother, 148.

43. *Language,* 64.

44. "Sur," 255.

45. *Ibid.,* 256.

46. *Ibid.,* 256.

47. *Ibid.,* 257.

48. *Ibid.,* 259.

49. *Ibid.,* 261.

50. *Ibid.,* 267.

51. *Ibid.,* 268.

52. *Ibid.,* 271.

53. *Dancing,* 172.

54. Spender, *For the Record,* 40.

55. *Dancing,* 4.

56. Quoted in *Dancing,* 19.

57. *Dancing,* 20.

58. Ibid.

59. Ibid.

60. *Dancing,* 76.

61. *In the Red Zone,* 19.

62. *Ibid.,* 26.

63. *Ibid.,* 27.

64. Erlich makes a similar analogy in *Coyote's Song.*

Chapter Three

1. Interview, O'Connell, 36–37.

2. "The Fisherwoman's Daughter," 212–237.

3. This is from the head note of an earlier version of the essay, "The Hand that Rocks the Cradle Writes the Book," 1.

4. A concept similar to Alice Walker's "patchwork quilting."

5. Woolf, *Room,* 76.

6. See Alice Walker, du Plessis and Rich's, *Of Woman Born,* on the feminist search for the mother.

7. In a letter dated 19 March 1991,

Le Guin wrote me that she first read *Orlando* then *Room* while in college. In "The Fisherwoman's Daughter," she refers to *Three Guineas* as her "treasure in days of poverty," 234.

8. Cited in *Dancing*, 227. Le Guin quotes from the first draft of this essay, included in Woolf's *The Pargiters* as edited by Mitchell Leaska. My summation of the essay as a whole comes from the final version, included in Woolf's *Collected Essays*.

9. *Dancing*, 222.

10. Le Guin disguised her gender once; at the request of the editors of *Playboy* she signed herself U. K. Le Guin. The story was "Nine Lives." Le Guin later adopted the playful nom de plume "Mom de Plume."

11. *Dancing*, 227.

12. Takver, in *The Dispossessed*, is a biologist and the mother of two children. The main character, however, is Shevek, her partner, who is science's equivalent of the heroic and solitary artist. See Chapter Two for more on Takver.

13. *Dancing*, 233–234.

14. "Write beyond the ending" is du Plessis' phrase; "write the body" is Woolf's; and "white writing" is Cixous'.

15. Carol Gilligan, *In a Different Voice*. Le Guin's comments on Lacan can be found in "The Fisherwoman's Daughter," *Dancing*, 225.

16. Le Guin's poem "For Hélène Cixous" plays with Cixous' pivotal line, "*Je suis là où ça parle.*" In *Wild Oats and Fireweed*, 60.

17. *Dancing*, 168.

18. *Dancing*, vii.

19. See, for example, Simone de Beauvoir, *The Second Sex*.

20. DuPlessis, x.

21. DuPlessis, 33.

22. Woolf, *Room*, 82.

23. DuPlessis, 32–34.

24. *Ibid.*, 34.

25. *Buffalo Gals*, 196.

26. *Ibid.*, 196.

27. *Dancing*, 161.

28. In a phone interview, March 1991.

29. *Home*, npn.

30. *Ibid.*, 489.

31. *Ibid.*, 45.

32. Rochelle relates that Le Guin wrote him that there are no "matriarchs" in *Always Coming Home* (*Communities*, 90). *Always Coming Home* has never received the level of critical attention it warrants. Useful articles include those by Crow, Cummins, Fitting, Franko, Harper, Khanna, Klarer, Jacobs, Jose. See also Erlich's *Coyote's Song* and White, 95–102.

33. *Home*, 15.

34. In a phone interview in March 1991, Le Guin indicated to me that she aligns herself with eco-feminism.

35. In Ortner, "Is Female to Male as Nature is to Culture?"

36. In King, "The Ecology of Feminism."

37. For an overview of ecofeminism, see King, "What is Ecofeminism?"

38. Davies, 6.

39. Chodorow, *The Reproduction of Mothering*, and Dinnerstein, *The Mermaid and the Minotaur*.

40. Griffin, *Woman and Nature*, and Daly, *Gynecology*.

41. Warren, "Feminism and Ecology," 15.

42. See Griscom, "On Healing the Nature/Culture Split in Feminist Thought."

43. *Home*, 179.

44. *Ibid.*, 189.

45. See Kolodny, *The Lay of the Land*, and Merchant, *The Death of Nature*, on the connection between women, exploitation, and the natural world.

46. *Home*, 73.

47. *Ibid.*, 29.

48. Letter to the author, 19 March 1991.

49. "A Non-Euclidean View of California as a Cold Place to Be," in *Dancing*, 90.

50. *Ibid.*, 90.
51. *Ibid.*, 93.
52. Related during a public reading in Berkeley, California, 4 May 1990.
53. Interview in *Locus*, 5.
54. *Tehanu*, 21.
55. *Ibid.*, 21.
56. *Ibid.*, 197.
57. *Searoad*, 1.
58. *Ibid.*, 106.
59. Letter to the author, 19 March 1991.
60. Disch, 125. In his dissertation on Le Guin, George Hersh, a friend and confidant of Le Guin's, attributes Disch's anger to a problem that arose with inclusion of one of his stories in the *Norton Anthology* Le Guin was compiling.
61. Barr, "*Searoad Chronicles of Klatsand* as a Pathway."
62. "Introducing Myself," in *Wave*, 5.
63. This story seems to be based on Le Guin's experience as a guest writer in 1985 at one of Bly's ironically named "Great Mother" conferences. This is backed up by Le Guin's comments in Hagan's *Women Respond to the Men's Movement*.
64. "Limberlost," 52.

Chapter Four

1. Alan Elms made this argument about the cat/scanner relationship in Cordwainer Smith's planoforming stories during a lecture he gave to my Literature of Science Fiction class in Spring 1999.
2. Phone conversation, 18 March 1991.
3. Westfahl, 39.
4. Quoted in "Introduction," in *Fisherman*, 10.
5. *Ibid.*, 9.
6. *Ibid.*, 9.
7. Lyotard is the starting point for consideration of the so-called "master narrative."
8. *Fisherman*, 102.

9. *Ibid.*, 104.
10. *Ibid.*, 112.
11. Deirdre Byrne observes that Hideo's story demonstrates the necessity of situatedness to identity formation, an intriguing idea in light of Le Guin's attention to place. Le Guin's piece on the house she was raised in ("Growing up in a Work of Art") offers some interesting avenues for investigating the effects of that home on her own art.
12. Byrne, "Truth and Story," 244–245.
13. Rochelle, 110.
14. See his book on this topic.
15. Le Guin claims these aren't the same as Yeowe and Werel in *Planet of Exile*, though it is tempting to see them this way; how seriously she makes this claim is hard to tell.
16. *Four Ways*, 11.
17. *Ibid.*, 29.
18. Sklar, 202.
19. *Four Ways*, 83.
20. *Ibid.*, 168.
21. *Ibid.*, 173.
22. In her "Introduction" to *Birthday of the World*, Le Guin notes that she modeled the plantation where Old Music is held on one she visited in the American South, xii.
23. *Birthday*, 192.
24. In Barr, *Future Females*, 59.
25. *Ibid.*, 61.
26. *Four Ways*, 199.
27. *Ibid.*, 120.
28. *Ibid.*, 205–206.
29. *Birthday*, ix–x.
30. Byrne addresses this idea in relation to feminist separatist sf but finds that Le Guin has not taken the story far enough.
31. *Earthsea Revisioned*, 9.
32. *A Wizard of Earthsea*, 5.
33. *Left Hand*, 63.
34. *Always Coming Home*, 488–492.
35. *Tehanu*, 97.
36. *Ibid.*, 97.
37. *Tales from Earthsea*, 64.

38. *Ibid.*, 125.
39. *Ibid.*, 295.
40. *Ibid.*, 81.
41. *Ibid.*, 93.
42. *Ibid.*, 152.
43. *Ibid.*, 159.
44. See *Madwoman.*
45. Interview, O'Connell, 37.
46. *Ibid.*, 37.
47. *Tombs*, 123.
48. *Other Wind*, 170.
49. *Ibid.*, 171.
50. *Tehanu*, 9.
51. *Earthsea Revisioned*, 24.
52. *Ibid.*, 23.
53. *Tehanu*, 223.
54. *Ibid.*, 37.
55. Cixous, "Laugh," 291.
56. *Ibid.*, 292.
57. *Ibid.*, 289.
58. *Other Wind*, 126.
59. *Ibid.*, 225–226.
60. *Ibid.*, 226.
61. *Ibid.*, 227.
62. Hollindale, 186.
63. *Other Wind*, 245.
64. Manlove, "Conservatism," 287.
65. *The Farthest Shore*, 122.
66. Suvin, "Earthsea and its Cognitions," 498.
67. In "What Became of God the Mother?" and *Beyond Belief*, Pagels describes a systematic undermining of women's authority by the leaders of the early Christian church. See also *The River of God* by Gregory Riley, and Bart Ehrman's *Lost Christianities.* Comoletti and Drout argue that Le Guin's depictions of wizards, their power and their celibacy, draw from a medieval model of the Christian priesthood.

Chapter Five

1. Le Guin's most recent work has not yet received much critical attention;
Mike Cadden has written about *Gifts*, the first Western Shore book. Marleen S. Barr's essay on *Changing Planes* appeared in the 2008 Le Guin issue of *Paradoxa.* Richard Erlich published an extended "Note" on *Lavinia* that appeared in *Science Fiction Studies.* But other writing on Le Guin can be applied here, for example Getz's essay on a peace studies approach to Le Guin or Suvin's article on the real world application of what Le Guin writes in the fantasy realms of Earthsea.

2. In *A Wave in the Mind*, 214.
3. *Ibid.*, 216.
4. *Ibid.*, 216.
5. Le Guin did attend protests, for example against the Patriot Act; she also says in the poem "In the Third Year of the War" (in *Incredible Good Fortune*) that she posted the number of the dead in a window of her home where passersby would see it.
6. Barr, "*Changing Planes.*"
7. *Ibid.*, 276.
8. Cadden, "Taking Different Roads."
9. *Voices*, 81.
10. *Ibid.*, 1.
11. *Ibid.*, 3.
12. *Ibid.*, 32.
13. *Ibid.*, 29.
14. In *Incredible Good Fortune*, 72.
15. *Voices*, 177.
16. Lavinia defines *fas* as "the right, what one must do" (62) while *nefas* means to act "against the order of things" (61–62).
17. *Lavinia*, 60.
18. Erlich, "Note," 349.
19. Both quotes are from *Lavinia*, 89.
20. LaFreniere, Interview, np.
21. Quoted from Le Guin's website.
22. Interview, Milo, np.
23. *Ibid.*

Bibliography

Works by Ursula K. Le Guin

Listed by year of first publication

1959

"Folksong from the Montayna Province." *The Prairie Poet* (Fall): 75.

1960

"An Expert in Youngness." *The Husk* 39 (May): 127.
"On Sappho's Theme." *The Husk* 39 (March): 87.

1961

"*An die Musik.*" *Western Humanities Review* 15 (Summer): 247–58. Reprinted in *Orsinian Tales*, 1976.

1962

"April in Paris." *Fantastic* 11 (September): 54–65. Reprinted in *The Wind's Twelve Quarters*, 1975.

1963

"Darkness Box." *Fantastic* 12 (November): 60–67. Reprinted in *The Wind's Twelve Quarters*, 1975.
"The Masters." *Fantastic* 12 (February): 85–99. Reprinted in *The Wind's Twelve Quarters*, 1975.

1964

"The Dowry of the Angyar." *Amazing* 38 (September): 46–64. Reprinted in *The Wind's Twelve Quarters* as "Semley's Necklace," 1975.
"The Rule of Names." *Fantastic* 13 (April): 79–88. Reprinted in *The Wind's Twelve Quarters*, 1975.
"The Word of Unbinding." *Fantastic* 13 (January): 67–73. Reprinted in *The Wind's Twelve Quarters*, 1975.

1966

Planet of Exile. New York: Ace.
Rocannon's World. New York: Ace.

1967

City of Illusions. New York: Ace.

1968

A Wizard of Earthsea. Berkley: Parnassus. Quotations from New York: Bantam, 1975.

1969

The Left Hand of Darkness. New York: Ace.
"Nine Lives." *Playboy*, 16 November. Reprinted in *The Wind's Twelve Quarters.*
"Winter's King." *Orbit 5*. Ed. Damon Knight, 67–88. New York: Putnam. Reprinted in *The Wind's Twelve Quarters*, 1975.

1971

The Lathe of Heaven. New York: Scribner's. Quotations from New York: Avon, 1973.
The Tombs of Atuan. New York: Atheneum. Quotations from New York: Bantam, 1975.

1972

"The Crab Nebula, the Paramecium, & Tolstoy." *Riverside Quarterly* 5 (February): 89–96.
The Farthest Shore. New York: Atheneum. Quotations from New York: Bantam, 1975.
"The Word for World Is Forest." *Again, Dangerous Visions*. Ed. Harlan Ellison, 30–108. Garden City, NY: Doubleday. Reprinted as *The Word for World Is Forest*. New York: Berkley-Putnam, 1976.

1973

"A Citizen of Mondath." *Foundation* 4. Reprinted in *Language of the Night*, 1979.
"Dreams Must Explain Themselves." *Algol* 21. Reprinted in *Language of the Night*, 1979.
"On Norman Spinrad's *The Iron Dream*." *Science-Fiction Studies* 1 (Spring): 41–44.
"The Ones Who Walk Away from Omelas." *New Dimensions III*. Ed. Robert Silverberg, 1–7. New York: Signet, 1973. Reprinted in *The Wind's Twelve Quarters*, 1975.
"Surveying the Battlefield." *Science-Fiction Studies* 1 (Fall): 88–90.

1974

"The Day Before the Revolution." *Galaxy* 35 (August): 17–30. Reprinted in *The Wind's Twelve Quarters*, 1975.
The Dispossessed: An Ambiguous Utopia. New York: Harper & Row. Quotations from New York: Avon, 1974.

1975

"The New Atlantis." *The New Atlantis and Other Novellas of Science Fiction.* Ed.
  Robert Silverberg, 57–88. New York: Hawthorn. Reprinted in *The Compass
  Rose*, 1982.
"A Week in the Country." *Little Magazine* 9 (Winter): 28–46. Reprinted in *Orsin-
  ian Tales*, 1976.
Wild Angels. Santa Barbara, CA: Capra.
The Wind's Twelve Quarters. New York: Harper & Row.

1976

"Conversations at Night." *Orsinian Tales.*
"The Diary of the Rose." *Future Power: A Science Fiction Anthology.* Ed. Jack Dann
  and Gardner R. Dozois, 3–31. New York: Random House. Reprinted in *The
  Compass Rose*, 1982.
"The Eye Altering." *The Altered I: An Encounter with Science Fiction by Ursula K.
  Le Guin and Others.* Ed. Lee Harding, 108–117. Carlton, Australia: Norstrilia.
  Reprinted in *The Compass Rose*, 1982.
"Ile Forest." *Orsinian Tales*, 19–35.
"The Lady of Moge." *Orsinian Tales*, 183–197.
Orsinian Tales. New York: Harper & Row.
"A Response to the Le Guin Issue." *Science-Fiction Studies* 3 (March): 43–46.
"Science Fiction and Mrs. Brown." *Science Fiction at Large.* Reprinted in *Language
  of the Night*, 1979.
"The Space Crone." *The Co-Evolution Quarterly* 10 (Summer): 108–111. Reprinted
  in *Dancing at the Edge of the World*, 1989.
Very Far Away from Anywhere Else. New York: Atheneum.
The Water Is Wide. Portland, OR: Pendragon. Reprinted in *The Compass Rose*, 1982.

1977

"Introduction." *Rocannon's World.* Reprinted in *The Language of the Night*, 1979.
"Gwilan's Harp." *Redbook* 149 (May). Reprinted in *The Compass Rose*, 1982.

1978

"The Eye of the Heron." *Millenial Women.* Ed. Virginia Kidd, 123–203. New York:
  Delacorte. Republished as *The Eye of the Heron.* New York: Bantam, 1984.

1979

The Beginning Place. Redbook (December). Republished by New York: Harper &
  Row, 1980. Quotations from New York: Bantam, 1981.
The Language of the Night. Ed. Susan Wood. New York: Putnam. Quotations from
  New York: Berkley, 1982.
Leese Webster. New York: Atheneum.
Malafrena. New York: Putnam. Quotations from New York: Berkley, 1980.
"Malheur Country." *Kenyon Review* 1 (Winter): 22–30. Reprinted in *The Compass
  Rose*, 1982.

"The Pathways of Desire." *New Dimensions 9*. Ed. Robert Silverberg, 2–32. New York: Harper & Row, 1979. Reprinted in *The Compass Rose*, 1982.

"Two Delays on the Northern Line." *The New Yorker*, 12 November, 50–57. Reprinted in *The Compass Rose*, 1982.

Tillai and Tylissos. With Theodora K. Quinn. St. Helena, CA: Red Bull, 1979.

1980

"It Was a Dark and Stormy Night; or, Why Are We Huddling about the Campfire?" *Critical Inquiry* 7 (Autumn): 191–199. Reprinted in *Dancing at the Edge of the World*, 1989.

"The White Donkey." *TriQuarterly* 49 (Fall): 259–61. Reprinted in *The Compass Rose*, 1982.

1981

Hard Words and Other Poems. New York: Harper & Row.

"On Writing Science Fiction." *The Writer*, February.

1982

"The Phoenix." *The Compass Rose*, 126–132.

"Sur," *The New Yorker*, 1 February, 38+. Reprinted in *The Compass Rose*, 1982.

The Adventures of Cobbler's Rune. New Castle, VA: Cheap Street.

The Compass Rose. New York: Harper & Row. Quotations from New York: Bantam, 1983.

1983

"A Non-Euclidean View of California as a Cold Place to Be," *The Yale Review* (Winter). Reprinted in *Dancing at the Edge of the World*, 1989.

In the Red Zone. Northridge, CA: Lord John.

Solomon Leviathan's Nine Hundred and Thirty-First Trip Around the World. New York: Philomel.

1985

Always Coming Home. New York: Harper & Row.

King Dog: A Screenplay. Santa Barbara, CA: Capra.

"She Unnames Them," *The New Yorker*, 21 Jan. Reprinted in *Buffalo Gals*, 1987.

1987

Buffalo Gals and Other Animal Presences. Santa Barbara, Capra, 1987.

A Woman Writing or The Fisherwoman's Daughter. New Orleans: Graduate School of Tulane University. Revised and republished as "The Fisherwoman's Daughter" in *Dancing at the Edge of the World*, 1989.

1988

"The Carrier Bag Theory of Fiction." *Women of Vision*. Ed. Denise du Pont, 1–12. New York: St. Martin's. Reprinted in *Dancing at the Edge of the World*, 1989.

Catwings. New York: Orchard–Franklin Watts.
"Introduction." *The Book of Fantasy.* Ed. Jose Luis Borges, Silvina Ocampo, A. Bioy Casares. 1940. New York: Carroll & Graf. 9–12.
"Legends for a New Land." *Mythlore* 56: 4–10.
A Visit from Dr. Katz. New York: Atheneum.
Wild Oats and Fireweed. New York: Perennial-Harper & Row.

1989

Catwings Return. New York: Orchard-Franklin Watts.
Dancing at the Edge of the World: Thoughts on Words, Women, Places. New York: Grove Press.
Fire and Stone. New York: Atheneum.
"The Hand that Rocks the Cradle Writes the Book." *New York Times Review of Books.* 22 January: 1+.
"Limberlost." *Michigan Quarterly Review* 28 (Winter): 63–70. Reprinted in *Unlocking the Air and Other Stories.*

1990

"The Shobies Story." *Universe 1.* Ed. Robert Silverberg and Karen Haber, 36–64. New York: Foundation-Doubleday. Reprinted in *A Fisherman of the Inland Sea,* 1994.
Tehanu: The Last Book of Earthsea. New York: Atheneum.
"Unlocking the Air." *Playboy,* December. Reprinted in *Unlocking the Air and Other Stories,* 1996.

1991

"First Contact with the Gorgonids." *Omni.* Reprinted in *A Fisherman of the Inland Sea,* 1994.
"Newton's Sleep." *Full Spectrum 3.* Reprinted in *A Fisherman of the Inland Sea,* 1994.
"Recreating Reality: Making It Happen for Your Reader." *The Writer.* 104.
Searoad: Chronicles of Klatsand. New York: HarperCollins.

1992

"Introducing Myself." *Left Bank.* Reprinted in *The Wave in the Mind,* 2004.

1993

"Dancing to Ganam." *Amazing.* Reprinted in *A Fisherman of the Inland Sea,* 1994.
Earthsea Revisioned. Cambridge, MA: Labute.
The Norton Book of Science Fiction: North American Science Fiction, 1960–1990. Ed. Ursula K. Le Guin and Brian Attebery. New York: Norton.

1994

"Another Story or A Fisherman of the Inland Sea." *Tomorrow.* Reprinted in *A Fisherman of the Inland Sea,* 1994.

A Fisherman of the Inland Sea. New York: HarperPrism.
Going Out with Peacocks and Other Poems. New York: HarperCollins.

1995
Four Ways to Forgiveness. New York: HarperPrism.

1996
Unlocking the Air and Other Stories. New York: HarperPerennial, 1997.

1998
Steering the Craft. Eighth Mountain.

1999
Sixty Odd. Boston: Shambhala.

2000
The Telling. New York: Harcourt.

2001
The Other Wind. New York: Harcourt.
Tales from Earthsea. New York: Harcourt.

2002
The Birthday of the World. New York: HarperCollins.

2003
Changing Planes. New York: Harcourt. Quotations from New York: Ace, 2004.

2004
"Cheek by Jowl: Animals in Children's Literature." 2004 Mary Hill Arbuthnot Lecture. *Children and Libraries* (Summer/Fall): 20–30.
Gifts. New York: Harcourt.
The Wave in the Mind: Talks and Essays on the Writer, the Reader, and the Imagination. Boston: Shambhala.

2006
"Imaginary Friends." *Newstatesman*, 18 December. http:www.newstatesman.com/print/200612380040.
Incredible Good Fortune. Boston: Shambhala.
Voices. New York: Harcourt.

2007

"Finding my Elegy." *Northwest Review* 45, no. 7.
Powers. New York: Harcourt.

2008

Lavinia. New York: Harcourt.
"Living in a Work of Art," *Paradoxa* 21 123–136.
"The Real Uses of Enchantment." Guardian.co.uk. March. http:www.guardian.co.
ud/books/2008/mar/29/fiction.salmanrushdie/pring.
"The Skin." Book View Café Blog, 15 November. Blog.bookviewcare.com/2008/
11/15/the-skin/.

Interviews

"Author Spotlight: Ursula K. Le Guin." Question and Answer. 18 March 2000. http://
www.mcdougalllittnell.com/guest/le_guin/ukans.htm.
Broughton, Irv. *The Writer's Mind: Interviews with American Authors.* By Irv Broughton,
309–338. Fayetteville: University of Arkansas Press, 1990.
"Hainish Tales: An Interview with Ursula K. Le Guin." *Amazon.com.* 13 October 2000.
amazon.com/exec/obidos/tg/feature/-/67941/104–5177770–9259117.
Lafreniere, Steve. "Ursula K. Le Guin." *Vice Magazine.* 20 April 2009. http://www.vice
land.com/int/v15n12/htdocs/ursula-k-le-guin-440.php.
McCaffery, Larry. "An Interview with Ursula K. Le Guin." *Across the Wounded Galax-
ies: Interviews with Contemporary American Science Fiction Writers.* Ed. Larry
McCaffery, 151–175. Urbana: University of Illinois Press, 1990.
Milo, Erika. "Life in the Wider Household of Being: An Interview with Ursula K. Le
Guin. *Northwest.org.* 21 November 2003. http:westbynorthwest.org/artman/pub
lish/printer_634.shtml.
O'Connell, Nicholas. "Ursula K. Le Guin." *At the Field's End: Conversations with Twenty
Northwest Writers.* Ed. Nicholas O'Connell, 19–38. Seattle: Madrona, 1987.
Rountree, Cathleen. "The Space Crone." *On Women Turning 60: Embracing the Age
of Fulfillment.* Ed. Cathleen Rountree, 56–69. New York: Harmony, 1997.
"Sci-Fi's 'Queen of Fantasy:' What Do You Do When Your Fiction Becomes Reality?"
Art Beat (August-September 1982): 36–37.
"Sing Muse, of the Woman Unsung." *The Inkwell Review.* 12 June 2008. inkwellreview.
blogspot.com/2008/06/sing-muse-of-woman-unsung-html.
"Ursula K. Le Guin: The Last Book of Earthsea." *Locus* (January 1990): 5.
"Ursula K. Le Guin: In a World of Her Own." *Mother Jones* 9 (January 1984): 23+.
Walsh, William. "I am a Woman Writer; I am a Western Writer: An Interview with
Ursula Le Guin." *Kenyon Review* 17, no.3/4 (1995): 192–205.

Secondary Sources

Abrash, Merritt. "Le Guin's 'The Field of Vision': A Minority View on Ultimate Truth."
Extrapolation 26, no. 1 (Spring 1985): 5–15.

Adams, Rebecca. "Narrative Voice and Unimaginability of the Utopian 'Feminine' in Le Guin's *The Left Hand of Darkness* and 'The Ones Who Walk Away from Omelas.'" *Utopian Studies* 2.1 and 2 (1991) 35–48.

Adkins, Lisa. "Passing on Feminism: From Consciousness to Reflexivity?" *European Journal of Women's Studies* 11, no. 4 (2004): 427–444.

Aldiss, Brian, and David Wingrove. *Billion Year Spree: The History of Science Fiction.* 1973 (as *Million Year Spree*). London: Gollancz, 1986.

Algeo, John. "Magic Names: Onomastics in the Fantasies of Ursula Le Guin." *Names* 30 (1982): 59–67.

Anderson, Kristine J. "Places Where a Woman Could Talk: Ursula K. Le Guin and the Feminist Linguistic Utopia." *Women and Language* 151 (1992): 7–10.

Annas, Pamela J. "New Worlds, New Words: Androgyny in Feminist Science Fiction." *Science Fiction Studies* 5 (July 1978): 148–156.

Arbur, Rosemarie. "Beyond Feminism, the Self Intact: Woman's Place in the Work of Ursula K. Le Guin," in *Selected Proceedings of the Science Fiction Research Association 1978 National Conference*, ed. Thomas J. Remington, 146–63. Cedar Falls, IA: University Northern Iowa Press, 1979.

_____. "Le Guin's 'Song' of Inmost Feminism." *Extrapolation* 21 (1980): 223–226.

Armitt, Lucie, ed. *Where No Man Has Gone Before: Women and Science Fiction.* London: Routledge, 1991.

Attebery, Brian. "*The Beginning Place*: Le Guin's Metafantasy." *Children's Literature* 10 (1982): 113–23.

_____. "Gender, Fantasy, and the Authority of Tradition." *Journal of the Fantastic in the Arts* 7, no. 1 (1996): 51–60.

_____. "On a Far Shore: the Myth of Earthsea." *Extrapolation* 21, no. 3 (1980): 269–77.

_____. "Science Fiction, Parables, and Parabolas." *Foundation* 95 (2005): 7–22.

Baggesen, Soren. "Utopian and Dystopian Pessimism: Le Guin's *The Word for World is Forest* and Tiptree's 'We Who Stole the Dream.'" *Science Fiction Studies* 14, no. 1 (1987): 34–43.

Bailey, Edgar C., Jr. "Shadows in Earthsea: Le Guin's Use of a Jungian Archetype." *Extrapolation* 21 (1980): 254–61.

Bain, Dena C. "*The Tao Te Ching* as Background to the Novels of Ursula K. Le Guin." *Extrapolation* 21, no. 3 (Fall 1980): 209–22.

Barbour, Douglas. "Wholeness and Balance: An Addendum." *Science Fiction Studies* 2 (1975): 248–9.

_____. "Wholeness and Balance in the Novels of Ursula K. Le Guin." *Science Fiction Studies* 1, no. 3 (Spring 1974): 164–73.

Barr, Marleen S. "Changing Planes: The First Post 9/11 Feminist SF Text Embraces When It Changed." *Paradoxa* 21 (2008): 271–292.

_____. *Lost in Space: Probing Feminist Science Fiction and Beyond.* Chapel Hill: University of North Carolina Press, 1993.

_____. "*Searoad Chronicles of Klatsand* as a Pathway Toward New Directions in Feminist Science Fiction; or, Who's Afraid of Connecting Ursula Le Guin to Virginia Woolf?" *Foundation* 60 (1994): 58–67.

_____, ed. *Future Females, The Next Generation: New Voices and Velocities in Feminist Science Fiction Criticism.* Lanham, MD: Rowman & Littlefield, 2000.

Barrow, Craig and Diana Barrow. "Le Guin's Earthsea: Voyages in Consciousness." *Extrapolation* 32, no 1 (1991): 20–44.

_____. "*The Left Hand of Darkness*: Feminism for Men." *Mosaic* 20, no. 1 (1987): 83–96.

Bassnett, Susan: "Remaking the Old World: Ursula Le Guin and the American Tradition." In Armitt, *Where No Man Has Gone Before*, 50–66.

Baym, Nina. *Women's Fiction: A Guide to Novels by and about Women in America, 1820–1870*. Ithaca, NY: Cornell University Press, 1978.

Beauvoir, Simone de. *The Second Sex*. Trans. H. M. Parshley. 1949. New York: Alfred A. Knopf, 1953.

Bernardo, Susan M., and Graham J. Murphy. *Ursula K. Le Guin: A Critical Companion*. Westport, CT: Greenwood, 2006.

Bickman, Martin. "Le Guin's *The Left Hand of Darkness*: Form and Content." *Science Fiction Studies* 4 (1977): 42–47.

Bierman, Judah. "Ambiguity in Utopia: *The Dispossessed*." *Science Fiction Studies* 2 (1975): 249–55.

Bittner, James W. *Approaches to the Fiction of Ursula K. Le Guin*. Ann Arbor: UMI Research Press, 1984.

_____. "Persuading Us to Rejoice and Teaching Us How to Praise: Le Guin's *Orsinian Tales*." *Science Fiction Studies* 5 (1978): 215–42.

Bloom, Harold. "Clinamen: Towards a Theory of Fantasy." *Bridges to Fantasy*. Ed. George E. Slusser, Eric S. Rabkin, and Robert Scholes. Carbondale: Southern Illinois University Press, 1982.

_____. *Ursula K. Le Guin's "The Left Hand of Darkness."* New York: Chelsea House, 1987.

_____, Ed. *Ursula K. Le Guin*. New York: Chelsea House, 1986.

Braidotti, Rosi. "A Critical Cartography of Feminist Post-postmodernism." *Australian Feminist Studies* 20, no. 47 (July 2005): 169–180.

Brandt, Bruce E. "Two Additional Antecedents for Ursula Le Guin's 'The Ones Who Walk Away from Omelas.'" *ANQ* (16:3) (2003): 51–56.

Brigg, Peter. "A 'Literary Anthropology' of the Hainish, Derived from the Tracings of the Species Guin." *Extrapolation* 38, no. 1 (1997): 15–24.

Brooks, Ann. *Postfeminisms: Feminism, Cultural Theory, and Cultural Forms*. London: Routledge, 1997.

Brown, Barbara. "Feminist Myth in Le Guin's 'Sur.'" *Mythlore* 16, no. 4 (1990): 56–59.

_____. "*The Left Hand of Darkness*: Androgyny, Future, Present, and Past." *Extrapolation* 21 (1980): 227–35. Reprinted. in Bloom, *Ursula K. Le Guin's "The Left Hand of Darkness,"* 91–99.

Brown, Wendy. "The Impossibility of Women's Studies." *differences: A Journal of Feminist Cultural Studies* 9, no.3 (1997): 79–101.

Bryant, Dorothy. *The Kin of Ata Are Waiting for You*. 1971. San Francisco: Moon, 1976.

Bucknall, Barbara J. "Androgynes in Outer Space." *Critical Encounters: Writers and Themes in Science Fiction*. Ed. Dick Riley, 56–69. New York: Ungar, 1978.

_____. "Rilke and Le Guin." *Mythlore* 16, no. 2 (1989): 62–65.

_____. *Ursula K. Le Guin*. New York: Ungar, 1981.

Burns, Tony. *Political Theory, Science Fiction, and Utopian Literature: Ursula K. Le Guin and "The Dispossessed."* Lanham, MD: Lexington, 2008.

Butler, Judith. *Gender Trouble: Feminism and the Subversion of Identity*. New York: Routledge, 1990.

Byrne, Deidre. "Truth and Story in Ursula K. Le Guin's Short Fiction and the South African Truth and Reconciliation Commission." In *Future Females*, 237–246.

Cadden, Mike. "Purposeful Movement Among People and Places: The Sense of Home in Ursula K. Le Guin's Fiction for Children and Adults." *Extrapolation* 41, no. 2 (2000): 338–50.

_____. "Speaking Across the Spaces Between Us: Ursula Le Guin's Dialogic Use of Character in Children's and Adult Literature." *Paradoxa* 2 (1996): 516–30.

_____. "Speaking to Both Children and Genre: Le Guin's Ethics of Audience." *The Lion and the Unicorn* 24, no. 1 (2000): 128–42.

_____. "Taking Different Roads to the City: The Development of Ursula K. Le Guin's Young Adult Novels." *Extrapolation* 47, no. 3 (2006): 427–44.

_____. *Ursula K. Le Guin Beyond Genre: Fiction for Children and Adults.* New York: Routledge, 2005.

Cassell, Ann L. "Civil Liberties and Science Fiction: The Civil Rights and Feminist Movements Reflected in Selected Writings of Ursula K. Le Guin." *Discovery: The Journal of the Humanities and Social Sciences of University College, Rutgers* (1975): 1–7.

Castillejo, Irene Claremont de. *Knowing Woman: A Feminine Psychology.* New York: Colophon-Harper & Row, 1974.

Chodorow, Nancy. *The Reproduction of Mothering: Psychoanalysis and the Sociology of Gender.* Berkeley: University of California Press, 1978.

Cixous, Hélène. "The Laugh of the Medusa." Trans. Keith Cohen and Paula Cohen. 1976. In *The Signs Reader: Women, Gender and Scholarship.* Ed. Elizabeth Abel and Emily K. Abel, 279–297. Chicago: University of Chicago Press, 1983.

_____, and Catherine Clément. *The Newly Born Woman.* Trans. Betsy Wing. 1975. Minneapolis: University of Minnesota Press, 1986.

Clareson, Thomas D. *Understanding Contemporary American Science Fiction: The Formative Period (1926–1970).* Columbia: University of South Carolina Press, 1990.

Clarke, Amy M. "Female Values in Ursula K. Le Guin's *Always Coming Home.*" Paper presented at the Philological Association of the Pacific Coast Conference, 1990.

_____. "Holidays on Ice: Arctic Narratives and the Utopian Moment." Paper presented at the Science Fiction Research Association Conference, New Lanark, Scotland, 2002.

_____. "Honor Thy Mother: Ecofeminist Perspectives in the Work of Ursula K. Le Guin." Paper presented at the Yosemite/Natural Areas Conference, Concord, CA, 1990.

_____. "Inhabitory Ethics: Old Ways, Women's Ways, and Yin Utopias in *Always Coming Home.*" Paper presented at the Western American Literature Association Conference, Reno, NV, 1992.

_____. "Is Ursula K. Le Guin a 'California' Author?" Paper presented at the Western Literature Association Conference, Sacramento, CA, 1999.

_____. "Real Mages Do It with Their Staffs: Revising the Erotic Life of Earthsea." Paper presented at Mythcon 38, Berkeley, CA, 2007.

_____. "The Return of the Native: Ishi and Ursula K. Le Guin." Paper presented at the International Conference on the Fantastic in the Arts, Fort Lauderdale, FL, 2000.

_____. "Tales from the Distaff: The Parallax View of Earthsea." *Paradoxa* 21 (2008): 63–74.

_____. "When It Changed: Feminism and Mrs. Le Guin." Paper presented at the International Conference on the Fantastic in the Arts, Fort Lauderdale, FL, 1999.

_____. *A Woman Writing: Feminist Awareness in the Work of Ursula K. Le Guin.* Ph.D. diss., University of California, Davis, 1992.

Cogell, Elizabeth Cummins. "Setting as Analogue to Characterization in Ursula Le Guin." *Extrapolation* 18 (1977): 131–41.

_____. *Ursula K. Le Guin: A Primary and Secondary Bibliography.* Boston: G. K. Hall, 1983.

Collins, James F. "The High Points So Far: An Annotated Bibliography of Ursula K.

Le Guin's *The Left Hand of Darkness* and *The Dispossessed.*" *Bulletin of Bibliography* 58, no. 2 (2001): 89–100.

Comoletti, Laura B., and Michael D. Drout. "How They Do Things with Words: Language, Power, Gender, and the Priestly Wizards of Ursula K. Le Guin's Earthsea Books." *Children's Literature* 29 (2001): 113–141.

Coppock, Vicki, Deena Haydon, and Ingrid Richter. *The Illusions of "Post-Feminism:" New Women, Old Myths.* London: Taylor & Francis, 1995.

Covington, Coline. "In Search of the Heroine." *Journal of Analytical Psychology* 34 (1989): 243–254.

Crow, Charles L. "Homecoming in the California Visionary Romance." *Western American Literature* 24, no. 1 (1989): 1–19.

Crow, John H., and Richard D. Erlich. "Words of Binding: Patterns of Integration in Earthsea." *Ursula K. Le Guin.* Ed. Joseph D. Olander and Martin Harry Greenberg. New York: Taplinger, 1979.

Cummins, Elizabeth. "The Land-lady's Homebirth: Revisiting Ursula K. Le Guin's Worlds." *Science Fiction Studies* 17, no. 2 (1990): 153–66.

_____. "'Praise then Creation Unfinished'": Response to Kenneth M. Roemer." *Utopian Studies* 2, no. 1 and 2 (1991): 19–23.

_____. "Taoist Configurations: '*The Dispossessed.*'" In De Bolt, *Ursula K. Le Guin, Voyager to Inner Lands and to Space,* 153–174.

_____. *Understanding Ursula K. Le Guin.* Columbia: University Press of South Carolina, 1990.

Daly, Mary. *Beyond God the Father: Toward a Philosophy of Women's Liberation.* Boston: Beacon, 1973.

_____. *Gyn/ecology: The Metaethics of Radical Feminism.* Boston: Beacon, 1978.

Davies, Katherine. "Historical Associations: Women and the Natural World." *Women and Environments* 9, no. 2 (1987): 4–6.

Davis, Laurence. "The Dynamic and Revolutionary Utopia of Ursula K. Le Guin." In Davis and Stillman, *The New Utopian Politics of Ursula K. Le Guin's "The Dispossessed,"* 3–36.

_____, and Peter Stillman, Eds. *The New Utopian Politics of Ursula K. Le Guin's "The Dispossessed."* Lanham, MD: Lexington, 2005.

De Bolt, Joe. "A Le Guin Biography." In De Bolt, *Ursula K. Le Guin, Voyager to Inner Lands and to Outer Space,* 13–28.

_____, Ed. *Ursula K. Le Guin: Voyager to Inner Lands and to Outer Space.* Port Washington, NY, and London: Kennikat. 1979.

Delany, Samuel R. *The Jewel-Hinged Jaw: Notes on the Language of Science Fiction.* Elizabethtown, NY: Dragon, 1977.

Dietz, Frank. "'Home is a Place Where You Have Never Been': The Exile Motif in the Hainish Novels of Ursula K. Le Guin." In *The Literature of Emigration and Exile.* Ed. James Whitlark, 105–13. Lubbock: Texas Tech University Press, 1992.

Dinnerstein, Dorothy. *The Mermaid and the Minotaur: Sexual Arrangements and Human Malaise.* New York: Perennial-Harper & Row, 1976.

Disch, Thomas M. *The Dreams Our Stuff Is Made Of: How Science Fiction Conquered the World.* New York: Free, 1998.

Donawerth, Jane. "The Feminist Dystopia of the 1990s: Record of Failure, Midwife of Hope." In Barr, *Future Females,* 49–66.

_____, and Carol A. Kolmerten, Eds. *Utopian and Science Fiction by Women: Worlds of Difference*. Syracuse, NY: Syracuse University Press; and Liverpool, UK: Liverpool University Press, 1994.

Dooley, Patricia: "Magic and Art in Ursula Le Guin's Earthsea Trilogy." *Children's Literature* 8 (1980): 103–10.

Dunn, Margaret M. "The Dragon is Not Dead: Le Guin's Earthsea Trilogy." In *Forms of the Fantastic*. Ed. Jan Hokenson and Howard Pearce, 175–180. Westport, CT: Greenwood, 1986.

DuPlessis, Rachel Blau. *Writing Beyond the Ending: Narrative Strategies of Twentieth-Century Women Writers*. Bloomington: Indiana University Press, 1985.

Ehrman, Bart. *Lost Christianities: The Battles for Scripture and the Faiths We Never Knew*. Oxford: Oxford University Press, 2003.

Eisenstein, Hester. *Contemporary Feminist Thought*. Boston: G. K. Hall, 1983.

Elam, Diane. "Sisters Are Doing It To Themselves." In *Feminisms and Generations*. Ed. Devoney Looser and E. Ann Kaplan. Minneapolis: University of Minnesota Press, 1997.

Erlich, Richard D. "*Always Coming Home*: Ethnography, unBible and Utopian Satire." *Paradoxa* 21 (2008): 137–166.

_____. *Coyote's Song: The Teaching Stories of Ursula K. Le Guin*. 1997. SFRA Digital Book, 2001. http://www.sfra.org/Coyote/CoyoteHome.htm.

_____. "Le Guin and God: Quarreling with the One, Critiquing Pure Reason." *Extrapolation* 47, no. 3 (2006): 351–79.

_____, and Diana Perkins. "Herons, Ringtrees, and Mud: Ursula K. Le Guin's *The Eye of the Heron*." *Extrapolation* 43, no. 3 (2002): 314–29.

Esmonde, Margaret P. "The Master Pattern: The Psychological Journey in the Earthsea Trilogy." In Olander and Greenberg, *Ursula K. Le Guin*, 15–35.

Evans, Sara. *Personal Politics: The Roots of Women's Liberation in the Civil Rights Movement and the New Left*. New York: Vintage, 1979.

Faludi, Susan. *Backlash: The Undeclared War Against American Women*. 1991. New York: Anchor, 1992.

Fayad, Mona. "Aliens, Androgynes, and Anthropology: Le Guin's Critique of Representation in *The Left Hand of Darkness*." *Mosaic* 30, no. 3 (1997): 59–73.

Feimer, Joel N. "Biblical Typology in Le Guin's *The Eye of the Heron*: Character, Structure and Theme." *Mythlore* 19, no. 4 (1993): 13–19.

Fekete, John. "'The Dispossessed' and 'Triton': Act and System in Utopian Science Fiction." *Science Fiction Studies* 6 (1979): 129–43.

Figes, Eva. *Patriarchal Attitudes*. New York: Stein and Day, 1970.

Finch, Sheila. "Paradise Lost: The Prison at the Heart of Le Guin's Utopia." *Extrapolation* 26 (1985): 240–248.

Firestone, Shulamith. *The Dialectic of Sex: The Case for Feminist Revolution*. New York: Bantam, 1970.

Fitting, Peter. "Readers and Responsibility: A Reply to Ken Roemer." *Utopian Studies* 2, nos. 1 and 2 (1991): 24–29.

Franko, Carol. "Acts of Attention at the Borderlands: Le Guin's *The Beginning Place* Revisited." *Extrapolation* 37, no. 4 (1996): 302–15.

_____. "Dialogic Narration and Ambivalent Utopian Hope in Lessing's *Shikasta* and Le Guin's *Always Coming Home*." *Journal of the Fantastic in the Arts* 2, no. 3 (1990): 23–33.

_____. "Self-conscious Narration as the Complex Representation of Hope in Le Guin's *Always Coming Home*." *Mythlore* 15, no. 3 (1989): 57–60.

Freedman, Carl. *Critical Theory and Science Fiction.* Hanover, NH: University Press of New England, 2000.

Friedan, Betty. *The Feminine Mystique.* New York: Dell, 1963.

Friend, Beverly. "Virgin Territory: Women and Sex in Science Fiction." *Extrapolation* 14 (December 1972): 45–58.

Galbreath, Robert. "Taoist Magic in the Earthsea Trilogy." *Extrapolation* 21, no. 3 (1980): 262–68.

Gal-Or, Jenny. "Articulating Ghost Stories: Haunted Humanity in 'Newton's Sleep.'" *Paradoxa* 21 (2008): 232–249.

Genz, Stéphanie. *Third Way/ve: The Politics of Postfeminism. Feminist Theory* 7, no. 3 (2006): 333–353.

Getz, John. "A Peace-Studies Approach to *The Left Hand of Darkness.*" *Mosaic* 21, nos. 2 and 3 (1988): 203–14.

Gilbert, Sandra M., and Susan Gubar. *The Madwoman in the Attic: The Woman Writer and the Nineteenth-Century Literary Imagination.* New Haven, CT: Yale University Press, 1979.

_____. *No Man's Land: The Place of the Woman Writer in the Twentieth Century,* I: *The War of the Words.* New Haven, CT: Yale University Press, 1988.

_____, Eds. *The Norton Anthology of Literature by Women: The Tradition in English.* New York: Norton, 1985.

Gilligan, Carol. *In A Different Voice.* Cambridge, MA: Harvard University Press, 1982.

Gillis, Stacy, Gillian Howie, and Rebecca Munford, eds. *Third Wave Feminism: A Critical Exploration.* 2nd edition. Hampshire, UK: Palgrave Macmillan, 2007.

_____, and Rebecca Munford, "Genealogies and Generations: the Politics and Praxis of Third Wave Feminism." *Women's History Review* 13, no. 2 (2004): 165–182.

Giusti, Angela. "Earthsea and Its Relationship to Christian and Occult Practices." *Arizona English Bulletin* 37, no. 2 (1995): 26–31.

Greer, Germaine. *The Female Eunuch.* 1971. New York: Bantam, 1972.

Griffin, Susan. *Woman and Nature: The Roaring Inside Her.* New York: Harper & Row, 1978.

Grimstad, Kirsten, and Susan Rennie, Eds. *The New Woman's Survival Sourcebook.* New York: Knopf, 1975.

Griscom, Joan L. "On Healing the Nature/Culture Split in Feminist Thought." *Heresies* 13, no. 4 (1981): 4–9.

Gubar, Susan. "What Ails Feminist Criticism?" *Critical Inquiry* 24, no. 4 (1998): 878–902.

Hall, Elaine J., and Marnie Salupo Rodriguez. "The Myth of Postfeminism." *Gender and Society* 17, no. 6 (2003): 878–902.

Haraway, Donna. "A Cyborg Manifesto: Science, Technology, and Socialist-Feminism in the Late Twentieth Century." In *Simians, Cyborgs and Women: The Reinvention of Nature,* 149–181. New York: Routledge, 1991.

Harper, Mary Catherine. "Spiraling Around the Hinge: Working Solutions in *Always Coming Home.*" In *Old West–New West: Centennial Essays.* Ed. Barbara Howard Meldrum, 241–257. Moscow: Idaho University Press, 1993.

Hartwell, David. *Age of Wonders: Exploring the World of Science Fiction.* 1984. New York: Tor, 1996.

Hatfield, Len: "From Master to Brother: Shifting the Balance of Authority in Ursula K. Le Guin's *Farthest Shore* and *Tehanu.*" *Children's Literature* 21 (1993): 43–65.

Hawkesworth, Mary. "The Semiotics of Premature Burial: Feminism in a Postfeminist Age." *Signs* 29, no. 4 (2004): 961–986.
Hayles, N. B. "Androgyny, Ambivalence and Assimilation in *The Left Hand of Darkness.*" In *Ursula K. Le Guin*, Eds. Joseph D. Olander and Martin Harry Greenberg. 1979.
Heilbrun, Carolyn G. *Toward a Recognition of Androgyny*. New York: Harper & Row, 1973.
Heldrech, Lillian M. "To Defend or to Correct: Patterns of Culture in *Always Coming Home.*" *Mythlore* 16, no. 1 (1989): 58–62.
Hemmings, Clare. "Telling Feminist Stories." *Feminist Theory* 6, no. 2: 115–139.
Henry, Astrid. *Not My Mother's Sister: Generational Conflict and Third Wave Feminism.* Bloomington: Indiana University Press, 2004,
_____. "Solitary Sisterhood: Individualism Meets Collectivity in Feminism's Third Wave." In *Different Wavelengths: Studies of the Contemporary Women's Movement.* Ed. Jo Reger, 81–96. New York: Routledge, 2005.
Hersh, George. *Making the Self: Aspects of the Life Cycle in the Works of Ursula Le Guin.* Ph.D. diss., Wright Institute Graduate School of Psychology, 1999.
Heywood, Leslie, and Jennifer Drake, Eds. *Third Wave Agenda: Being Feminist, Doing Feminism.* Minneapolis: University of Minnesota Press, 1997.
Holliday, Valerie. "Delany Dispossessed." *Extrapolation* 44, no. 4 (2003), 425–36.
Hollindale, Peter. "The Last Dragon of Earthsea." *Children's Literature in Education* 34, no. 3 (2003): 183–193.
Hollinger, Veronica. "Feminist Science Fiction: Breaking Up the Subject." *Extrapolation* 31, no. 3 (1990): 229–239.
_____. "(Re)reading Queerly: Science Fiction, Feminism, and the Defamiliarization of Gender." In *Future Females, The Next Generation.* Ed. Marleen S. Barr, 197–215. Lanham, MD: Rowman & Littlefield, 2000.
hooks, bell [Gloria Watkins]. *Ain't I a Woman: Black Women and Feminism.* Boston: South End, 1981.
_____. *Feminist Theory: From Margin to Center.* Boston: South End Press, 1984.
Hostetler, Margaret. "'Was It I that Killed the Babies?': Children as Disruptive Signifiers in Ursula K. Le Guin's *Always Coming Home.*" *Extrapolation* 42, no. 1 (2001): 27–36.
Hubel, Teresa. "In Pursuit of Feminist Postfeminism and the Blessings of Buttercup." *English Studies in Canada* 31, nos. 2 and 3 (2005): 17–21.
Hull, Keith N. "What Is Human? Ursula Le Guin and Science Fiction's Great Theme." *Modern Fiction Studies* 32, no. 1 (1986): 65–74.
Huntington, John. "Public and Private Imperatives in Le Guin's Novels." *Science Fiction Studies* 2 (1975): 237–43.
Jackson, Kasi. "Feminism, Animals, and Science in Le Guin's Animal Stories." *Paradoxa* 21 (2008): 206–231.
Jackson, Rosemary. *Fantasy: The Literature of Subversion.* London: Methuen, 1981.
Jacobs, Naomi. "The Frozen Landscape in Women's Utopian and Science Fiction." In *Utopian and Science Fiction by Women: Worlds of Difference.* Ed. Jane L. Donawerth, 190–202. Syracuse, NY: Syracuse University Press, 1994.
Jago, Wendy. "'A Wizard of Earthsea' and the Charge of Escapism." *Children's Literature in Education* 8 (1972): 21–9.
James, Edward. *Science Fiction in the 20th Century.* Oxford: Oxford University Press, 1994.
Jameson, Fredric. "World-reduction in Le Guin: The Emergence of Utopian Narrative." *Science Fiction Studies* 2 (1975): 221–30. Reprinted in Bloom, 1987.

Jose, Jim. "Reflections on the Politics of Le Guin's Narrative Shifts." *Science Fiction Studies* 18, no. 2 (1991): 180–197.

Junko, Yoshida. "'Masculine Mystique' Revisioned in the Earthsea Quartet." In *The Presence of the Past in Children's Literature*. Ed. Ann Lawson Lucas, 187–193. Westport, CT: 2003.

Kaplan, Alexander G., and Joan P. Bean, Eds. *Beyond Sex-Role Stereotypes: Readings Toward a Pscyhology of Androgyny*. Boston: Little, Brown & Co., 1976.

Kavka, Misha. "Feminism, Ethics, and History, or What Is the 'Post' in Postfeminism?" *Tulsa Studies in Women's Literature* 21, no. 1 (2002): 29–44.

Kelso, Sylvia, Ed. *Ursula K. Le Guin. Paradoxa* (21) 2008.

Ketterer, David. *New Worlds for Old: The Apocalyptic Imagination, Science Fiction and American Literature*. Bloomington: Indiana University Press, 1976.

Khader, Jamil. "Race Matters: People of Color, Ideology, and the Politics of Erasure and Reversal in Ursula Le Guin's *The Left Hand of Darkness* and Mary Doria Russell's *The Sparrow*." *Journal of the Fantastic in the Arts* 16, no. 2 (2005): 110–27.

Khana, Lee Cullen. "Women's Utopias: New Worlds, New Texts," in *Feminism, Utopia, and Narrative*. Eds. Libby Falk Jones and Sarah Webster Goodwin, 134–140. Knoxville: University of Tennessee Press, 1990.

Khouri, Nadia."The Dialectics of Power: Utopia in the Science Fiction of Le Guin, Jeury, and Piercy." *Science Fiction Studies* 7 (1980): 49–59.

King, Ynestra. "The Ecology of Feminism and the Feminism of Ecology." *Healing the Wounds: The Power of Ecological Feminism*. Ed. Judith Plant, 18–28. Boston: New Society, 1989.

_____. "What is Ecofeminism?" *Zeta Magazine* 1 (1988): 124–127.

Klarer, Mario. "Gender and the 'Simultaneity Principle': Ursula Le Guin's *The Dispossessed*." *Mosaic* 25, no. 2 (1992): 107–21.

Klein, Gérard. "Le Guin's 'Aberrant' Opus: Escaping the Trap of Discontent." Trans. Richard Astle. *Science Fiction Studies* 4 (1977): 287–95.

Kolodny, Annette. *The Lay of the Land: Metaphor as Experience and History in American Life and Letters*. Chapel Hill: University of North Carolina Press, 1975.

Kroeber, Alfred. *Anthropology*. 1923. New York: Harcourt, Brace, 1948.

_____. *Handbook of the Indians of California*. Bureau of American Ethnology Bulletin 78. Washington, D. C.: Smithsonian, 1925.

Kroeber, Karl. *Romantic Fantasy and Science Fiction*. New Haven, CT: Yale University Press, 1988.

_____. "Sisters and Science Fiction." *The Little Magazine* 10.1 and 2 (1976): 87–90.

Kroeber, Theodora. *Alfred Kroeber: A Personal Configuration*. Berkeley: University of California Press, 1970.

_____. *The Inland Whale: Nine Stories Retold from California Indian Legends*. Berkeley: University of California Press, 1959.

_____. *Ishi in Two Worlds: A Biography of the Last Wild Indian in North America*. Berkeley: University of California Press, 1961.

LaBar, Martin. "The Left Hand of Sexism? Women as the Alien Species on Gethen." *Extrapolation* 21 (1980): 187–189.

Lake, David J. "Le Guin's Twofold Vision: Contrary Image-sets in *The Left Hand of Darkness*." *Science Fiction Studies* 8 (1981): 156–64.

Lamb, Patricia Frazer, and Diana L. Veith. "Again, *The Left Hand of Darkness*: Androgyny or Homophobia?" *Erotic Universe: Sexuality and Fantastic Literature*. Ed. Donald Palumbo. New York: Greenwood, 1986.

Lefanu, Sarah. *Feminism and Science Fiction*. London: Women's, 1988.

Lem, Stanislaw. "Lost Opportunities: Part II: *The Left Hand of Darkness*," *SF Commentary* 24 (1971): 22–24.

Lewis, R.W. B. *Innocence, Tragedy, and Tradition in the Nineteenth Century*. Chicago: University of Chicago Press, 1955.

Lewis, [Percy] Wyndham. 1934. *Men Without Art*. New York: Russell and Russell, 1964.

Lindow, Sandra K. "Becoming Dragon: The Transcendence of the Damaged Child in the Fiction of Ursula K. Le Guin." *Extrapolation* 44, no. 1 (2003): 32–44.

_____. "Wild Gifts: Anger Management and Moral Development in the Fiction of Ursula K. Le Guin and Maurice Sendak." *Extrapolation* 47, no. 3 (2006): 445–56.

Littlefield, Holly. "Unlearning Patriarchy: Ursula Le Guin's Feminist Consciousness in *The Tombs of Atuan* and *Tehanu*." *Extrapolation* 36, no. 3 (1995): 244–58.

Lodge, David, Ed. *Twentieth Century Literary Criticism: A Reader*. London: Longman, 1972.

Lothian, Alexis. "Grinding Axes and Balancing Oppositions: The Transformation of Feminism in Ursula K. Le Guin's Science Fiction." *Extrapolation* 47, no. 3 (2006): 380–95.

Love, Rosaleen. "Ursula K. Le Guin and Therolinguistics." *Paradoxa* 4, no. 10 (1998): 231–236.

Lyotard, Jean-François. *The Postmodern Condition: A Report on Knowledge*. 1979. Trans. Geoff Bennington and Brian Massumi. Minneapolis: University of Minnesota, 1984.

Maddern, Phillipa. "True Stories: Women's Writing in Science Fiction." *Meanjin* 44, no. 1 (1985): 110–123.

Malkki, Tarya. "The Marriage Metaphor in the Works of Ursula K. Le Guin." In *Modes of the Fantastic: Selected Essays from the Twelfth International Conference on the Fantastic in the Arts*. Eds. Robert A Latham and Robert A. Collins, 100–109. Westport, CT; and London: Greenwood, 1995.

Manlove, C. N. "Conservatism in the Fantasy of Le Guin." *Extrapolation* 21, no. 3 (1980): 287–97.

_____. *Modern Fantasy: Five Studies*. Cambridge: Cambridge University Press. 1975.

Marks, Elaine, and Isabelle de Courtivron, Eds. *New French Feminisms: An Anthology*. Amherst: University of Massachusetts Press, 1980.

Maslen, Robert. "Towards an Archaeology of the Present: Theodora Kroeber and Ursula K. Le Guin." *Foundation* 67, no. 21 (1996): 62–74.

McCaffery, Larry. "Introduction." *Across the Wounded Galaxies: Interviews with Contemporary American Science Fiction Writers*. Ed. Larry McCaffery, 1–8. Urbana: University of Illinois Press, 1990.

McGuirk, Carol. "Optimism and the Limits of Subversion in *The Dispossessed* and *The Left Hand of Darkness*." In Bloom, 1987.

McLean, Susan. "'The Beginning Place': An Interpretation." *Extrapolation* 24 (1983): 130–42.

_____. "The Power of Women in Ursula K. Le Guin's *Tehanu*." *Extrapolation* 38, no. 2 (1997): 110–18.

McRobbie, Angela. "Post-Feminism and Popular Culture." *Feminist Media Studies* 4, no. 3 (2004): 255–264.

McWhorter, Carrie B. "Brandishing Shifgrethor: Le Guin's *The Left Hand of Darkness*." *Notes on Contemporary Literature* 28, no. 1 (1998), 11–12.

Merchant, Carolyn. *The Death of Nature: Women, Ecology, and the Scientific Revolution*. San Francisco: Harper & Row, 1980.

Mielenhausen, Eileen M. "Comings and Goings: Metaphors and Linear and Cyclical Movement in Le Guin's *Always Coming Home.*" *Utopian Studies* 3 (1991): 99–105.

Miller, Jean Baker. *Toward a New Psychology of Women.* Boston: Beacon, 1976.

Millett, Kate. *Sexual Politics.* 1970. New York: Avon, 1971.

Mitchell, Juliet. "Women: The Longest Revolution." *New Left Review* 40 (1966).

Moers, Ellen. *Literary Women: The Great Writers.* New York: Doubleday, 1976.

Moi, Toril. *Sexual/Textual Politics: Feminist Literary Theory.* London: Methuen, 1985.

Moore, John. "An Archaeology of the Future: Ursula Le Guin and Anarcho-Primitivism." *Foundation* 63 (1995): 32–39.

Moraga, Cherríe, and Gloria Anzaldúa, Eds. 1981. *This Bridge Called My Back: Writings by Radical Women of Color.* New York: Kitchen Table: Women of Color, 1984.

Morgan, Elaine. *The Descent of Women.* New York: G. P. Putnam's Sons, 1971.

Morgan, Robin, Ed. *Sisterhoood is Powerful: An Anthology of Writings from the Women's Liberation Movement.* New York: Vintage, 1970.

Moskowitz, Sam. "When Women Rule." *When Women Rule.* Ed. Sam Moskowitz. New York: Walker, 1972.

Moylan, Tom. "Beyond Negation: The Critical Utopias of Ursula K. Le Guin and Samuel R. Delany." *Extrapolation* 21 (1980): 236–53.

_____. *Demand the Impossible: Science Fiction and the Utopian Imagination.* New York: Methuen, 1986.

Murphy, Patrick D. "The High and Low Fantasies of Feminist (Re)Mythopoeia." *Mythlore* 60 (1989): 26–31.

_____. "The Left Hand of Fabulation: The Poetry of Ursula K. Le Guin." In *The Poetic Fantastic: Studies in an Evolving Genre.* Eds. Patrick D. Murphy and Vernon Hyles, 123–126. New York: Greenwood, 1989.

Nicholson, Linda. "Interpreting Gender." *Signs* 20 (Autumn 1994): 79–105.

Nodelman, Perry. "Reinventing the Past: Gender in Ursula K. Le Guin's *Tehanu* and The Earthsea Trilogy." *Children's Literature* 23 (1995): 179–201.

Nudelman, Rafail. "An Approach to the Structure of Le Guin's SF." Trans. Alan G. Myers. *Science Fiction Studies* 2 (1975): 210–20.

Nurka, Camille "Postfeminist Autopsies." *Australian Feminist Studies* 17, no. 38 (2002): 177–189.

Olander, Joseph D., and Martin Harry Greenberg. *Ursula K. Le Guin.* New York: Taplinger, 1979.

Ortner, Sherry. "Is Female to Male as Nature is to Culture?" In *Women, Culture and Society.* Eds. Michelle Zimbalist Rosaldo and Louise Lamphere, 67–86. Stanford, CA: Stanford University Press, 1974.

Pagels, Elaine H. *Beyond Belief: The Secret Gospel of Thomas.* New York: Random House, 2003.

_____. "What Became of God the Mother?: Conflicting Images of God in Early Christianity." In *Womanspirit Rising.* Eds. Carol P. Christ and Judith Plaskow, 107–119. New York: Harper & Row, 1979.

Paglia, Camille. *Sexual Personnae.* New Haven, CT: Yale University Press, 1990.

Parrinder, Patrick. "The Alien Encounter: Or, Ms. Brown and Mrs. Le Guin." *Science Fiction: A Critical Guide.* Ed. Patrick Parrinder. London: Longman, 1980.

_____. *Science Fiction: Its Criticisms and Teaching.* London: Methuen, 1980.

Patteson, Richard F. "Ursula K. Le Guin's Earthsea Trilogy: The Psychology of Fantasy." In *The Scope of the Fantastic.* Eds. Robert Collins and Howard D. Pearce, 239–247. Westport, CT: Greenwood, 1985.

Payne, Tonia L. "'Home Is a Place Where You Have Never Been': Connections with the Other in Ursula Le Guin's fiction." *AUMLA: Journal of the Australasian Universities Language and Literature Association* 96 (2001): 189–206.

Pennington, John. "Exorcising Gender: Resisting Readers in Ursula K. Le Guin's *Left Hand of Darkness*." *Extrapolation* 41, no. 4 (2000): 351–358.

Person, Leland S. *The Cambridge Introduction to Nathaniel Hawthorne*. New York: Cambridge University Press, 2007.

Petersen, Zina. "Balancing Act: Ursula Kroeber Le Guin." In *Impossible to Hold: Women and Culture in the 1960s*. Eds. Avital H. Bloch and Lauri Umansky, 65–77. New York: New York University Press, 2005.

Philmus, Robert M. "Ursula Le Guin and Time's Dispossession." Eds. Rhys Garnett and R. J. Ellis. 125–150. In *Science Fiction Roots and Branches: Contemporary Critical Approaches*. Basingstoke, UK: Macmillan, 1990.

Piercy, Marge. *Woman on the Edge of Time*. Greenwich, CT: Fawcett, 1976.

Plank, Robert. "Ursula K. Le Guin and the Decline of Romantic Love." *Science Fiction Studies* 3 (1976): 36–43.

Porter, David L. "The Politics of Le Guin's Opus." *Science Fiction Studies* 2 (1975): 243–248.

Rabkin, Eric S. *The Fantastic in Literature*. Princeton, NJ: Princeton University Press, 1976.

Ransom, Amy J. "Recent Scholarship on Ursula K. Le Guin." *Science Fiction Studies* 36, no. 1 (2009): 144–153.

Rashley, Lisa Hammond. "Revisioning Gender: Inventing Women in Ursula K. Le Guin's Nonfiction." *Biography* 30, no. 1 (2007): 22–47.

Reger, Jo, Ed. *Different Wavelengths. Studies of the Contemporary Women's Movement*. New York: Routledge, 2005.

Reid, Suzanne Elizabeth. *Presenting Ursula K. Le Guin*. New York: Twayne, 1997.

Remington, Thomas J. "A Time to Live and a Time to Die: Cyclical Renewal in the Earthsea Trilogy." *Extrapolation* 21, no. 3 (1980): 278–86.

Rhodes, Jewell Parker. "Ursula Le Guin's *The Left Hand of Darkness*: Androgyny and the Feminist Utopia." In *Women and Utopia: Critical Interpretations*. Eds. Marleen S. Barr and Nicholas D. Smith, 108–120. Lanham, MD: University Press of America, 1983.

Rich, Adrienne. *Of Woman Born: Motherhood as Experience and Institution*. New York: W. W. Norton, 1976.

_____. "When We Dead Awaken: Writing as Re-Vision." In *On Lies, Secrets, and Silence: Selected Prose 1966–1978*, 33–49. New York: Norton, 1979.

Riley, Gregory J. *The Rivers of God: A New History of Christian Origins*. New York: HarperCollins, 2001.

Rilke, Ranier Maria. *The Duino Elegies*. Trans. David Young. New York: Norton, 1978.

Roberts, Robin. "Post-Modernism and Feminist Science Fiction." *Science Fiction Studies* 17 (1990): 136–152.

Robinson, Christopher L. "The Violence of the Name: Patronymy in Earthsea." *Extrapolation* 49, no. 3 (2008): 385–409.

Rochelle, Warren G. "Choosing to be Human: The American Romantic/Pragmatic Rhetoric in Ursula K. Le Guin's Teaching Novel, *Gifts*. *Extrapolation* 48, no. 1 (2007): 84–95.

_____. *Communities of the Heart: The Rhetoric of Myth in the Fiction of Ursula K. Le Guin*. Liverpool, UK: Liverpool University Press, 2000.

_____. "The Emersonian Choice: Connections Between Dragons and Humans in Le Guin's Earthsea Cycle." *Extrapolation* 47, no. 3 (2006): 417–26.

_____. "The Story, Plato, and Ursula K. Le Guin." *Extrapolation* 37, no. 4 (1996): 316–29.

Roemer, Kenneth M. "Dissensus Achieved, Apologies Offered, and a Hinge Proclaimed: A Response to the Responses." *Utopian Studies* 2, nos. 1 and 2 (1991): 59–62.

_____. "The Talking Porcupine Liberates Utopia: Le Guin's Omelas as Pretext to the Dance." *Utopian Studies* 2, nos. 1 and 2 (1991): 6–18.

Rosinsky, Natalie M. *Feminist Futures: Contemporary Women's Speculative Fiction*. Ann Arbor, MI: UMI Research Press, 1984.

Russ, Joanna. *The Female Man*. New York: Bantam, 1975.

_____. *How to Suppress Women's Writing*. Austin: University of Texas Press, 1983.

_____. "The Image of Women in Science Fiction." In *Images of Women in Fiction: Feminist Perspectives*. Ed. Susan Koppelman Cornillon, 79–92. Bowling Green, OH: Bowling Green University Popular Press, 1972.

_____. "The Subjunctivity of Science Fiction." *Extrapolation* 15 (December 1973): 51–59.

_____. "'What if...?' Literature." In *The Contemporary Literary Scene*. Ed. F. V. Magill, 197–201. Englewood Cliffs, NJ: Salem, 1974.

Sargent, Pamela. "Women and Speculative Fiction." In *Women of Wonder: Science Fiction Stories by Women about Women*. Ed. Pamela Sargent, 1977. New York: Vintage-Random House, 1978.

Sawyer, Andy. "Ursula Le Guin and the Pastoral Mode." *Extrapolation* 47, no. 3 (2006): 396–416.

Scheiding, Oliver. "An Archeology of the Future: Postmodern Strategies of Boundary Transitions in Ursula K. Le Guin's *Always Coming Home* (1985)." *Amerikastudien / American Studies* 41, no. 4 (1996): 637–56.

Scholes, Robert. "The Good Witch of the West." *Hollins Critic* 11 (1974): 1–12.

_____. *Structural Fabulation: An Essay on Fiction of the Future*. South Bend, IN: University of Notre Dame Press, 1975.

Segal, Lynne. Interview with Isobel Armstrong. "Keeping Optimism Alive." *Women: A Cultural Review* 12 no. 3 (2001): 269–275.

Selinger, Bernard. *Le Guin and Identity in Contemporary Fiction*. Ann Arbor: UMI Research Press, 1988.

Senior, W. A. "Cultural Anthropology and Rituals of Exchange in Ursula K. Le Guin's Earthsea." *Mosaic* 29, no. 4 (1996): 101–13.

Shelley, Mary. *Frankenstein or the Modern Prometheus*. Oxford: Oxford University Press, 1969.

Shippey, T. A. "The Magic Art and the Evolution of Words: Ursula Le Guin's Earthsea Trilogy." *Mosaic* 10, no. 2 (1977): 147–64.

Showalter, Elaine. *A Literature of Their Own: British Women Novelists from Brontë to Lessing*. Princeton, NJ: Princeton University Press, 1977.

_____. *The New Feminist Criticism: Essays on Women, Literature and Theory*. New York: Pantheon, 1985.

Singer, June. *Androgyny: Toward a New Theory of Sexuality*. Garden City, NY: Anchor-Doubleday, 1976.

Sklar, Howard. "Sympathy as Self-Discovery: The Significance of Caring for Others in 'Betrayals.'" *Paradoxa* 21 (2008): 185–205.

Slusser, George E. *The Farthest Shores of Ursula K. Le Guin*. San Bernardino, CA: Borgo, 1976.

Smith, Cordwainer [Paul Linebarger]. "Alpha Ralpha Boulevard." *The Best of Cordwainer Smith*. Ed. J. J. Pierce. Garden City, NY: Nelson Doubleday, 1975.

Sobat, Gail Sidonie. "The Night in Her Own Country: The Heroine's Quest for Self in Ursula K. Le Guin's *The Tombs of Atuan*." *Mythlore* 21, no. 3 (1996): 24–32.

Somay, Bülent. "From Ambiguity to Self-reflexivity: Revolutionizing Fantasy Space." In *The New Utopian Politics of Ursula K. Le Guin's* The Dispossessed. Eds. Laurence Davis and Peter Stillman, 233–47.

Spacks, Patricia Meyer. *The Female Imagination*. 1972. New York: Alfred A. Knopf, 1975.

Spencer, Kathleen L. "Exiles and Envoys: The SF of Ursula K. Le Guin." *Foundation* 20 (1980): 32–43.

Spender, Dale. *For the Record: The Making and Meaning of Feminist Knowledge*. London: Women's, 1985.

_____. *Man Made Language*. London: Routledge and Kegan Paul, 1980.

_____. *Women of Ideas and What Men Have Done to Them*. London: Routledge and Kegan Paul, 1982.

Spivack, Charlotte. *Ursula K. Le Guin*. Boston: Twayne, 1984.

Spivak, Gayatri Chakravorty, "Feminism and Critical Theory." 1978. Reprinted in *Contemporary Literary Criticism: Literary and Cultural Studies*. Eds. Robert Con Davis and Ronald Schleifer, 519–534. New York: Longman, 1994.

Sturgeon, Theodore. *Venus Plus X*. New York: Pyramid, 1980.

Suvin, Darko. "Cognition, Freedom, *The Dispossessed* as a Classic." Paradoxa 21 (2008): 23–49.

_____. *Metamorphoses of Science Fiction: On the Poetics and History of a Literary Genre*. New Haven, CT: Yale University Press, 1979.

_____. "On U. K. Le Guin's 'Second Earthsea Trilogy' and Its Cognitions: A Commentary." *Extrapolation* 47, no. 3 (2006): 488–504.

_____. "Parables of De-Alienation: Le Guin's Widdershins Dance." *Science Fiction Studies* 7, nos. 2 and 3 (1975): 265–74.

Tasker, Yvonne, and Diane Negra, Eds. *Interrogating Postfeminism: Gender and the Politics of Popular Culture*. Durham, NC: Duke University Press, 2007.

Tavormina, M. Teresa. "Physics as Metaphor: The General Temporal Theory in *The Dispossessed*." *Mosaic* 13, nos. 3 and 4 (1980): 51–62.

Thomas-Card, Traci. "Ursula K. Le Guin's 'Sur:' Defamiliarizing the Frontier." *Paradoxa* (21): 250–270.

Thompson, Christine K. "Going North and West to Watch the Dragons Dance: Norse and Celtic Elements in Ursula Le Guin's Earthsea Trilogy." *Mythlore* 15, no. 1 (1988): 19–22.

Todd, Janet. *Feminist Literary History*. New York: Routledge, 1988.

Todorov, Tzvetan. *The Fantastic: A Structural Approach to a Literary Genre*. Trans. Richard Howard. 1970. Ithaca, NY: Cornell University Press, 1975.

Tolkien, J. R. R. "On Fairy Stories." In *The Monsters and the Critics and Other Essays*. Ed. Christoper Tolkien, 109–161. London: George Allen & Unwin, 1983.

Tompkins, Jayne P. *Sensational Designs: The Cultural Work of American Fiction 1790–1866*. New York: Oxford University Press, 1985.

Tschachler, Heinz. "'How to Walk with My People': Ursula K. Le Guin's Futuristic Frontier Mythology." *Western American Literature* 33, no. 3 (1998): 254–72.

_____. *Ursula K. Le Guin*. Boise, ID: Boise State University Press, 2001.

Turner, Victor. *The Forest of Symbols*. Ithaca, NY: Cornell University Press, 1967.

_____. "Variations on a Theme of Liminality." *Secular Rituals.* Eds. Sally F. Moore and Barbara G. Meyerhoff, 36–70. Amsterdam, the Netherlands: Van Gorcum, 1977.

Urbanowicz, Victor. "Personal and Political in *The Dispossessed.*" *Science Fiction Studies* 5 (1978): 110–17.

Van Gennep, Arnold. *The Rites of Passage.* Trans. Monika Vizedom and Gabrielle L. Caffee. Chicago: Chicago University Press, 1960.

Vavrus, Mary Douglas. "Putting Ally on Trial: Contesting Postfeminism in Popular Culture." *Women's Studies in Communication* 23, no. 3 (2000): 413–429.

Walker, Alice. *In Search of Our Mother's Gardens: Womanist Prose.* New York: Harcourt Brace Jovanovich, 1983.

Walker, Jeanne Murray. "Myth, Exchange and History in *The Left Hand of Darkness.*" *Science Fiction Studies* 6 (1979): 180–189.

_____. "Rites of Passage Today: The Cultural Significance of *A Wizard of Earthsea.*" *Mosaic* 13, nos. 3 and 4 (1980): 179–91.

Walker, Rebecca. "Riding the Third Wave." Interview with Sangamithra Iyer. *Satya Magazine* (January 2005).

Warren, Karen J. "Feminism and Ecology: Making Connections." *Environmental Ethics* 9 (1987): 3–21.

Wayne, Kathryn Ross. *Redefining Moral Education: Life, Le Guin, and Language.* Bethesda, MD: Austin & Winfield, 1995.

Webb, Sarah Jo. "Culture as Spiritual Metaphor in Le Guin's *Always Coming Home.*" In *Functions of the Fantastic: Selected Essays from the Thirteenth International Conference on the Fantastic in the Arts.* Ed. Joe Sanders, 155–160. Westport, CT and London: Greenwood, 1995.

Wendell, Carolyn. "The Alien Species: A Study of Women Characters in the Nebula Award Winners, 1965–1973." *Extrapolation* 2, no. 4 (1979): 343–354.

Westfahl, Gary. *The Mechanics of Wonder: The Creation of the Idea of Science Fiction.* Liverpool, UK: Liverpool University Press, 1998.

Whelehan, Imelda. *Modern Feminist Thought: From the Second Wave to Post-Feminism.* Edinburgh, Scotland: Edinburgh University Press, 1995.

White, Donna R. *Dancing with Dragons: Ursula K. Le Guin and the Critics.* Columbia, SC: Camden House, 1999.

Wolf, Naomi. *The Beauty Myth.* London: Chatto & Windus, 1990.

Woolf, Virginia. *The Pargiters.* 1932. Ed. Mitchell Leaska. New York: Harcourt Brace Jovanovich, 1978.

_____. "Professions for Women." In *Collected Essays.* 1925. Ed. Leonard Woolf, 284–289. London: Hogarth, 1966.

_____. *A Room of One's Own.* 1928. Harmondsworth, UK: Penguin, 1973.

Women's Studies 2.2 (1974). Special issue on androgyny.

Wright, Linda. "Reconciliation in 'The Matter of Seggri.'" *Paradoxa* 21 (2008): 167–184.

Wymer, Thomas L. "Text and Pre-texts in Le Guin's *The New Atlantis.*" *Extrapolation* 44, no. 3 (2003): 296–303.

Wytenbroek, Jacqueline Robin. "*Always Coming Home*: Pacifism and Anarchy in Le Guin's Latest Utopia." *Extrapolation* 28, no. 4 (1987): 330–39.

Yoke, Carl. "Precious Metal in White Clay." *Extrapolation* 21 (1980): 197–208.

Yoshioka, Kumiko. "Welcome to the Future: *Always Coming Home.*" *Paradoxa* 4, no. 11 (1998): 460–76.

Zaki, Hoda. *Phoenix Revisited: The Survival and Mutation of Utopian Thought in North American Science Fiction, 1965–1982.* San Bernardino, CA: Borgo, 1988.

Index

201

205